# *Wild* WINES

## Creating Organic Wines From Nature's Garden

# DAWN MARIE

SQUARE ONE
P U B L I S H E R S

COVER DESIGNER: Jeannie Tudor
COVER PHOTO : Getty Images, Inc.
PART ONE ILLUSTRATOR: Jeannie Tudor
PART TWO ILLUSTRATOR: Vicki Renoux
TYPESETTER: Gary A. Rosenberg
EDITOR: Joanne Abrams

**Square One Publishers**
115 Herricks Road • Garden City Park, NY 11040
(516) 535-2010 • (877) 900-BOOK
www.squareonepublishers.com

**Library of Congress Cataloging-in-Publication Data**

Marie, Dawn.
    Wild wines : creating organic wines from nature's garden /
Dawn Marie.
        p. cm.
    Includes index.
    ISBN-13: 978-0-7570-0292-2 (quality pbk.)
    ISBN-10: 0-7570-0292-7 (quality pbk.) 4238 3058 ⅒
    1. Organic wines. 2. Wine and wine making. I. Title.

TP548.6.O74M37        2008
641.8'72—dc22
                                                2006100673

Printed in the United States of America

10   9   8   7   6   5   4   3   2   1

# Contents

## 9. Root Wines, 123

## 10. Flower Wines, 137

## 11. Leaf Wines, 163

## 12. Other Wines, 181

*To my husband, Leonard,*
*who has supported me in every way*
*throughout the creation of this book.*
*You are my inspiration and my intoxication.*

# Acknowledgments

Thanks go to the following vineyards, wineries, and wine importers for providing information about their products and/or the organic and Biodynamic wine industry:

- Phil La Rocca from La Rocca Vineyards
- Martha Barra from Girasole Vineyards and Barra of Mendocino Winery
- Kristen Barnhisel from Handley Cellars
- Ann Thrupp, Ph.D., from Fetzer Vineyards
- Bill Kremer, Director of Winemaking, King Estate Winery
- Nathan from Frey Organic Wine
- Bart Alexander from China Bend Winery
- Katrina from Ceago Vinegarden
- Doug Tunnell from Brick House Vineyards
- Shari Staglin from Staglin Family Vineyard
- Rich Tanguay from Heller Estate
- Jennifer Gallagher from Robert Sinskey Vineyards
- Tony Coturri from Coturri Winery
- Stacy from Hallcrest Vineyards
- Yorkville Cellars
- Tony Norskog from Nevada County Wine Guild, Our Daily Red, Orleans Hill Winery, and Heartswork
- Darcy Pendergrass from Amity Vineyards
- Michelle from Frog's Leap Winery
- Mickey Dunne from Badger Mountain Vineyard
- Dr. Michael Ginoulhac from the Organic Wine Company

Thanks to Elizabeth B. Singh at Florida Crystals Refinery for the sugar refining information.

Thanks to Maury Wills from the Department of Agriculture Organic Program for providing his willing expertise regarding organic criteria for vineyards and wineries.

Thanks to Theresa McCarthy (for Francis W. Foote) from the United States Department of the Treasury's Alcohol and Tobacco Tax and Trade Bureau for clarifying this agency's role in wine labeling and testing for fining agents in wine.

Thanks to Rudy Shur, publisher of Square One Publishers, for his willingness to give a writer an opportunity to become a published author.

Thanks to Mishie (Mini-Me) and Jaymeister (Johnny-Five) for supporting my early writing endeavors when life was so frenzied, and for partaking in many wild food delights, sometimes knowingly and sometimes unknowingly.

# Introduction

W ho doesn't love a good glass of wine? Each year, more and more people learn to appreciate this delightful beverage and make it a part of their dining experience. But did you know that you don't have to limit yourself to grape wines made by vintners? The fact is that it's easy to make your own wine at home. Better yet, there's no need to go to your local supermarket or farm stand for the fruit needed to make your wine. You can just take a trip outside and "shop" from Nature's bounty for the plants needed to craft pure, distinctive, flavorful wines—wild wines!—right in your kitchen.

Wild wines are created by combining ingredients selected and hand-picked by you, the Great Gatherer—fruits, roots, flowers, leaves, and other plant parts foraged from your city or suburban backyard, the surrounding neighborhood, or anywhere plants grow unaided and unimpeded by human intervention. Making wild wines can link you to past peoples by reviving age-old winemaking techniques, using unadulterated, foraged vegetation as the primary ingredient. And, of course, making wild wines will allow you to give friends and family a gift that is both natural and unique—a hand-crafted wine that is available nowhere else.

Nature's bounty embraces you even when you feel too hurried to notice it or are looking through untrained eyes. These pages will help you to identify more than sixty wild edible plants—from apples to thimbleberries to red clover—that can be transformed into wild wine. You will also learn to find wholesome secondary components to use in your wine. Wild grapes and wild plums can be changed into raisins and prunes, which can add fullness and flavor to otherwise weak wines. Some citrus fruits can be grown indoors as houseplants to be added to wines that are naturally low in acid. Wild grains such as oats and rice can enhance the body of weaker wines, as can store-bought wheat berries and dried corn kernels. You'll be pleased to learn that there is no need to add the various chemical compositions and animal-based products used in commercial wines—and even in some organic wines. Your wines can use ingredients made strictly from Nature's flora, not its fauna. And the results can surpass any wines you've ever enjoyed.

Part One of *Wild Wines* provides you with the basics of winemaking, starting with commercial wines. In the first few chapters, you'll learn about different types of wine, and you'll discover what actually goes into a standard bottle of store-bought wine. Later chapters offer a close look at the world of organic wines, again showing you what actually goes into these specialty vintages. Finally, Part One introduces you to the world of wild winemaking. You'll learn how to forage for Nature's bounty; how to choose additional winemaking ingredients; and how to equip your wild wine kitchen at relatively little expense. Perhaps most important, you'll explore the step-by-step process for making wine at home, from the preparation of the plant matter to the corking of your first bottle.

Part Two presents wild wine recipes, with each chapter focusing on a different type of wine—fruit, root, flower, leaf, and more. For every plant explored, you'll find wild plant collection tips, a helpful description of the wine that can be made with that plant, and a detailed recipe. In short, you'll find everything you need to choose a wine that suits your tastes, and to create your own Wild Blackberry Wine, Wild Ginger Wine, or even Wild Rose Petal Wine.

I feel that the more you learn about winemaking, the more you'll want to learn. That's why this book ends with a helpful Glossary of terms; a Resources section that will guide you to fruit-picking supplies, winemaking supplies, and more; an Evaluation of Organic Wineries; and an extensive Suggested Reading List. These appendices will extend your knowledge, help you locate any assistance you might need, and aid you in further appreciating the world of organic wines.

As someone who has created and enjoyed wild wines for many years, I can assure you that the rewards of winemaking are endless. In warm weather, you can fully immerse yourself in Nature as you gather wonderful fruits, flavorful leaves, and exotic roots. Yet you can make wine on even the coldest of days by using plants picked earlier in the year, and preserved through drying or freezing. Not only can a glass of wild wine provide a warm glow on a chilly night, but starting a new batch of dried fruit or tea leaf wine can fill your home with earthy cheerfulness during the blustery winter months.

Won't you join me now on an adventure into the fruitful, root-filled, flowery, and leafy world of wild edible plants? Let us plunge into the long neck of a transparent green bottle and see where the wild wine takes us!

# PART ONE

---

# *The Basics*

B efore concocting your first batch of wild wine, you should have some general knowledge of wine, both wild and commercial, under your belt. Knowing what lurks within the contoured green glass of a store-bought vintage (besides grapes) will inspire you to make your own wine using wild plants and natural ingredients.

Here, in Part One, you'll learn all about commercial wine and its many ingredients. The common grape is the fruit most often associated with wine, and it is the standard ingredient for commercial vintages. The grape on its own is healthy and wholesome. Winemakers often take this vitamin-filled orb and process it to the point of no return. Nonorganic wine may be modified with more additives and chemical "enhancers" than such a lovely berry deserves, resulting in a fruit product that is so altered it becomes unrecognizable.

I'll also introduce you to organic wine and its components (which may surprise you), as well as to the wonders of wild wine. You'll learn all about the benefits of wild wine, and about the ingredients, supplies, and techniques required to make it. I think you'll be pleased by how easy it is to create your own wine.

All around you are renewable gifts of the earth—gifts that can be transformed into pure wine. Let us begin our journey into Nature!

# 1

# *Hello, Grape*

Ah, wine. There are many aisles devoted to this simple libation at most liquor stores. The shelves of libraries and bookstores are stocked with scads of colorful books about wine. And acres of prime soil are dedicated to the growing and harvesting of wine grapes. Why is the humble grape—its clusters, its arbors, and its vining tendrils—such a large part of art, beauty, and history? It's because we, the consumers, invest our time, interest, and money in the consumption of fermented fruit.

Perhaps you have been confused by all of the intimidating varieties of wine offered in clear glass, colored glass, and, alas, large cardboard boxes. This chapter provides the briefest of introductions to commercial wine by discussing its color, sweetness, and types, and providing tips on serving and tasting.

## THE COLOR OF WINE

For the most part, red wines are made from red grapes and white wines are made from green grapes, although there are some exceptions to this rule. The color of wine comes from exposure or lack of exposure to the pigments in the skins of the grape. Regardless of the outward color of the grape skins, the "innards" of all grapes are the same pale green color. If red skins intermingle with the nearly colorless pulp during the early stages of wine production, the wine takes on a reddish hue. If the skins are not allowed to maintain contact with the pulp, however, the result is a white wine.

Rosé, or blush, wine originates from the red grape, but the fruit skins are permitted to be in contact with the grape pulp for only a short period of time—generally twenty-four hours—and then are removed. The short period of contact the colored part of the fruit has with the juice imparts a pinkish hue.

The length of time grape skins remain in contact with the fruit pulp determines the color of the finished wine, ranging from white to blush to deep red.

## THE SWEETNESS OF WINE

The sweetness of wine is largely determined by the natural sweetness of the grape. Great care is taken to pick the grapes at their prime level of ripeness to ensure the correct balance of acid and sugar. Many factors affect the sweetness of grapes from year to year, including temperature, rainfall, amount of sunshine, and fertility of the soil, to name a few. These conditions make up the microclimate of a grape-growing region, and this is why wine grapes are not grown commercially in all areas of the country. During select years, some vintages command a high price, as that particular season's grape harvest stands out as being superior in quality.

Some vintners stop the fermentation of their grapes when the desired level of sweetness is achieved. Often, if the grapes are not sweet enough, the vintner adds sugar or grape juice concentrate. Although this is costly to the vineyard, it is sometimes necessary. In the state of California, however, it is illegal to add sugar to wine; Californian vintners can add only grape juice concentrate to their grapes to attain the level of sweetness needed to make a fine wine.

## TYPES OF WINE

White wines are most typically served with seafood, poultry, pork, and other light fare, while red wines complement red meat and other strong-tasting foods.

Table wines are the most common type of wine, and, as their name implies, are typically served during a meal. The standard rule is to serve white table wine with fish, fowl, pork, and light-colored or blander-tasting food; and to offer red wine when serving red meat and strong-tasting foods. Rosé, being part red and part white, is considered a neutral wine, and may be served with any kind of food.

An apéritif is a slightly sweet, fruity wine that may be served as an appetizer. It is called a fortified wine because alcohol is added to bring the alcohol content up to 15 to 20 percent. Typically, the alcohol content of table wine does not exceed 14 percent by volume. However, the consumer's demand for wines with higher alcohol content has caused grape growers to allow the grapes to hang on the vines longer so that the fruit develops more sugar. That sugar begins converting to alcohol before the fruit has been picked, so some wine can be naturally fermented to 15 to 17 percent alcohol by volume. This means that some table wines now contain the same high level of alcohol typical of apéritif wines.

Dessert wine, or after-dinner wine, is also sweet and is intended to be served with the last course of the meal, either with dessert or during the cheese course.

Sparkling wine is a carbonated wine, and can be white, red, or something in between. Champagne is a type of sparkling wine. By French law, sparkling wine can be called champagne only if it is made from grapes of the Champagne region of France, and then, only if the grapes are processed using the traditional champagne method—*method champenoise*. When wine is fermenting, there is a naturally occurring release of carbon dioxide. If wine is bottled when fermentation has not ceased, or if fermentation is reactivated by adding yeast and sugar to a finished still wine, it will transform itself into a carbonated wine. It takes a very thick glass bottle and a sturdy cork to keep the carbon dioxide gases from popping a top or exploding a bottle, which is why champagne is corked with a specially designed cap and a metal tie-down. The pressure within a bottle of champagne can be equal to three times the amount of pressure in the tires of your automobile—as high as ninety pounds per square inch!

Ice wine is a lesser-known type of wine that was created unintentionally in an effort to salvage a harvest of grapes after an unexpected freeze in eighteenth-century Germany. It has been commercially produced in Germany since the 1960s, and in the United States, since the 1980s. After late-season grapes have been naturally exposed to freezing temperatures, the juice is pressed from them before the fruit thaws, and wine is made from this expressed juice. Only the concentrated juice that has *not* turned into ice—about 20 percent of the juice—is used to make wine. The remaining 80 percent of the juice has formed ice crystals. Because such a small amount of the grape harvest is used, this product is most often sold in half bottles (375 milliliters), and commands a high price. Note that "iced wine" is made from fruit that has been artificially frozen. "Ice wine," on the other hand, can be legally labeled as such only if the grapes were frozen naturally on the vine.

## SERVING WINE

There is a rule of thumb about serving wines. Whites should be chilled for one to two hours, depending on the vintage, and reds should be served closer to room temperature, or at about 60 to 65 degrees. When a wine is chilled, the flavors and aromas may be less remarkable during the actual drinking of the wine. Think about other beverages you consume both cold and at room temperature. The colder drink does not have the same intensity of flavor as the warmer drink. The same is true for wines. Wines that are served too warm may taste thin, and those served too chilled may lack full aroma and flavor. If you are serving a questionable vintage, cooling it first will reduce any unpleasantness in the aroma and taste, but if you are serving a superior wine, you will want every nuance in bouquet and flavor to dance upon your palate.

It is recommended that white wines be chilled for an hour or two prior to serving, and that red wines be served close to room temperature.

Another step in serving wine is allowing it to breathe—uncorking the wine before serving to expose it to air with the assumption that this will improve the flavor. The wine-breathing ritual is a controversial issue among wine experts. Those who support this practice believe that young wines, in particular, need to breathe to allow the bitter taste of tannins to be mellowed through oxidation (exposure to the air). Others do not believe it is necessary for the wine to breathe, or think that the wine may actually suffer as a result of this practice. Wines that do not require aging may not benefit from this additional exposure to air. Most whites and many reds are ready to drink as soon as they are opened. If you try breathing a wine that is fully mature, it may be fragile with age and give up its spirit soon after it is poured.

**Exposing a young wine to the air can soften and improve its flavor. If the wine is mature and at its peak, though, exposure to air can actually spoil it.**

Should you allow your wine to breathe? If you sip your wine and find it harsh, push your glass away, allow it to be exposed to the air, and enjoy it after dinner. Some young red wines that show little of their potential aroma or flavor may mellow when the bottle is opened one to two hours prior to serving. Sometimes a wine is best after it has remained uncorked overnight.

If you determine that your wine is improved through exposure to air, you may want to further encourage this process by pouring the wine into a glass or actually decanting it. Decanting wine simply means transferring it from the bottle into another container, such as a carafe or a decanter. Doing so will expose more surface area of the wine to the air. Another advantage of decanting wine is the removal of any sediment—plant matter, spent yeast cells, and tannins that separated from the wine during fermentation. To decant successfully, first place the bottle of wine upright (not on its side) to allow the sediment to settle to the bottom. Then, when the wine is decanted, the sediment will remain at the bottom of the bottle, and you can easily stop pouring when particles become visible. Sediment is not harmful to the wine drinker; however, it can impart some bitterness and an unpleasant mouthfeel.

Once the wine is in the decanter, it should not be left there indefinitely, especially if the decanter is made of lead crystal (the lead may leach into the wine over time). Too much exposure to air for too long will result in overoxidation, which will change the wine's color and taste. Use the decanter only for serving, and return any unconsumed wine to the bottle for storage. Some folks like to filter the wine during decanting, but in doing so, they may lose some of the flavors and aromas.

In addition to serving wine at the proper temperature and allowing it to breathe, there's the issue of the glass. I doubt that I am the only person who ever drank a glass of wine from a coffee mug or an iced-tea glass, but I do admit that I prefer consuming wine from a wineglass. Wineglasses can be short or tall, wide-mouthed or narrow-mouthed, with varying capacities and stem heights. For those of you who are stemware aficionados, the Resources section in the back of this book lists a mail-order wine catalog that sells a wide variety of specialty wineglasses and other wine-related items. (See page 198.) Using the proper glass will help you fully appreciate your wine.

## TASTING WINE

The senses used in appreciating wine include sight, smell, and taste. To inspect the appearance of wine, first tilt the glass away from you to reveal the width and hue of the rim. The rim is the ring of wine circling the surface of the glass, and is best observed against a white surface, such as a tablecloth. Now check the clarity and color. Aging red wines may be ruby or brown-red; young wines might be bright purple. An undesirably oxidized red or white wine will appear brown and dull.

While continuing to hold the glass by its stem, swirl the wine to release its aroma and bouquet. The aroma is the smell from the fruit, and the bouquet is the more subtle scent that develops as the wine matures. Now sniff the wine, focusing on its smell and the feeling it evokes. It may be floral, spicy, fruity, or woody.

Finally, sip the wine. Roll it around in your mouth for several seconds. (This is called chewing.) More flavors should be detected in this way. Then take another sip. In addition to chewing, purse your lips and suck a little air through the wine a few times before swallowing. You will be able to taste and smell even more of the wine because you have released its flavors.

Now that you've been introduced to the condensed version of "Wine 101: Selecting, Serving, and Appreciating Wine," let's see if that bottle of fermented fruit you bought was truly worthy of your most innocent and wholesome admiration. We will proceed to dig a little deeper and see which ingredients actually go into a bottle of purchased wine.

Appreciation of wine is achieved primarily through three of the five senses—sight, smell, and taste. Additionally, the sensation of touch within the palate can help distinguish a full-bodied wine from a weak wine.

# 2

## *What Are You Really Drinking?*

Although fruit, yeast, and time are the most basic components needed to create wholesome and delicious wine, a number of other components are included in over-the-counter vintages. Commercial vintners alter their wine with any number of additives to balance sweetness and increase shelf life, to feed the yeast and adjust the acid, and to improve the clarity, flavor, and color of the wine they mass produce.

Many people are under the misconception that if a bottle of wine is more expensive or if it has a European label glued to the face of the slender green glass, the contents within are purer. High-priced or imported wine does not necessarily mean wholesome, pure, or natural. Let's take a look at some of the ingredients that often go into commercially made wine. These are the less-than-glamorous secrets of wine production that are not advertised and are seldom talked about, but are ever present in the wine you drink.

## GRAPES

Grapes would appear to be quite wholesome and harmless as far as health issues are concerned; however, they cling tightly to a very sinister secret. They are an extremely pesticide-laden fruit. There are at least seventeen different insecticides, pesticides, and fumigants used in grape-growing, and many contain possible carcinogens. According to Californians for Pesticide Reform, grape production accounts for a third of all pesticide-associated illnesses in California, the state where 90 percent of domestic wines are produced. Workers who tend the vines typically experience dermatitis at a rate ten times higher than other agricultural workers. There may be a link between pesticide use and increased birth defects among farmer and nonfarmer residents of winemaking regions. Pesticides have also been linked to nerve damage and genetic mutation. Minute traces of toxins find their way into your wineglass and, ultimately, into your body's tissues, where they accu-

Commercial grapes are grown using at least seventeen different weed and pest control products, some of which have been linked to cancer, birth defects, nerve damage, and genetic mutation.

mulate. It is speculated that these toxins may be the reason that some people get headaches after drinking wine.

In addition to the chemicals sprayed on or applied to wine grapes to increase the harvest, there is another hazard lurking at the end of each row of grape vines— the dreaded creosote-soaked end post. Creosote is a wood preservative containing more than 300 chemicals, including fungicides, insecticides, miticides, and sporicides. It is a distillation of high-temperature coal tar and is the same chemical used to pressure-treat railroad ties. Creosote in groundwater and soil biodegrades over many months or even years. Long-term external exposure (via skin contact) to creosote chemicals has resulted in skin and scrotum cancer. Eating food or drinking water contaminated with creosote may cause mouth burning and stomach pains. Other possible symptoms include skin or respiratory-tract irritation, convulsions, mental confusion, kidney or liver problems, unconsciousness, or even death.

Every day we are exposed to countless potentially harmful human-made chemicals. Awareness of these dangers in the foods we eat and the beverages we drink allows us to make informed decisions about what we consume.

I'm sure you have put two and two together by now to realize that harmful chemicals aren't just directly applied to the grapes. Unhealthy substances also affect the grapes indirectly through soil absorption, airborne contact, and water pollution. When chemicals are heaped on one another, the result is a sterile soil, and sterile soil is unhealthy soil. Fertile soil is alive, filled with microorganisms, worms, insects, and a thriving habitat for tiny but necessary life. Earth that is teeming with life is able to provide the nutrients and living energy that are needed for a productive fruit harvest.

The process of making a simple glass of wine may be endangering farm workers, negatively impacting people residing near the vineyard, and altering or injuring flora and fauna. Exposure to the treated air, water, soil, and grape vines may be doing irreparable damage to the innocent. Imagine what it could be doing to *you!*

## YEAST

*Wild yeast is everywhere—in the air, soil, and water, and on fruits, flowers, and leaves. Because this yeast is unpredictable, though, most winemakers rely on commercial yeast for fermentation.*

Yeast is the ingredient that initiates the transformation of fruit juice into wine. There are about 6,000 yeast cells in one ounce of actively fermenting must (the combination of grape skin, juice, and seeds). It's the action of yeast cells consuming sugar that results in the release of alcohol and carbon dioxide, which causes the frothing and foaming associated with fermentation. This single-celled fungus can be found on many wild fruits, including grapes, apples, plums, elderberries, and blueberries. Windborne wild yeasts may also be found on leaves and flowers and in soil or salt water. However, most vineyards would not risk a full season's harvest of grapes by relying on wild, unpredictable yeast to ferment a batch of wine.

Commercial yeast was originally developed from the naturally occurring wild yeast on the skins of wine grapes. The yeast was collected, cultured, and sold in packets. Some commercially available yeast ferment fast and hot and are suited to full-bodied wines with strong flavor or for wines with complex aromas. Some yeasts ferment more slowly and bring out fruity or spicy characteristics in the wine. Many different types of yeast have been developed for their ability to create different bouquets; to form compact lees; to develop fruit and floral aromas; to reduce foaming, thereby lessening the need for defoaming agents; to produce high-alcohol wines; and to prevent wild yeast growth, which can produce "off" flavors. For the home brewer, though, the type of yeast is most simply chosen by the color of the wine you will be making, either red or white. There is also a multipurpose yeast that can be used for all types of wine. Yeast can be purchased in liquid or dry form.

## SUGAR

As you learned in Chapter 1, vintners often find that grapes are not as sweet as desired, in which case, they add sugar or grape juice concentrate to the wine to achieve the desired level of sweetness. Although the statutes in the federal government's Code of Federal Regulations allow the addition of sugar to correct the sweetness of wines, California forbids the addition of sugar to the state's wines. In California, if a wine is lacking sweetness, a winery may add grape juice concentrate, which is sweeter and more intense than regular grape juice, to bring the wine up to the desired level of sweetness.

## SULFITES

Synthetic sulfites were pioneered by a European winemaker about two hundred years ago and are a common addition to wine today. They are added to wine must in the form of either sulfur dioxide ($SO_2$) or Campden tablets (potassium metabisulfite). Sulfites act as preservatives and antioxidants—substances that inhibit the destructive effects of oxidation.

Sulfites allow winemakers to increase the shelf life of wine by inhibiting the growth of wild yeast and bacteria, and preventing flavor and color changes caused by oxidation.

As a preservative, sulfites inhibit wild yeast growth, as well as the growth of destructive organisms—such as the bacteria that can turn a wine into vinegar—by binding with and removing them. As an antioxidant, sulfites can preserve the flavor and color of the wine by preventing oxidation. Since sulfites produce an environment that is hostile to yeast and deadly to most other microorganisms, when a wine has achieved its desired flavor and aroma, sulfites may be added to stop the fermentation. If wine that has attained a desirable level of sweetness were allowed to continue fermenting, the resulting beverage could be too dry, as the yeast would continue to consume the sugar, possibly to the point of making the wine unpalatable.

It is not known if sulfites are responsible for some people's adverse or allergic responses to wine, most often experienced as headaches or respiratory difficulties. A small number of people are believed to be deficient in the enzyme that breaks down sulfites, and for them, consuming additional sulfites can pose a problem. But sulfites can be found in much higher amounts on dried fruits such as apricots. Sulfites are also sprayed on lettuce and other produce to keep them from turning brown. If a person had sensitivity to these other sulfite-treated products, it is possible that sulfites may cause their headaches. However, if a like response is not experienced with dried fruits or treated lettuce, sulfites may not be the problem.

*The human body produces about one gram of sulfites daily through normal metabolism. Sulfites are also a natural byproduct of the fermentation process.*

The human body naturally produces about a gram of sulfites daily through normal metabolism. For comparison, one Campden tablet, containing about a half gram of metabisulfite, is typically dissolved in one gallon of wine. One gallon of wine equals about five (750 milliliter) bottles. So you can see that the amount of sulfites in a glass of wine would be far less than what would be metabolized naturally by the human body on a daily basis. Even wine that has not been adulterated with added sulfites will contain small amounts of this substance, as it is a naturally occurring part of the fermentation process.

Sulfites can have negative consequences for wine as well. They can reduce the aroma, create "off" tastes, and suppress fruit flavors. White wines contain about twice the amount of sulfites found in red wines, because whites are more prone to oxidation and spoilage. Additionally, cheaper wines may contain more sulfites than more expensive wines.

## What's Behind Those Pesky Red-Wine Headaches?

There are hundreds of compounds in addition to sulfur dioxide in a glass of wine. One of these compounds is amines, which can either constrict or dilate the blood vessels in your body. Histamines dilate the blood vessels, and tyramines constrict the blood vessels. The constriction of blood vessels from tyramines may cause headaches; however, the amounts of amines found in wine may be too small for headaches to result. Tyramines are also present in various aged or preserved foods such as aged cheese, and in chocolate, cola, and beer. Those who respond unfavorably to these products may also experience negative effects from the amines present in wine.

The reason some people react negatively to a glass of wine is still up for speculation. Some say with complete certainty that the problem is pesticides, sulfites, or something in the pigment of red grape skins. Experts, however, are still searching for a conclusive cause.

# FINING AGENTS

Fining agents are additives that are used to remove sediment and unwanted solids from wine. Some of those unwanted substances include tannin, which causes bitterness in wine; proteins, which can cause cloudiness; and other particles that can prevent a wine from clearing.

Fining agents work on the principle that all particles have either a positive or negative electrical charge. A positively charged fining agent can attract negatively charged particles, and a negatively charged fining agent can attract positively charged particles. When finings bind with the tiny particles in wine, their weight increases, and they settle to the bottom in the form of lees. Lees are nothing more than a combination of solid particles in wine that settle, leaving a clear wine free of sediment.

Some common fining agents are egg shells and egg whites; gelatin, which is derived from animal bone, tendons, skin, and connective tissue; casein, which is a protein found in milk; and isinglass, which is made from sturgeon (fish) bladders. If you prefer not to include animal products in your diet, then wine containing most of the above named fining agents would probably be undesirable to you. Store-bought wine is filled with curiosities, and animal-based fining agents are at the top of that list.

Bentonite is a clay fining agent that comes from volcanic ash. Since it is clay, it can be used by vegans. Also known as montmorillonite, smectite, and liquid clay, it is mined in Wyoming, Montana, South Dakota, and Germany. Bentonite is also commonly used to detoxify the human body by adsorbing toxins and delivering mineral nutrients. It's also used in mining as a viscosity and filtration control, and in oil, gas, and water well drilling. It has applications in hazardous waste treatment, cat litter, cosmetics, and pharmaceuticals, as well. Table 2.1 lists common fining agents, identifying their electrical charge, naming their source, and providing explanatory comments.

> Fining agents are used to remove sediment from wine. They can consist of animal-based products such as egg shells, egg whites, and gelatin, or of nonanimal products such as charcoal and clay.

# YEAST NUTRIENT

Yeast nutrient is used in winemaking to ensure active fermentation. This additional yeast fuel gives yeast the best opportunity to work at its full potential and supplements any components that may be lacking in the wine. It is composed of a variety of ingredients, including B-complex vitamins; nitrogen; minerals; diammonium phosphate (DAP), which supplies extra nitrogen; and pasteurized yeast cells. Defatted soy flour may also be used as a yeast nutrient to further encourage fermentation of the wine.

## TABLE 2.1.   COMMON FINING AGENTS

| Fining Agent | Electrical Charge | Source | Comments |
| --- | --- | --- | --- |
| Bentonite | Negative. | Colloid clay. | Bentonite is named after the town of Benton, Montana, where it is mined. Breathing bentonite dust can cause respiratory disease. |
| Casein | Positive. | Protein found in milk. | Cassein is also known as sodium caseinate or potassium caseinate. |
| Egg whites | Positive. | Chicken eggs. | Two or three egg whites can clarify 55 gallons of wine. |
| Gelatin | Positive. | Bones, tendons, skin, and connective tissues of animals. | Gelatin is one of the most powerful animal-based fining agents. |
| Irish moss | Negative. | Common at low tide on all shores of the North Atlantic Ocean. | Irish moss is a red-brown marine algae. It's also used as an emollient and nutritive, and to combat pulmonary and urinary afflictions. |
| Isinglass | Positive. | Sturgeon bladders. | Isinglass is collagen-based. It is also known as "fish glue." |
| Kieselsol | Negative. | Silica gel. | Kieselsol is often used in conjunction with gelatin. |
| Sparkalloid (silica gel) | Positive. | Crystalline silica from the preserved skeletons of marine animals found in dry sea beds. | Also known as calcined diatomaceous earth and siliceous rock, sparkalloid must be filtered out after use. |

## PECTIC ENZYME

Pectin is a carbohydrate that is present in all fruits to varying degrees. Apples, in particular, contain above-average amounts of pectin. Pectic enzyme, which breaks down pectin, is used in winemaking to reduce the naturally occurring pectins in fresh fruit. Although pectins are advantageous in other applications, such as jelly making, they are less desirable in winemaking. Pectin molecules are large, and they can gel in musts and wines, resulting in a hazy beverage. Additionally, because of the larger size of pectin molecules, they tend to clog wine filters more rapidly, resulting in much more effort being expended during filtration. When pectic enzyme is added, the clearing wine develops more compact lees. With the lees separating from the wine more readily, it is easier to extract a clear wine more quickly.

The addition of pectic enzyme during the crushing phase of fruit processing permits a greater abundance of juice to be extracted from each pound of fruit. Wines processed with pectic enzyme may retain a richer color and a finer clarity than wines that are not so treated. Because this enzyme can cause the wine to age more rapidly, pectic-enzyme-treated wine may peak sooner than nontreated wines and would, therefore, have a shorter shelf life.

## ACID

Acid is used to give wine a crisp, slightly tart taste. Acid also retards the growth of potentially harmful microorganisms, and can positively contribute to the creation of complex tastes that occur during aging.

Acid blend—a combination of citric, malic, and tartaric acids—is sometimes used to adjust the acid level in the grapes. Other times, individual acids are used, depending on the desired results. Citric acid, the principal acid in citrus fruits such as lemons, limes, grapefruits, and oranges, is the most widely used winemaking acid. In addition to adding crispness to wine, citric acid is also used to treat fermentation barrels. It is used as an acidifier to lower pH, and in combination with sulfur dioxide, is employed as a rinsing solution to sterilize barrels. Malic acid is the primary acid in apples. It can create an apple taste in the wine, and may cause a secondary fermentation known as malolactic fermentation, both of which may be undesirable. Tartaric acid is the principal acid in grapes, and can contribute to a wine's color and stability. When grapes are used, tartaric acid may be added to reduce the pH level of the juice or wine. One disadvantage of tartaric acid is that it can form undesirable crystals in the wine.

> Acid contributes to a wine's complex flavors. Acid also retards the growth of potentially harmful microorganisms.

Lactic acid and fumaric acid are used less often to adjust the acid level in wines. Lactic acid is found in muscles and in sour milk, while fumaric acid occurs naturally in certain plants and molds. Sorbic acid may be used in winemaking, not to alter the acid in the wine, but to inhibit mold growth and to activate a secondary fermentation, which converts the harsher malic acid into a combination of softer lactic acid and carbon dioxide. If a secondary fermentation continues for too long, this can result in an unpalatably dry wine.

## ACID REDUCERS

Calcium carbonate reduces the excess natural acids in high-acid wines or in the juice prior to or during fermentation. This compound is derived from limestone and is made up of animal shells and bones. A negative side effect of using calcium carbonate is that it can change the flavor of the wine. Because grapes grown in warm weather climates are usually low in acid, carbonates are seldom added to warm climate fruit.

Calcium sulfate (gypsum) is used to lower the pH level in sherry wine. Gypsum is a colorless or white mineral that is also used to make plaster of Paris, chalk, and agricultural fertilizers. Another acid reducer is potassium carbonate, which is also an ingredient in soap. It is often used in combination with potassium bicarbonate to lower wine acid.

## TANNIN

Tannin, a naturally occurring plant chemical, lends wine depth, complexity, and "bite." Too much tannin, though, can cause bitterness.

Tannins are phenol-based plant acids found in the skins, seeds, and stems of fruits. Too little tannin can cause a wine to be weak and bland, while too much of this zesty acid can cause bitterness and excessive astringency. The correct amount of tannin results in wine with structure, depth, complexity, and age-worthiness, as well as "bite."

When grapes are crushed, the naturally occurring tannins are automatically released into the fruit juice. Sometimes crushed fruit is not allowed to be in long-term contact with the tannin-emitting plant parts, so the addition of tannin is necessary. Oak is high in tannin, and when wine is aged in oak barrels, tannin is released into the wine. Many vineyards now use stainless-steel vats for the fermentation and storage of wine, and this reduces some of the occurrence of tannins. Oak chips may be added to those vats to achieve the correct tannin level in the finished product.

## FILTERS

Wine is filtered to remove unwanted microscopic particles. Although filtering results in a clearer finished wine, the process may remove some desirable components, such as color and aroma. And though wine is not a significant source of protein, filtered wines may also be somewhat lower in protein than unfiltered wines. Although filtering the wine may result in an aesthetically pleasing and "clean" wine, it can also render it lifeless, devoid of the vital essences present in yeast, bacteria, and fruit debris.

For depth or sheet filtration, the wine passes through a thick layer of fine material, which traps and removes small particles. Algae-based products, like diatomaceous earth, carrageenan, or agar-agar, are used as filters. Plant-based filters may be made from cellulose powder, or can consist of perlite, which is volcanic glass in pearl-like grains.

For surface or membrane filtration, the wine passes through a thin film of plastic polymer. Sterile filtration uses micropore filters, which are fine enough to remove yeast cells. Filtering out the yeast cells stops the fermentation process. By halting the fermentation process, wines that have attained their desired level of sweetness are not in danger of a revived fermentation, which could result in excessive dryness.

## DECOLORIZING AGENTS

Sometimes oxidation makes the wine turn brownish. To eliminate this unappealing color, commercial wine may be decolorized through the use of activated carbon or polyvinylpolypyrrolidone (PVPP). PVPP (sold as Polyclar) is an adsorbent (a substance that adheres to the surface of solids or liquids), that is insoluble in water. The color-containing residues attach themselves to the PVPP, thus reducing the overall color of the wine.

## DEFOAMING AGENTS

Fermentation produces foaming and frothing. However, commercial winemakers are allowed to add defoamers to their fermenting wine to reduce this action. Defoamers prevent foam from overflowing containers during active fermentation. Approved defoaming agents include polyoxyethelene (40) monostearate, silicon dioxide (an important material in microchip manufacturing), dimethylpolysiloxane, sorbitan monostearate, glyceryl monooleate, and glyceryl dioleate. Unfortunately, these items look like they belong in an ingredients list on a box of overprocessed, artificially colored breakfast cereal—not like components of a fine bottle of wine.

## OTHER WINE INGREDIENTS

A number of other ingredients are allowed to be added to wine. Copper sulfate is a poisonous blue compound used in dyeing and as a fungicide. In winemaking, it is used to remove hydrogen sulfide from the finished wine. Hydrogen sulfide is a compound that produces a rotten-egg smell. The residual level of copper in wine cannot be in excess of 0.5 parts per million (0.5 mg/L).

Dimethyl dicarbonate can be used to sterilize, stabilize, and reduce the alcohol content of wine when the alcohol becomes too strong and overwhelms the flavor of the wine. Ethyl maltol is used to stabilize a wine. A wide variety of enzymes can be added to wine to convert starches into fermentable carbohydrates, to clarify and stabilize wine, to facilitate separation of the juice from the fruit, and to reduce or remove proteins.

Ferrocyanide, a salt that is used to make blue pigments, contains iron and six cyanide groups. In winemaking it is used to remove trace metals and objectionable levels of sulfides. Ferrous sulfate (an iron, oxygen, and sulfur salt) is used to clarify and stabilize wine. It is also used in tanning leather.

About eighty additives may be included in a bottle of wine. Although a few of these additives have been used for centuries to retain a wine's color and freshness,

About eighty additives may be included in a bottle of wine, most of which do not have to be individually listed anywhere on the label.

the overuse of such a multitude of substances has become the norm only in the past fifty years.

## COMPONENTS OF FINISHED WINE

So, when all is said and done, what actually ends up in that bottle of wine you so carefully selected? Finished wine contains ethyl alcohol; sugar; pigments from skins and juice; about a half dozen vitamins, including thiamin, riboflavin, and niacin; fifteen or more minerals; acids; and protein. There is a small amount of solids, including lees, that may or may not be visible, and, unfortunately, there is residue from the chemicals, fining ingredients, and additives that were used in the wine-making process.

Viticulture—the cultivation of grapes for winemaking—seems to be less about tending the vine and more about altering the environment surrounding the vine. Winemaking has fallen victim to mass production, food sterilization, and industrial agriculture. Vintners focus on extending shelf life so that wine can endure all hardships of temperature changes, motion, and exposure to light during transport. In doing so, they have created wines that are stable, yet lifeless.

What are our choices as modern-day consumers? We could avoid indulging in the pleasures of the vine, or we could find a more acceptable alternative—a libation that is not a product of industrial agriculture and carefully balanced chemical additives. One choice we can make is to try organic wine!

# 3

---

# *Organic Wine*

If you shop in the "organic wine" section of your local whole foods or liquor store, you will find many phrases on the beautifully designed wine bottle labels. You may see statements such as, "100-Percent Organic," "Organic," "Made with Organically Grown Grapes," "No Sulfites Added," "No Fining Agents," and "Biodynamically Grown Grapes." Confused? Well, there is quite a disparity in what entitles a bottle of wine to rest on the shelves of an organic wine rack. When you were buying nonorganic wine, you simply went to the bottles that were filled with either red or white wines and selected a product that seemed appealing. Organic wine selection is perhaps a bit less simple.

## WHAT DOES "ORGANIC" MEAN?

If a wine is labeled "organic," it must have 95 percent organic ingredients by weight or volume and no added sulfites. The 5 percent nonorganic ingredients can include nonorganic grapes, nonorganic sugar, or substances like yeast, which has no organic counterpart.

There currently is no commercially available organic yeast. This is the reason that many wines which otherwise would be considered 100-percent organic are not. If winemakers follow all of the other criteria for organic winemaking, and the only nonorganic ingredient is yeast, then technically they are producing a 99.99-percent organic wine. Unfortunately, the current National Organic Program (NOP), which establishes national standards for the production and handling of organically produced products, does not permit this type of labeling. A product that contains a fraction of one percent nonorganic ingredients must be labeled the same as a product containing up to 5 percent nonorganic ingredients.

Wild yeast (which is naturally occurring on the skins of grapes) is organic; however, it is unpredictable as far as fermentation goes. The resulting wine could be unpleasant. In fact, unfavorable wild yeast can completely ruin a batch of wine.

According to federal organic standards, the use of chemically treated materials that come in contact with the soil is prohibited for new installations or replacement purposes. This bars the installation of potentially hazardous creosote-soaked end posts, but not posts already in place at the time of this mandate. Only when those existing treated posts are replaced will they be made of a more suitable and non-soil-contaminating material like redwood, cement, or metal. Until that time, the roots from certified organic wine grapes may be exposed to the dangers and ill effects of soil-leaching creosote.

## WHAT DOES "MADE WITH ORGANICALLY GROWN GRAPES" MEAN?

On a bottle of wine, the label "Made with Organically Grown Grapes" means that the grapes meet organic fruit production standards. This includes the growing of cover crops—crops planted in the fall and then mowed and tilled into the soil the following spring to help control weeds, attract beneficial insects, protect the soil from erosion, and improve the grapes' sugar content by enhancing the vine's water-holding capacity. It also includes crop rotation, the addition of soil nutrients, the combating of insect infestations with beneficial insects, mulching, and hand weeding. If weed or pest control substances are applied, they must meet the criteria of organic crop maintenance. When organic practices are used, the vineyard is work-

## What About 100-Percent Organic Wine?

Organic wine is a tricky little bugger and not so simple to decipher. Only a wine that is labeled "100-percent organic" can be considered completely organic—that is, made from 100-percent organically produced ingredients. The grapes would have to be organically grown, harvested, and processed, and the yeast would have to be wild or natural. There would be no added sulfites, and the amount of detectable, naturally occurring sulfites would not exceed 10 parts per million (ppm). A lab test would have to be done to prove this low level of sulfites before a vintner could apply a label stating that a wine is 100-percent organic. If fining agents were used, these substances, too, would have to be organic.

Unfortunately, at this time, a 100-percent organic commercially made wine does not exist on the shelves. Technically, the addition of commercially produced yeast, for which there is no organic counterpart, precludes a vineyard's wine from truly being considered organic. For vineyards to meet the government standards for labeling organic wine "100-percent organic," they would have to rely upon the wild yeasts on grape skins. Wild yeast could wreak unpredictable havoc on an unsuspecting batch of wine and on a tearful winemaker. So until a vineyard wishes to take the wild yeast risk, or someone devises a reliable organic yeast, the best we will be able to find in the stores is "organic" wine.

ing in harmony with Nature, rather than involving massive doses of agrichemicals. It is a more labor intensive, yet back-to-basics approach to raising crops.

Farm workers who handle organically grown grapes and those folks who reside near the organic vineyard are not exposed to the harmful effects of pesticides and harvest-increasing chemicals. Organic farming practices prevent soil erosion and protect groundwater. The soil may be treated with ground-up fish bones or infusions of plants such as nettles and chamomile. The rows between grapevines may be planted with wildflowers, attracting insects and encouraging local wildlife to graze.

Unfortunately, once the certified-organic grapes have been plucked from their tender vines, other things may be added to make the harvested fruit less wholesome. Wine made from organically grown grapes may contain added sulfites, but not to exceed 100 parts per million. When sulfites are added, the USDA-certified-organic seal cannot be stamped on the wine bottle. Up to 30 percent of the contents of wine labeled "made with organically grown grapes" can be nonorganic. See the inset "Requirements for Organic Wine Label Claims" on page 24 for a summary of the different organic labeling claims. (To learn exactly what nonorganic substances are permitted, visit the National Organic Program website at www. ams.usda.gov/NOP/.)

> Instead of using chemical substances that alter and pollute our air, water, and soil, organic farming works in harmony with Nature.

## WHAT DOES "NO SULFITES ADDED" MEAN?

Remember that sulfites occur naturally through the process of fermentation, and that all wine contains some amount of them. When wine tests at a level of zero sulfites, it merely means that the equipment used today does not detect the very small amounts present in that wine. When a label states "No Sulfites Added," it means that manmade chemical sulfur dioxide has not been added to stabilize and preserve the wine. The only sulfites in that bottle are the ones created naturally through fermentation, and the level should not exceed 10 parts per million.

## WHAT DOES "NO FINING AGENTS ADDED" MEAN?

The statement "No Fining Agents Added" means that the vineyard did not use any agents to remove sediment and help clarify the wine. When fining agents are not used, there is a greater chance that a small amount of solid material will be found within that bottle of wine. One organic wine producer actually acknowledges this in its advertising, letting the consumer know that the possibility exists for a few unexpected "floaties" to appear in the wine. In addition to these wines' including one less unnecessary ingredient, they may be somewhat higher in protein.

The interesting point about the "No Fining Agents" statement is that there is no governing body to verify such a claim. When there is no monitoring system in

# Requirements for Organic Wine Label Claims

## "100% Organic"

The product:    Must contain 100% organically produced ingredients, not counting added water and salt.

The label *must*:

☐ Show below the name and address of the producer, bottler, importer, etc., the statement. "Certified organic by _____" or similar phrase, followed by the name of the Certifying Agent. Certifying Agent seals may not be used to satisfy this requirement.

The label *may show*:

☐ The term "100% organic" to modify the product name.

☐ The term "organic" to identify the organic ingredients. Water and salt included as ingredients must not be identified as organic.

☐ The USDA organic seal and/or certifying agent seal(s).

☐ The certifying agent business/Internet address or telephone number.

## "Organic," or Similar Statement

The product:    Must contain at least 95% organic ingredients, not counting added water and salt.

Must not contain added sulfites.

May contain up to 5% of:

a. nonorganically produced agricultural ingredients that are not commercially available in organic form and/or

b. other substances, including yeast, allowed by 7 CFR 205.605.

The label *must*:

☐ List the organic ingredients as "organic" when other organic labeling is shown. Water and salt included as ingredients must not be identified as organic.

☐ Show below the name and address of the producer, bottler, importer, etc., the statement. "Certified organic by _____" or similar phrase, followed by the name of the Certifying Agent. Certifying Agent seals may not be used to satisfy this requirement.

The label *may show*:

☐ The term "Organic" to modify the product name.

☐ "X% organic" or "X% organic ingredients."

☐ The USDA Organic seal and/or certifying agent seal(s).

☐ The certifying agent business/Internet address or telephone number.

## "Made with Organic Ingredients," or Similar Statement

The product:Must contain at least 70% organic ingredients, not counting added water and salt.

Must not contain added sulfites, though wine may contain added sulfur dioxide in accordance with 7 CFR 205.605.

May contain up to 30% of:

a. nonorganically produced agricultural ingredients that are not commercially available in organic form; and/or

b. other substances, including yeast, allowed by 7 CFR 205.605.

The label must:☐ List the organic ingredients as "Organic" when other organic labeling is shown. Water and salt included as ingredients must not be identified as organic.

☐ Show below the name and address of the producer, bottler, importer, etc., the statement. "Certified organic by _____" or similar phrase, followed by the name of the Certifying Agent. Certifying Agent seals may not be used to satisfy this requirement.

The label may show:☐ The term "Made with organic _____ (specified ingredients or food group)."

☐ "X% organic" or "X% organic ingredients."

☐ The certifying agent seal(s).

☐ The certifying agent business/Internet address or telephone number.

The label must not show: The USDA Organic seal.

## "Some Organic Ingredients"

The product:May contain less than 70% organic ingredients, not counting added water and salt.

May contain more than 30% of:

a. nonorganically produced agricultural ingredients; and/or

b. other substances, without being limited to those in 7 CFR 205.605.

The label must:Show "X% organic ingredients" when organically produced ingredients are identified in the ingredient statement.

The label may show:☐ The organic status of ingredients in the ingredients statement.

The label must not show:☐ Any other reference to organic contents.

☐ The USDA organic seal.

☐ The certifying agent seal.

Reprinted with permission from the NOP.

place, how is the consumer to believe with certainty that these claims are, in fact, true? If a wine were labeled "100-Percent Organic," it would be subject to a lab test to prove the level of naturally occurring sulfites. It would seem only fair that a vintner alleging that fining agents were not added be held to the same standard.

The Alcohol and Tobacco Tax and Trade Bureau (TTB) now regulates wine labeling, which was previously under the jurisdiction of the Bureau of Alcohol, Tobacco, and Firearms (BATF). The TTB states that vineyards are required to maintain records to substantiate their labeling practices. TTB investigators make periodic inspections of winery operations. Although they do collect wine samples for analysis by the TTB laboratory, their lab cannot test for fining agents. For this reason, the TTB relies on the winemaker's required records to determine if fining agents have been used.

Because wine companies do not have to provide proof of their "No Fining Agents" claims, and because they are not accountable to any agency capable of corroborating these claims, it is difficult to believe the "No Fining Agents" statement. The consumer can only hope that vintners are being truthful in this regard.

## WHAT IS BIODYNAMICS?

Biodynamic gardening treats the whole farm like a living organism. Like organic gardening, it uses no herbicides or other chemical substances, but it also involves unique farming techniques intended to work with the rhythms of the Earth.

Biodynamics is a metaphysical approach to agriculture that involves bridging agriculture with a higher spiritual wisdom. This system of farming was introduced in the 1920s by Rudolf Steiner, a highly respected Austrian-born philosopher and scientist. In biodynamic farming there are different considerations for soil preparation and the use of plant-enhancing natural sprays. There are also favorable and unfavorable days for farm activities, including pruning and harvesting, determined by the astrological calendar.

Certified organic farming and biodynamic farming are two separate things. To be certified as biodynamic, a farm must undergo biodynamic stewardship for a minimum of two years. Biodynamic processors and handlers must demonstrate compliance with their respective standards, but for them, the two-year minimum is not required. Demeter, an organization named after the Greek goddess of agriculture, is the international certifying body for biodynamic farming. Demeter believes its standards exceed those of the NOP. Because the USDA does not recognize standards that exceed its own, Demeter has opted out of USDA certification.

The philosophy of Demeter includes managing the whole farm as a living organism and maintaining a healthy, diverse ecosystem. In addition to a farm's supporting a broad ecological perspective, it must also support the cosmic influences and rhythms of which the Earth is a part. The farm must practice nutrient self-sufficiency; maintain balanced soil that possesses a good amount of organic matter, does not contain too much clay or too much sand, and has the ability to hold water; and build soil health through enlivened compost and the stimulation of plant health. Livestock must be integrated, and 80 percent of the livestock feed must come from the farm. The use of genetically modified organisms is prohibited, and the use of irradiation, synthetic fertilizers, insecticides, fungicides, herbicides, and hormones during growing, processing, handling, and storage are prohibited, as well.

## WHO REGULATES ORGANIC WINE?

The National Organic Program is the designated entity that establishes regulations for producing organic wine and for ensuring that the product meets organic standards according to the letter of the law. The NOP is under the jurisdiction of the United States Department of Agriculture (USDA), and took over the process of certification of organic food production from the Bureau of Alcohol, Tobacco, and Firearms (BATF) in 2002. At that time, the BATF retained responsibility for organic wine labeling. Although the terminology used is sometimes confusing, it is mandated in an effort to give consumers the most accurate description of the contents of a bottle of organic or additive-restricted wine without being misleading.

The BATF has since relinquished responsibility for organic labeling claims to the Alcohol and Tobacco Tax Trade Bureau. The TTB is currently in charge of approving the certificates for label approval, and coregulates the organic claims on wine bottles. So although the contents of the product and the organic nature of the product are under the jurisdiction of the NOP, the TTB has control over the actual label. This includes statements pertaining to fining agents; organic and biodynamic claims; and statements that identify the vineyard and winery, the appellation (winegrowing region), the variety, and the vintage. The vintage—the year the wine was produced—may appear only on labels of grape wine, not wine made from other fruits.

There are both private and federal certifiers who verify that vineyards and wineries maintain the organic standard set forth by the NOP. These certifiers—who are credentialed by the USDA—oversee crop production, pest control, and handling of the fruit. Currently, there are fifty-five accredited certifying agents who confirm the organic status of certified organic wine grapes. Some states do not have their own certifiers, and in those cases, certifiers from other states may implement the NOP standards.

As you can see, many different types of wine can be found in the organic section of your local store. Understanding the terminology used to label these wines should help you make a more informed choice when selecting a beverage to meet your personal standards for food quality. But if the available wines are still not as pure and natural as you would like them to be, then turn the page and join me as I enter the world of wild winemaking!

# 4

---

# *Wild Wine*

Wild wine is made with plants that grow naturally without human intervention, including trees, shrubs, and aquatic and herbaceous plants, many of which are viewed as "weeds." A great number of wild edible plants are considered by some to be invasive, marring the human-proclaimed beauty of a manicured lawn or infringing on the border of a lavishly landscaped park. But these are the plants that give substance, character, and uniqueness to our Earth, and ultimately lend the same qualities to our wild wines.

Many wild plants can be transformed into wild wine. Some are less common, while others are easily recognizable to nearly everyone. One such common plant is the lawn groomer's dreaded dandelion. Rather than digging one up for addition to the compost pile, why not harvest the golden yellow flowers and make some blossom wine? Blackberries are another tenacious and sometimes unpopular shrub found across most of the United States. The canes form thick, thorny, impenetrable masses that look less than appealing. But instead of trying to eradicate this robust plant, why not collect its fruit to make blackberry wine and harvest the leaves for tea leaf wine? There are many more distinctly wonderful edible plants that go unnoticed or despised by all but the trained eyes of a forager.

Society seems insistent on shaping the world in which we live by taming or obliterating Nature and replacing it with urbanization. Keeping Nature at arm's length seems to be the goal, rather than immersing ourselves in it, as indigenous peoples and past societies once did. Isn't it possible to allow Nature to thrive as it is intended to do—as it is compelled to do? Why do we continue to force order and structure in the natural world when wonderful and chaotic growth thrives all around us? At least we can pair the tame with the wild so that both the structure of orderliness and the treasures of wildness can grow symbiotically upon the surface of our Earth. Let's embrace this green circle of life and make the most of Nature's gifts. Let's make some wild wine!

## WHY MAKE WILD WINE?

Believe it or not, a bottle of wild wine can cost as little as thirty cents to make!

In addition to helping us live in harmony with Nature by accepting the gift of edible wild plants, making wild wine can be quite economical. The cost of a bottle of homemade wild wine can be as low as thirty cents. I doubt that anyone can truthfully claim to have ever paid such a pittance for a bottle of commercial wine. But inexpensive wine created from foraged wildings can offer a good deal more than financial savings.

Wild wine can be healthy for the body, mind, and spirit. Remember the ingredients allowed in a bottle of store-bought wine as described in Chapter 2? Whether chemicals or nonorganic additives, many of those ingredients are not fit for human consumption, and may present health risks. Some of these substances' physical and mental effects may not even be fully known at this time. Conscientious consumers want food and beverages that are most closely aligned with Nature. Proximity to earthliness equates with enlightenment of self, resulting in an all-encompassing melding of the body, mind, and soul.

Although it may be difficult to see the spiritual aspect of making wild wine, imagine the following. You spend a wonderful day in Nature, breathing fresh, clean air into your lungs. You are warmed by the rays of the sun, and are gently caressed by a soft breeze. Splashes of floral color are everywhere—amidst the ground-loving herbs, on the limbs of spring fruit trees, and dangling from the bushy branches of blossoming shrubs. You are surrounded by soft, green grass. If you gaze up into the satiny blue sky, you can watch the clouds dance to the sweet harmony of Nature's singing, buzzing, and croaking creatures. As you drink in the sights, sounds, fragrances, and sensations of our sweet Mother Earth, you can gather flowers, fruit, leaves, and roots to create your own taste sensation—wild wine!

When you create wild wines, you are making a libation that is wholly without additives and unnecessary ingredients. Your wines can be made without sulfites, fining agents, and other chemicals used to stabilize and preserve the wine. The plants you collect are completely organic—there are no pesticides or wood-preserving chemicals, like those found in creosote-soaked end posts. Because the plants were not treated with pesticides, nor did anyone tend to the plants you collect, there is no danger posed to farm workers and nearby residents through exposure to hazardous chemicals. The groundwater beneath the earth has not been affected by unnatural substances, and the air all around you is without agricultural pollutants.

When you buy nonorganic wine, many people are negatively affected by your purchase. When you buy organic wine, fewer people are negatively affected. But when you make your own wine, no one is negatively affected, and you can create a beverage that is just as wholesome as you want it to be. Beyond this important benefit is the wonderfully wide range of plants from which you can choose. In the store, although some wines are made from fruits such as blueberries, the majority of vintages are derived from grapes. It's true that there are countless types of grapes and blends and levels of sweetness and choices of still wine versus carbonated wine, but they all sprout from primarily one plant—the grape. When making your own wild wine, you can choose from a huge array of plants. You can make wine from fruits, roots, leaves, flowers, shoots, plant spikes, sap, seeds, and bark. You are limited only by your knowledge of edible wild plants and your own imagination.

## FORAGING

Foraging is defined as the search for food or provisions. Most people "forage" at their local grocery store. There is no Zen in that! When you are perusing the aisles of the supermarket, you encounter not one iota of enlightenment. What you find is structure. Products are arranged by food type, by brand, by ethnic distinction, or by an item's need to be refrigerated or frozen. This is quite a cold and generic experience. The true Nature-seeker cannot find any pleasure, balance, or completeness within the confines of a supermarket.

The naturalist seeks out Nature, wherever it may be. The naturalist homes in on the greens and browns of the outdoors and on the varied colors of blooming flowers. Whenever the naturalist is outdoors—which is a good deal of the time—he or she is spotting this or that potential plant for food, for aesthetics, or for knowledge. There are about two hundred wild plants known to me to be edible and growing in the United States. Many of these plants can be fermented into delicious wild wine.

Some of the plants listed in this book have cultivated counterparts, and if you do not relish the thought of foraging, these plants can be purchased in the store. The fruits that can be found both in the wild and in stores include apples, blackberries, blueberries, cherries, cranberries, currants, gooseberries, grapes, plums, raspberries, and strawberries. Wild roots for which you can buy a cultivated counterpart include burdock and carrot. Both of the wild grains—wild oats and wild rice—are also commonly sold in stores. In some cases, the cultivated plant is much like the wild version. In others, differences between wild and cultivated varieties may make it necessary for you to slightly modify the wine recipe to achieve the desired flavor and level of sweetness. The individual descriptions of the plants found in Part Two highlight these similarities and differences, helping to ensure winemaking success.

Although some wild plants can be replaced by their cultivated counterparts, be aware that in other cases, the store-bought version is very different from the wilding. The information provided in Part Two will guide you in modifying recipes as necessary to compensate for these differences.

## WHERE CAN I FIND THE PLANTS?

Wild edible plants grow everywhere, although some plants are more adaptable to certain climates or specific habitats. It's probably best for you to start close to home—in your own backyard or in nearby woods, meadows, valleys, or mountains—to collect the goodness that Mother Earth welcomes us to share. The wild wines you create are limited only by the range of plants growing in your region, your ability to travel to new places where wildings can be found, and your knowledge of which wild plants may or may not be consumed.

As you know, climate varies as you move from one region of the country to another. A few of the plants listed in this book can be more easily found along the Pacific coast, the Rocky Mountains, or east of the Mississippi. Fortunately, though, many of the plants can be found from coast to coast in a wide geographical area.

If you live in a city, you may think you have a limited amount of plants to choose from because nothing much seems to be growing besides concrete. The small patches of noncemented ground may be few and far between. You will be surprised to learn how many plants are growing in the cracks of sidewalks, in open places like softball fields, around lakes or ponds, or just a short drive away. If you have a small plot of land or are a spectator of outdoor sports, you have probably seen dandelions, chickweed, burdock, wild carrot, thistle, clover, daisies, and violets. These plants all have a very wide growing range, and can be found just about anywhere you go.

If you live in the country, or if you can take a short drive to a recreational area such as a forest preserve, bicycle path, camping area, park, or lake, you will probably increase the number of wild edible plants available to you. Trees found in the woods and around forest fringes include wild apple, wild plum, hawthorn, oak, maple, mulberry, and wild cherry. Some shrubs common to the same area include blackberry, elderberry, currant, gooseberry, raspberry, wild rose, and New Jersey tea. You might even stumble upon the wild counterpart of the most well-known wine-making ingredient—the grape. Common wild-growing herbaceous plants include aniseroot, day lily, wild ginger, goldenrod, dead nettles, self-heal, wild strawberry, and wild oats. If you are near water, you might even find cattails or wild rice.

The best way to find plants in Nature is to *be* in Nature. The discussions below will acquaint you with the different habitats Nature provides for wild plants. It's a good idea to become familiar with the terms used to describe these habitats so that when you get to Part Two—which presents foraging information on specific plants—you'll understand where you are most likely to locate each plant in which you're interested.

## Forests

Forested areas include rich woods, deciduous forests, shaded areas, shaded woods, and open woods. *Rich woods* are generally densely populated with trees, and the soil is moist and teeming with underground organisms. It is common to find shade-lov-

> Begin looking for wild plants close to home—in your own backyard or in nearby "wild places" such as woods, meadows, bike trails, and hiking paths.

ing mushrooms in this habitat alongside wild plants that prefer the dampness and darkness of the forest. Most of the trees in a *deciduous forest* lose their leaves during the autumn and winter. These trees include oak, maple, ash, elm, and wild nut trees such as black walnut and hickory. Any woods that have a mat of colorful leaves in October are probably deciduous. *Shaded areas, shaded woods,* and *open woods* are similarly wooded habitats that receive a little more sunlight than rich woods. These are areas where the forest is sparser, and you actually are able to "see the forest through the trees."

Forest fringes and thickets are the areas adjacent to wooded areas. *Forest fringes* include the line of demarcation that separates the rim of the forested area from the more open or grassy area next to it. *Thickets* are made up of smaller trees and shrubs that may bridge the gap between the actual forest and herbaceous plants. This is usually an area that receives partial sunlight during the day, with the shadows of trees casting intermittent darkness over the plants.

*Lowlands* are low-altitude areas that are not much higher than sea level, as well as areas that are lower than adjacent terrain. An area described as *lowland wet forest* is a low-lying forest that receives an accumulation of moisture from rainfall or nearby waterways. Another description of this habitat might be *rich, moist soils.* If the area is located beside the woods rather than within them, it might be referred to as *damp borders.*

*Dry open woods* are arid regions that may be populated more with evergreen trees such as pines than with leaf-bearing trees. These forests often have greater spacing between the trees, which may be interspersed with other deep-rooted plants in search of water, such as sagebrush. The range of this habitat includes parts of the Southwest and the high mountain deserts. When the dry woods make up the side of a mountain or hill, they are called *dry, rocky slopes.*

## Fields and Meadows

*Grassy clearings* are meadowlike areas where you could imagine a great softball game taking place or a group of children playing Ring Around the Rosie while wearing flowers in their hair. These fields of grass receive full sunlight throughout the day. *Sunny borders* are the areas of the meadow that are beside a wooded or shrubby area. A *hillside* could be any part of an open area that is on a slope. *Dry fields* are clearings that are less moist. Some plants thrive in full sunlight and have a lesser need for water than other plants.

## Waterways

Plants that have greater needs for water are usually found near *waterways,* such as lakes and streams, or in valleys and flood plains. *Freshwater marshes* are those areas where there is slow-moving or standing water. In addition to ponds, areas of standing water could include roadside ditches and low areas where water accumulates and is present throughout most of the year.

## Roadsides and Waste Areas

In general, it's best to avoid roadsides when foraging for plants. If you do decide to collect in these areas, stick to seldom-used roads and avoid those plants closest to the pavement.

Two very common places to find wild plants are along roadsides and in waste areas. Since *roadsides* are exposed to toxic substances from the exhaust of cars and other vehicles, the plants that grow along them are generally an unwise choice for transforming into wine. If you are collecting in these areas, it's better to do so on a seldom-used road and to avoid gathering those plants closest to the pavement, as they would have greater exposure to pollutants.

While the term "waste place" sounds unpleasant, it is much the same as cultivated ground. *Waste places* are patches of earth that are a bit scrappy, unused, or abandoned, resembling overgrown vacant lots. They can include places of disturbed ground because wild plants love to establish roots in newly mulched soil. If you are a gardener, I'm sure you have experienced the sprouting of weeds in your newly tilled flower or vegetable beds.

## Less Common Areas

Some of the less common areas where plants can be found are very specific. *Sandy clearings* are open areas of sand, possibly near the ocean. Although *rocky terrain* could apply to many rocky areas across the country, it more often pertains to mountainous rocky areas. If you are near some mountains, you may want to look for plants indigenous to *mountain roadsides*. Areas described as having *poor soil* contain soil that is not black or brown and nutrient-rich with worms, microbes, and beneficial insects. Instead, it is dry, dense, clay-like, and golden or reddish brown. Although uninviting in appearance, this type of soil is home to a number of beautiful, edible native plants.

## Areas to Avoid

Now that you know some of the places to collect wild plants for winemaking, let me share with you those places where wild plants should *not* be collected. Besides avoiding high-traffic areas close to streets and roads, you'll want to stay away from plants found near railroad tracks. In addition to being contaminated with the creosote that leaches out of railroad ties, areas along the tracks are often maintained with chemicals to keep the tracks clear of weeds. Even in your own backyard, there exists the possibility of chemical dangers lurking in the unseen depths of your soil.

Have you ever sprayed a weed control product on your lawn? If you haven't lived in your home for more than three years, do you know if the lawn was treated by the previous owners? What about your neighbors? Do they douse their lawns with petrochemicals, some of which might meander over to your untreated lawn?

Any area that has been or *may* have been treated in any way should not be utilized as a wild plant source. In public places, the general rule is that if an area is people-used, someone has probably maintained it with chemicals for the aesthetic enjoyment of its visitors. If an area is remote or seldom visited by humans, there is less danger of contamination. To be sure, you can contact whomever has jurisdiction over the park or other area in which you are interested, and learn with certainty if people have merely mowed the lawn or if they have abated the weeds —which are often wild edible plants—using nonnatural methods.

Table 4.1 shows general areas where winemaking plants are most likely to be found. Remember that some forest-loving plants are able to grow in open areas or direct sunlight, and some sunlight-loving plants manage to sprout in forests. The table is meant only to guide you to the most *common* habitats of the plants used in wild winemaking. Some plants that are found in both moist and dry areas are listed only under the areas in which they are most often found. An exception is the wild rose, which is listed in both the forest and meadow columns because this plant is so versatile that it grows in a variety of habitats.

## WHEN CAN I FIND THE PLANTS?

Wild edible plants are available throughout the year, although readers who live in milder climates may have a greater selection of plants available in the cold weather months. Most plants can be collected for about a two-month period, starting at the time listed in Table 4.2. This means that if the plant is first found in the spring, it may continue to be found through part of the summer. Some plants have a much longer period of availability, and can be collected continuously for many months once they have been identified.

Wild roses have edible parts available in all four seasons. In the spring, the early growth leaves can be collected to make rose-leaf wine. In the summer, the petals from the flowers can be transformed into rose-petal wine. During the autumn, the rose hips, which are the fruiting body of the wild rose, can be used to make a very good rose-hip wine. And in the winter, the rose hips can still be found clinging tightly to the now-dormant wild rose canes.

When wild fruit is used to make wine, the fruit should be ripe and at its peak of sweetness. Fruits picked past their prime may lack both the moisture and the sugar needed to make a desirable beverage. Plant preparation is easiest when you

Do not collect plants found growing near railroad tracks or on any ground that has been treated with chemicals. Even plants found *near* chemical-doused lawns should be avoided.

Most plants used to make wild wine can be collected for a two-month period. Roots are available for even longer periods of time, starting when the plant's greenery allows it to be identified.

| TABLE 4.1. | WHERE TO LOOK FOR WILD PLANTS | | |
|---|---|---|---|
| **Forest- or Shade-Loving Plants** | Aniseroot<br>Blueberry<br>Currant | Ginger, wild<br>Gooseberry<br>Huckleberry, evergreen | Maple<br>Oak<br>Oregon grape | Rose<br>Salal<br>Violet |
| **Moisture-Loving or Swamp Plants** | Cattail<br>Coltsfoot<br>Cranberry | Japanese knotweed<br>Rice, wild | Salmonberry<br>Silverweed | Thimbleberry<br>Wisteria |
| **Dry-Loving or Arid Plants** | Arrowleaf balsamroot | Chokecherry | Yucca | |
| **Meadow or Sun-Loving Plants** | Apple<br>Black locust<br>Blackberry<br>Burdock<br>California poppy<br>Carrot, wild<br>Cherry, wild<br>Chickweed<br>Clover | Daisy, ox-eye<br>Dandelion<br>Day lily<br>Dead nettles<br>Elderberry<br>Fennel<br>Fireweed<br>Goldenrod<br>Gorse | Grape, wild<br>Hawthorn<br>Huckleberry, red<br>Mulberry<br>New Jersey tea<br>Oat<br>Plum<br>Raspberry | Rose<br>Scotch broom<br>Self-heal<br>Serviceberry<br>Snowbrush<br>Strawberry<br>Sumac<br>Thistle |
| **Plants Found in Other Habitats** | Kinnikinnick—sand | Madrone—hot, rocky slopes | Manzanita—dry, rocky slopes | Mountain ash—rocky slopes |

select fruit that is unblemished and has not been entered by the smaller creatures of our world. Although I have made excellent apple wine using bruised fruits, to do so, I had to painstakingly remove all problem areas.

When making wine with leaves, be sure to collect the earliest, newest growth. Besides the fact that supple green leaves are much more appealing than dry, dull, debris-covered leaves, some wild plants—raspberry plants, for instance—form an unhealthy element in their leaves as they age. Fresh leaves do not contain this harmful substance.

Collect flowers midday when the morning dew has evaporated from their petals. And make sure you collect them on a sunny day—or at least on a day when it has not rained. Moisture on leaves and blossoms makes the accurate measurement of plant matter more difficult, and also renders the plants hard to handle because they tend to stick together. Flowers are best suited for winemaking when they are at their peak of color and fragrance—in full bloom, and gathered before any browning or deterioration is apparent on the petal edges. Be aware that blossoms are delicate and decay more quickly than other plant parts. During the summer months, do not keep them in a hot spot such as a locked vehicle.

If you are collecting roots, there are fewer rules to follow. Even woody, wrinkled, unattractive roots can be made into great wine. In fact, sometimes the most ancient and sad-looking taproots produce the finest beverage. To make at-home preparation a little easier, shake the roots to remove as much earth as possible while still at the collection site.

Edible leaves and roots are most easily identified by their flowers, so if you are new to plant identification, collect plants when they are in bloom to make sure you have found the right plant. When your plant recognition skills improve, you will be able to identify wild edible plants by their overall silhouette, fragrance, height, and leaf shape or vein pattern. As you refine your skills even more, you should be able to identify the brown, lifeless plant matter or the skeletal remains of last year's growth, which is visible throughout the cold weather months. This will aid you in locating wild plant patches for the following year's foraging endeavors.

Table 4.2 shows which plants generally become available during each month of the year. Be aware that because of climate variations, some plants may be available earlier or later in your area. Remember, too, that once a plant pops up, you will have about a two-month window of opportunity. Also, if a plant is found in the mountains at lower elevations, you will quite likely find more of the same plant at a higher elevation in the following weeks. Plants mature first closest to sea level, where it is warmer, and mature upslope later in the season. Finally, note that when plants such as certain roots are available throughout the year, they are listed under the month in which they first become easy to identify through the appearance of the plant's leaves or flowers.

## WHAT PLANTS CAN I USE?

There are so many wild edible plants available that you may wonder why all native food plants are not listed as being transformable into wine. The fact is that not all plants are suitable for winemaking. Some seeds and nuts are edible, but are so high in tannin that they would produce an unpalatable wine. Some wild foods contain bitter components that become less pungent when cooked, but remain unpleasantly apparent in wine. Some plant components can even cause extreme burning of the mouth and throat. And many wild foods make excellent salads and side dishes, but do not produce an enjoyable table wine.

On the other hand, I have been pleasantly surprised by wines made from unlikely sources, such as chickweed. A wild lettucelike plant with very small leaves, chickweed is a main ingredient of wild salads in my house throughout most of the

For best results, collect flowers when they are dry—after the morning dew has evaporated, and only on dry days. Moisture will make the petals stick together and prevent you from accurately measuring the blooms.

Be aware that not all wild edible plants are suitable for winemaking. Some plants are great for cooking or for use in raw salads, but would make an unpalatable wine.

# TABLE 4.2.   WHEN TO LOOK FOR WILD PLANTS

## January

**Maple sap.** Can be collected from January through April.

## February

**Apple blossoms.** Bloom from February through June.

**California poppy flowers.** Bloom from February through September.

**Coltsfoot flowers.** Bloom from February through June.

**Coltsfoot root.** Blooms from February through June; roots can be collected through September.

## March

**Blackberry leaves.** New leaf growth available from March through August.

**Chickweed.** Nearly a year-round plant; start looking for new growth as soon as winter weather clears.

**Oregon grape flowers.** Bloom from March through May.

**Violet flowers (common blue).** Bloom from March through June.

## April

**Aniseroot.** Leaves visible April through October; blooms May through June; roots can be collected year-round if proper identification can be made.

**Arrowleaf balsamroot.** Blooms from April through July; roots can be collected through September once identification is made.

**Dead nettle leaves.** Bloom from April through October.

**Ginger root (wild).** Blooms from April through May; nearly a year-round plant in moderate climates, where it can be found in winter months.

**Hawthorn flowers.** Bloom from April through May.

**Japanese knotweed shoots.** Best collected from April through June.

**Scotch broom flowers.** Bloom from April through June.

**Strawberry leaves.** Bloom from April through June; leaves can be collected earlier if proper identification is made.

**Violet flowers (yellow).** Bloom from April through June.

**Wisteria flowers.** Bloom from April through June.

**Yucca flowers.** Bloom from April through July.

## May

**Black locust flowers.** Bloom in May and June.

**Carrot (wild).** Blooms from May through August.

**Cattail spikes.** Husks appear from May through July.

**Clover flowers.** Bloom from May through October.

**Day lily flower and root.** Blooms from May through July; roots can be collected earlier if proper identification is made.

**Fennel flowers and leaves.** Bloom from May through September; leaves can be collected earlier if proper identification is made.

**Fireweed leaves.** Bloom from May through September; leaves can be collected earlier if proper identification is made.

**Grape leaves (wild).** Available from May through October; early leaves are better. Fruiting is in August and September for easier identification.

**Mulberries.** Fruit from May through July.

**New Jersey tea leaves.** Bloom from May through July; leaves can be collected throughout the growing season if proper identification is made.

**Oak leaves.** Available from May through October; early leaves are better.

**Oats (wild).** Mature in May and June.

**Ox-eye daisies.** Bloom from May through August.

**Rose flowers and leaves (wild).** Bloom from May through August; leaves can be collected earlier if proper identification is made.

**Salmonberries.** Fruit from May through August.

**Self-heal leaves.** Bloom from May through September; leaves can be collected earlier if proper identification is made.

**Silverweed leaves.** Bloom from May through August; leaves can be collected earlier if proper identification is made.

**Snowbrush leaves and flowers.** Bloom from May through August; leaves can be collected year-round if proper identification is made.

**Thistle root.** Leaves visible May through October; blooms from June through September; roots can be collected nearly year-round if proper identification is made.

## June

**Burdock root.** Leaves visible in June; blooms from July to October; roots can be collected until November.

**Cherries (wild mazzard).** Fruit in June and July.

**Dandelion flowers.** Bloom from June through October.

**Elderberry (blue) flowers.** Bloom in June and July.

**Strawberries (wild).** Fruit in June and July.

**Thimbleberries.** Fruit in June and July.

## July

**Blackberries.** Fruit in July and August.

**Blueberries.** Fruit in July and August.

**Currants.** Fruit in July and August.

**Goldenrod flowers.** Bloom from July through September.

**Gooseberries.** Fruit in July and August.

**Huckleberries (evergreen).** Fruit from July through December.

**Huckleberries (red).** Fruit in July and August.

**Madrone bark.** Available year-round, but bark curls from trunk in July, making it accessible.

**Manzanita berries.** Fruit from July through September.

**Oregon grape berries.** Fruit from July through September.

**Raspberries.** Fruit in July and August.

**Serviceberries.** Fruit from July through September.

**Sumac berries.** Fruit from July until the following year's new growth begins.

## August

**Cherries (wild rum).** Fruit in August and September.

**Chokecherries.** Fruit from August through October.

**Cranberries (lowbush/mountain).** Fruit in August and September.

**Elderberries (blue).** Fruit in August and September.

**Grapes (wild).** Fruit in August and September.

**Hawthorn fruit.** Fruit from August through October.

**Kinnikinnick berries.** Fruit from August through October.

**Plums (wild).** Fruit in August and September.

**Rice (wild).** Ripe in August and September.

**Salal fruit.** Fruit in August and September.

## September

**Mountain ash berries.** Fruit in September and October.

## October

**Apples (wild).** Fruit in October and November.

**Cranberries.** Fruit in October.

## November

**Rose hips.** Fruit from November through the winter.

## December

**Gorse flowers.** Bloom nearly year-round. Can be found in the winter months.

year. I once created a rather simple wine from the above-ground plant parts, and when the wine was ready to be bottled, I gave it a try. It was not terrible, but it was unpleasantly green-tasting with lettucelike undertones. Initially, I was going to omit that recipe from this book, but thought I could save the wine and use it for cooking. After letting the wine age for about six months, I went to refill my cooking wine bottle with the chickweed brew, and decided to take a little sip. It turned out that the half year of aging had improved the flavor, and it resumed its status as a fine and interesting table wine. It's all really a matter of trial and error. You'd be surprised by some of the plants that make the most delightful wines, and by the same token, by refreshing fruits that make rather distasteful wines.

One year I tried making blue camass wine from that plant's tasty underground bulb. This was a somewhat daring endeavor into the unknown. The cooked roots are quite enjoyable; however, there is a very apparent mucilaginous quality about them, and I was unsure how that trait would translate into a finished wine. After waiting three weeks for fermentation to cease (which it did not), I strained my mini batch of blue camass wine, and the liquid poured like room-temperature honey—slow and syrupy! Although the taste was quite pleasant, I abandoned that recipe because the consistency was so flawed.

Some wild plants would probably make excellent wine, yet they are not included here due to their scarcity. If plants cannot be found growing in abundance, or if they are considered a rare species, they should not be collected in the large quantities necessary for making wine. Spring beauty and mariposa tulip are two examples of less common perennial plants whose bulbs would both seemingly be excellent winemaking ingredients. Because these flowers grow sparsely, and harvesting the underground plant parts would limit or destroy their ability to reproduce, I have not attempted to transform their bulbs into wine.

## HOW CAN I IDENTIFY THE PLANTS?

The ability to properly identify wild plants begins with an interest in Nature, and is developed through practice and the use of good reference books. Eventually, you will be able to name many plants as soon as they emerge from the ground.

Identifying wild edible plants requires knowledge and practice. The best way to obtain the knowledge is by reading books about wild edible plants. The books in my personal library are listed in the Suggested Reading List in the back of this book. I recommend that you first check out the regional books that are specific to your area of the country. For example, if you reside in Colorado, you will have better luck identifying wild edible plants in your area by referring to *Edible Native Plants of the Rocky Mountains* than you will by using *Edible Wild Plants of Eastern North America*.

Not all of the plants you are looking for will be referenced in a single book. Books with very specific geographical ranges are not all-inclusive, and will not list every plant you are seeking. One reason for this is that plant area ranges are changing all the time. Perhaps at the time of publication, a particular plant was not known to be found in a certain area. It's possible that twenty or thirty years later, that plant has migrated to a new region. Plants also have the ability to adapt, with moisture, sunlight, and climate needs sometimes changing over time. There are a number of general guidebooks that cover much of the United States and provide more coast-to-coast and border-to-border areas of edible plant growth.

As you can see by reviewing the titles in my own personal library collection, I do not rely on one book alone as a guide for identifying wild plants. By cross-referencing a potential edible plant with two or more individual books, not only do I feel more assured that I have identified the correct plant, but I confirm that a particular plant is indeed edible.

Illustrations and photographs depict plants with varying degrees of accuracy, depending on the book you choose. By comparing a number of pictures and photographs, you will have the tools necessary to ensure proper plant identification. After all, each plant possesses its own "essence," or inner spirit that embodies the whole plant and not just the visual components of it.

It is important to compare all facets of a plant, including the leaf shape and pattern; the general plant structure; the color, shape, and size of the flowers; and other characteristics that may not be found in illustrations. Are the stems round or square, hollow or solid? Is the plant shrublike or herbaceous, and does it have a distinctive overall silhouette? Is there a characteristic fragrance or odor? In what habitat and at what time of year does the plant grow or bloom? These are all key points used to identify wild plants.

Over time, you will be able to identify plants with only the slightest hint of their presence. You may catch a glimpse of a fuzzy heart-shaped leaf growing out of the forest floor and know that it is wild ginger, or you may be driving along a West Coast road and see a shrubby fan of yellow flowers and instantly know that plant is Scotch broom. In the spring, you may spot the white blossoms that will become the future fruit of a cherry, apple, or plum tree, and the call of a red-winged blackbird might beckon you to a patch of cattails growing as a border around a hidden pond.

> When identifying plants out in the wild, do not examine just one element, such as the flower. Instead, look at all of the plant's components—the shape and arrangement of the leaves; the color, shape, and size of the flowers; and the structure of the stem. This will help ensure that you collect the right plant.

## HOW SHOULD I COLLECT THE PLANTS?

Now that you know when and where to collect the plants, let's talk about how to collect them. To start, I need to make an important plea. Please do not collect more than a twelfth of any plant growing in a single area. By collecting only a fraction of the available plant material, you will leave enough green life to allow these plants to procreate, and will allow other gatherers, observers, and pleasure-seekers the opportunity to enjoy the same plants. Also try to collect plants at a distance

Do not harvest more than a twelfth of any one plant growing in a single area. Doing so could negatively affect the wildlife that relies on the plant for sustenance.

from designated human access. By removing wild plants from areas less frequented by people, you will not lessen the pleasure of others who enjoy the more traversed paths of Nature.

If you have collected the designated twelfth of plant matter but still need a bit more to satisfy the amount required for your wild wine recipe, broaden your search around the area where the plant was found. By locating a similar habitat, you are bound to find more of the same plant. When you have succeeded in finding what you seek, it will become increasingly clear that the plant is all around you, and not just in that small pocket of earth where you first spotted it growing.

When you venture out into the forest, meadows, mountains, or waterways in search of winemaking plants, there are certain tools you will want to bring with you, depending on the type of plant you will be collecting. It's good to be prepared for an unexpected plant find, as well, as you will sometimes locate plants for which you are not even looking.

Bring a container large enough to hold whatever plant you are seeking. Roots, shoots, flowers, and leaves transport well in grocery bags or baskets. Larger or heavier fruits are best collected in buckets, and berries are best placed in solid, formed, but lightweight containers.

A one-gallon plastic vinegar jug makes a great container when collecting berries. By looping the handle through your belt or fanny pack, you'll leave both hands free to pick the fruit, and the jug's rigid walls will provide protection for the delicate berries.

The ideal collection container for delicate fruits such as berries is a clean one-gallon plastic vinegar jug. Cut a hole opposite the handle near the top, making it big enough to reach your hand inside the bottle. Then loop the handle through a belt or fanny pack so that you have two free hands for berry picking. This is quite handy when you want to hold a branch with one hand and pluck the fruit with the other. If you are concerned about berry juice stains, bring a pair of rubber gloves along. *Never* collect berries in a shopping bag, as they turn into a pulpy mass if not handled properly.

If you are collecting flowers, leaves, or seeds, for the most part, you won't need any tools. Flowers and leaves can be stripped by hand, and seeds can be collected by shaking or pulling. Most shoots can be handled like asparagus: Just snap them off at the base near the ground. Sometimes a pocketknife comes in handy, though.

If you are going after tree fruit such as apples, cherries, or plums, and you'd prefer not to climb the tree to collect your fruit, a fruit picker is a good idea. A fruit picker is a wire cage tipped with clawlike wire grippers. The device attaches to any handle, such as a telescoping pole or the end of a shovel, extending the natural reach of your arms and allowing you to retrieve fruit in the upper branches of the tree. The claw plucks the fruit, which then drops into the wire basket. Your treasured high-limb fruit can then be emptied into your collection container. Fruit picker heads are available at most hardware stores. If you can't locate one, a gardening supply catalog that sells this device is listed in the Resources section of this book. (See page 194.)

A less expensive means of picking hard-to-reach fruit is a limb puller. To make this device, take an old shovel handle, a sturdy dowel, a broken pool cue, or any pole-length piece of wood or metal. Fashion a hook at one end, and use this contraption to pull the fruit-laden branches down to your level so you can pluck the ripe fruit.

To collect roots, you will need either a hand or full-length shovel, or a spade. The hand shovel, which is more convenient because it fits compactly into a backpack or fanny pack, is just fine if you're pushing around loose dirt. If you have to dig a deep root out of compacted soil, though, a full-size tool will be needed.

## WHAT PART OF THE PLANT SHOULD I USE?

Each recipe in this book specifies the plant part needed to make that wild wine. Sometimes, though, multiple plant parts can be used. The leaves, flowers, and fruit (the hips) of the wild rose are all winemaking ingredients, and fennel wine can be made with the flowers and/or the leaves from that plant. Know that when using both leaves and blooms, the flavor and aroma of the flowers is the most potent, so you may want to adjust your recipe accordingly if you are using a proportionately larger amount of blossoms. Aniseroot wine can be made from a combination of the roots and leaves; using more roots will impart more of an earthy undertone, while using more leaves will present a more herblike flavor.

Not all parts of all wild edible plants are edible, so if the recipe doesn't specify that a substitution can be made, do not, on your own, replace one plant part with another. Knowing how to properly prepare wild plants and which plants or plant parts to avoid can spare you the disappointment of a poor-tasting wine or, worse, danger to yourself and others.

Use only the parts of the plants listed in the wild wine recipes. Edible plants sometimes include inedible parts that can ruin the taste of your wine, or even pose a danger to those who drink it.

## HOW SHOULD I PREPARE THE PLANTS?

When you return home from your foraging expedition, only a little more effort will be needed to make your food items "winemaking-ready." Large fruit should be rinsed with a little splash of cold water to remove any debris. Firm fruit such as apples can even be scrubbed with a vegetable brush to eliminate things like cobwebs and dirt. Discard any fruit that is blemished, or cut out the undesirable sections before weighing or measuring your fruit.

When working with fragile fruit, such as thimbleberries, do not use any water at all; doing so would wash all of the fruit, juice, and seeds right through the sieve. Later in the winemaking process, you will be straining your fruit juice, so any minor unwanted materials will ultimately be removed. The recipes in Part Two will alert you to other plants that must be handled with special care.

If you collect the freshest, newest growth of leaves, cleaning should not be necessary. If it is, though, leaves can be shaken, wiped with a dry cloth, or dusted. If you are compelled to give your greenery a rinse, make sure you measure the quantity of leaves needed for the recipe—either by weight or by volume—before you get the leaves wet. Once they are damp, leaves will stick together, which could make accurate measurement impossible.

Roots require a light scrubbing with a vegetable brush to remove the dirt from their skins, as well as a rinse in cold water. Roots do not, however, need to be peeled unless the recipe specifies so. Cut the top of the root where it meets the greenery of the plant, just as you would prepare a carrot. Weigh the roots after they are clean and you have shaken most of the water from them. Then chop, slice, or grate the roots as indicated in the recipe.

*Flowers are delicate and should not be rinsed with water. Just hold your blooms upside-down and give them a little shake to dislodge any hidden insects.*

The fragrance of flowers, petals, and blossoms is fragile, so it is best to avoid wetting or cleaning these plant parts in any way until the soaking process begins. To do so would wash away some of their wonderful aroma. If you pick only clean flowers from clean sites, you should feel fine about using them without washing them first. Most flower heads grow well above the ground, and do not come in contact with ground-borne debris. Some multipetaled flowers like daisies and dandelions are host to blossom-loving insects. In those cases, just turn the flower upside-down after you pick it, and shake the flower until the critters drop out.

Some flower wine recipes instruct you to remove the greenery at the base of the petals before using the blooms. There are two possible reasons for this direction. In some cases, the greenery would make the wine bitterly unpalatable, as is the case with dandelions; in other cases, a blood-thinning substance could form during fermentation of the greenery, as is the case with clover. So even if you think the instructions create unnecessary work, be sure to follow them!

Shoots, such as Japanese knotweed, can be rinsed in water if you desire. I find that because the shoots are the newest growth emerging from the earth, they are generally pretty clean, though, and need no washing. Cattails, which are plant spikes, are enclosed in a corn husk-like sheath, and are naturally protected from dirt and debris. Therefore, they do not have to be washed. Sap (maple) comes from within the tree trunk, and is as pure as water from a spring. If you have tapped a tree using a large-mouthed container, some material may accidentally fall onto the surface of your otherwise clean sap, but straining the sap will remove this material. Madrone bark requires no preparation once it has been rubbed from the tree trunk.

Seeds—wild rice and oats—are covered with a protective sheath, which should be removed before you begin winemaking. Once the chaff has been removed, it may be winnowed from the seeds. This means you are going to separate the scraps of papery covering from the usable seeds. If you pour the combined chaff and seeds from one container to another on a breezy day, the naturally lighter, unwanted debris will blow off on the wind current, leaving you with the naked grain. On a stagnant, windless day, a room fan can be used to accomplish the same task.

## PRESERVING PLANTS FOR FUTURE USE

If you have time to collect wild fruit when it is in season, but you do not have the time needed to start your winemaking immediately after the fruit has been picked, your wildings can be frozen for use later in the year. Always clean, remove blemishes from, and measure the amount of fruit you will need for the recipe before you freeze it. Once fruit has been frozen and defrosted, there will be a marked change in the physical size and condition of your fruit. With berries, the juice may separate from the fruit when it is thawed. If you were to freeze unknown measurements of fruit, and then measure it once it has been thawed, the resulting wine could be out of balance, with too much plant and not enough water. Be aware that the measurements listed in the recipes are for *fresh* fruit.

Another method of preserving your harvest is dehydration. Two wild fruits are particularly good candidates for preservation through drying. Wild grapes can be converted into raisins, and wild plums can be made into prunes. Not only can raisins and prunes be used as primary winemaking ingredient, but they can be added to other wines to lend body and natural yeast to your concoction. The seeds and pits of the fresh fruit need not be removed before drying. Pierce your fresh fruit with a fork to allow air to escape during dehydration. Then place the fruit in a single layer on a cookie sheet in the oven at the lowest temperature, or on the trays of a commercial dehydrator. Dry the fruit for a couple of hours to overnight, depending on its size and water content. Check the fruit's progress every hour or two to determine how close it is to drying. Be aware that if fruit is heated at too high a temperature, the yeast may be destroyed, and the if fruit will no longer be useful for its yeast-bearing properties.

Tea wine—wine made from tea leaf plants, including aniseroot, blackberry, dead nettles, fennel, fireweed, New Jersey tea, rose leaf, self-heal, silverweed, snowbrush, and strawberry leaf—can be prepared with fresh or dried leaves, but not frozen. I much prefer the taste of tea wine made with dried leaves, because dehydration makes the greenery lose its cut-grass flavor and develop a richer and more aromatic quality. To dry leaves, you can lay them in a single layer on a screen—such as an old screen door—and allow the moisture to evaporate naturally. This process will take several days, and sometimes more than a week if the leaves are thick and bulky. You can also dry leaves on a cookie sheet in an oven set at the lowest temperature for an hour or two. Or you can use a stacking electric dehydrator. If you

Freezing and dehydration are good ways to preserve wild plants until you have time to make them into wine.

have chosen to make your tea wine using fresh leaves, multiply the amount of plant matter by four. For example, if one cup of dried plant matter is called for, use four cups of fresh leaves. Dried leaves can be stored in glass jars until ready to use, and will keep for a very long time.

Roots can be either dried or frozen—once again, after they have been cleaned, measured, and sliced, chopped, or grated. Dried roots can be stored in glass jars for extended periods of time. To freeze, place them in freezer bags, being sure to label the bags so that you know both the type of plant frozen and the amount. Once frozen, many foods are impossible to identify.

As already mentioned, most flowers are fragile. Freezing would wilt them and reduce the blooms from their original magnificent flavor and color to withered, brown, odorless vegetation. For this reason, only the heartiest and most fragrant flowers—fennel, snowbrush, clover, goldenrod, and elder—can be preserved, not through freezing, but through dehydration.

Through preservation, plants can be stored in your freezer or in jars until you are ready to convert them into wine. I have made delicious wild wine using plants that have been dried or frozen for *years*. Even though dried plants tend to fade in flavor over time, I have not found that the flavor diminishes. However, to maximize flavor and color, I suggest using your preserved plants within about a year.

Weeds that grow in the cracks of sidewalks, brambles that border forests, and flowers that flourish in grassy meadows can all make their way into your kitchen. By scouring your neighborhood, wading in ponds, frequenting fields, and stalking the darkened forests, you will find many delicious wild wine components. If you are a child of Nature, you will find that you relish the fun of being outdoors collecting wild foods, and enjoy spending a relatively short amount of time converting your plant stuffs into wine.

Voluntary simplicity is the conscious choice to tread softly on this Earth. After all, we are just visitors here, and we are merely tending the land for future generations of people, plants, and animals. Let us choose to live more simply, to enjoy earthly pleasures rather than possessions, and to appreciate the bounty Nature provides us in the supermarket of the natural world.

Now that you know a bit more about foraging and preparing your wild plants, you're ready to learn about the other ingredients that go into wild wine. I think you'll be pleased to discover how few additions are needed to make a libation that is both wholesome and delicious.

# 5

---

# *Wild Wine Ingredients*

More goes into a bottle of wild wine than just wild plants, but the additional ingredients are natural. They are not synthetic components that detract from the wholesomeness of your creation.

You may be wondering why wild wines can't be made with plants alone. The fact is that most wild plants do not contain enough natural sugar, water, yeast (and yeast nutrients), acids, and tannin to create an appealing wine, so these ingredients must be added to achieve the correct strength, body, tartness, and sweetness. The natural grape is a magnificent fruit. It is sweet, it is juicy, and it has just the right amount of acid, body, flavor, and aroma to yield a great wine. Wild edible plants may be superior in one or more of these categories, but the plants are incomplete by comparison. We must add the components they lack.

## WATER

Water is the first ingredient to think about when discussing wild wine additions. Many fruits are juicy, containing their own natural liquid. But other plant parts, such as leaves and roots, are quite dry. Imagine trying to make wine from a carrot without the addition of water—it would be quite a task. So we add water to wild wine to supplement the moisture that may be lacking in wild plants.

Years ago, there would have been no further need for discussion of water, but today, a little more has to be said. A century ago, water would have been retrieved from either a well or a freshwater source; end of story. Today, we have tap water that is enhanced for our safety and health with additives like chlorine and fluoride. Our rivers and streams are far too polluted to drink from as our country's first Americans and American forefathers once did to quench their thirst. So now, supermarket shelves are stocked with numerous types of bottled water that give the illusion that the contents originated in a mountain spring, a mineral source, or an erupting geyser. Water is much more than just water today. How, then, do we sort out which H₂O should or should not be used to make wine?

The simplest and most convenient source of water available to people in developed nations is the faucet. One of the biggest fears of collecting water from the faucet is that of consuming unknown chemicals and inorganic substances. When I lived in Chicago, drinking water was pumped from Lake Michigan. Imagine what is illegally dumped into that body of water, and imagine what leaches into that water from its shores. Despite these potential threats, I have always made my wine from tap water. Did I suffer any ill effects from drinking wine composed in part of Great Lakes water? If so, they have not manifested themselves yet. Was an "off" taste apparent in my finished wine? Not to my knowledge, but I drank Chicago water for nearly forty years, so I was probably quite oblivious to its subtleties.

Tap water can be hard or soft. Hard water contains dissolved salts, such as calcium and magnesium, and has a high pH, meaning that it is alkaline. This does not pose a health risk, but can cause aesthetic problems, such as a bitter alkali taste. Hard water creates buildup of scale on pipes and fixtures, which can lead to lower water pressure and a reduction in the efficiency of your hot-water heater. It also creates buildups of deposits on dishes, utensils, and laundry basins, and slows the ability of soaps and detergents to foam. If your tap water is hard, it can be softened by treating it with lime or by passing it over an ion-exchange resin. Be aware, though, that some of the beneficial minerals are removed through the process, and that softened hard water sometimes tastes saltier than naturally soft water, and will affect the taste of your wine.

**Soft water is preferable for winemaking. Hard water can be softened, but the process sometimes imparts a salty taste that can affect the flavor of the wine.**

Soft water contains little or no dissolved salts. Although desirable for winemaking, soft water has its own pitfalls. It can be acidic and corrosive, and can leach metal—such as copper, lead, iron, manganese, and zinc—from pipes and fixtures, resulting in elevated levels of toxic metals and a metallic or sour taste. It can also cause damage to the pipes and create blue-green staining in sinks and drains.

The United States Environmental Protection Agency (EPA) does not regulate the pH level in drinking water because it's classified as a secondary drinking water contaminant whose impact is considered aesthetic. The EPA does, however, recommend that public drinking water systems maintain a pH between 6.5 and 8.5. If you would like to test your water before you use it for winemaking, you can order a pH testing kit from the supplier listed under "Water Quality" in the Resources section. (See page 201.) This company also sells kits that identify other harmful elements in drinking water, such as lead and copper, should you decide to pursue more in-depth water testing.

If you prefer to avoid tap water, you can use store-bought water to make your wild wine. Of course, you will want to use only plain bottled water—not water that contains flavors, extracts, or essences. It is estimated that about 25 percent of bottled water is derived from municipal water supplies, although it undergoes treatment or filtration before being bottled. If you buy bottled or dispensed water, be certain the flavor is not distasteful to you before you use it for home brewing. Distilled water should not be used, as trace minerals that are needed for yeast growth have been removed.

## SUGAR

Sugar is an interesting and complex ingredient. It can make your wine too sweet, too dry, or absolutely perfect.

Most sugar that is available in supermarkets today was exposed to contaminants during the growing process. Both sugar beet and sugar cane crops are sprayed with a multitude of chemicals and pesticides, just like other nonorganic crops. This is done to increase crop productivity and to eliminate insect pests. Synthetic fertilizers modify and enhance the soil while at the same time reducing the viability of the sugar crop.

Besides adding contaminants to your wine, sugar can decrease the purity of your brew by converting a vegan wine into one that is not. How, exactly, does simple sugar perform this amazing feat? It has to do with the way the sugar is processed. Bone char is often used as a filtering and decolorizing agent in the processing of white sugar. This product comes from cattle bone that has been dried, crushed, and heated to a high temperature. But not all commercial sugar uses bone char. Color and "impurities" may also be removed through use of a granular, activated carbon that is wood-based, coconut-shell-based, or coal-based; or through an ion-exchange system.

The bleaching process, which removes the molasses color and flavor from the sugar, also takes away the healthful minerals and vitamins that are naturally present in unprocessed sugar. In addition to removing the beneficial components of sugar, cane-processing companies may add foreign substances. Granulated sugar may be treated with phosphoric acid, formic acid (a colorless acid found in ants), preservatives, flocculants (substances that separate unwanted particles, which can then be filtered out), surfactants (foam-controlling substances), and viscosity modifiers (substances that adjust the thickness of the sweetener).

So how do you know whether a sugar is heavily processed, and whether it is vegan? If you can find beet sugar, you can feel confident that it at least does not contain bone char, as only cane sugar is processed using bone char. Generic and store-brand sugar producers, however, buy their sugar from many different sources, so there's no way of knowing whether their sugar is vegan at any given time. I wrote

Granulated white sugar has been bleached, which eliminates not only flavor and color, but also healthful vitamins and minerals. In addition, the sugar can be processed with animal products. If you want a purer product, opt for organic sugar.

to the major American sugar corporations, asking how their sugars are refined. Table 5.1 shows the results of my inquiries.

American sugar companies are clearly intertwined. If not completely under a single ownership, they are partly owned by one primary sugar corporation. The future direction of these sugar companies remains unclear. Will the corporations all convert to one form of filtration over the others, or will they continue to process sugar as separate entities? Whether, in the future, you will be able to easily tell if your choice of sweetener is with or without animal products remains to be seen. Until then, if you wish, you can opt to buy a purer form of sugar.

Organic sugar is less processed than granulated white sugar and comes in a variety of forms. Because this product doesn't undergo filtration and decolorization, its color ranges from light brown to tan in color. The darker the sugar, the less altered it is. Aside from gnawing on a raw sugar beet or taking your machete to a tall cane of sugar, the least processed organic sweetener you'll find is Sucanat. It is light brown, and rather than being crystal-like, it looks like small beads of yeast. Turbinado and demerara sugars are tied in second place as being the next least processed. They both bear a closer resemblance to processed sugar than Sucanat does because they are both granulated. Turbinado, sold under the brand name "Sugar in the Raw," is slightly tan, and demerara, which is a popular tea sweetener in England, is slightly yellow.

| TABLE 5.1   PROCESSES USED IN REFINING COMMERCIAL SUGAR | | | | |
|---|---|---|---|---|
| Sugar Company | Bone Char Used | Activated Carbon Used | Ion Exchange Technology Used | Comments |
| C&H Sugar (Crockett, CA) | Yes—made from the bones of non-European cattle. | No. | No. | Florida Crystals acquired C&H Sugar in 2005. Although the sugar product passes through a bone char filter, C&H maintains that there are no animal products in its sugar, and that it is certified kosher. |
| Domino/American Sugar Refining (Yonkers, New York) | Yes. | Yes. | Yes. | All three processes are utilized; therefore any Domino/American brand sugar may or may not be vegan. |
| Florida Crystals (South Bay, Florida) | No. | Yes. | No. | Florida Crystals also owns Refined Sugars, Inc. (Yonkers, NY) and it acquired C&H Sugar in 2005. Florida Crystals also owns 64 percent of Domino/American Sugar Refining. |

The three organic sweeteners may be used interchangeably. Because organic sugar is not pure white, it will impart a darker color to your wine and a slight molasses flavor. These characteristics are most apparent in wine made with Sucanat, the least-processed and most mineral- and color-rich of the organic sweeteners. I make wine with organic sugar—either Sucanat or turbinado—so my finished wine may be a little darker in color than the lighter results you would obtain using refined sugar. I cannot detect much difference in taste between the various sugars, but if you're opposed to the much darker color of the finished wine, you will want to choose your sweetener accordingly. The hearty flavor that Sucanat imparts is not at all unpleasant, although sensitive palates may object to the masking of a plant's natural flavor with the potency of the molasses taste.

> Because organic sugar is not bleached, it will impart a slightly darker color and a hint of molasses flavor to your wine.

It seems almost sacrilegious to venture out into the natural world to collect fine fruits, herbs, and vegetables, and then sweeten the must with what I consider a "dirty" sugar. The wine must be carefully balanced with the most natural sugary goodness available, and organic, less processed sugar is the sweetener most worthy of this honor.

## YEAST

Yeast is the ingredient that gets all of the winemaking action going by consuming sugar and transforming it into carbon dioxide and alcohol. Any yeast can start this process, but wine yeast is best suited to the task. For the home brewer, wine yeast is sold in small packets, each of which can make about five gallons of wine. In my early winemaking days, I used baker's yeast, which is commonly used to leaven bread. Although the wine fermented just fine, it had a heavy yeast flavor, which was less than desirable. The price of wine yeast is under a dollar per packet, and the superior results are worth the few extra pennies.

Wine yeast is sold anywhere winemaking and brewing supplies are sold. This includes natural food stores, some hardware stores, and winemaking supply companies found on the Internet. A website for one such supplier is listed under "Winemaking Supplies" in the Resources section in the back of this book. (See page 197.)

As I mentioned earlier in the book, certified organic yeast is not yet commercially available. To obtain the most natural, albeit unpredictable results, you can whip up a batch of wine using fruits that are likely to have dried yeast on their skins—mainly wild grapes, wild plums, and blueberries. (Some people say that the whitish bloom on the surface of these fruits is actually wild yeast.) If you attempt to ferment wine using these yeast-laden fruits, make sure to add the fruit to water that is no hotter than lukewarm. If the wild yeast is combined with a hot liquid, the yeast will be killed by the heat, and fermentation will not take place. If dried fruits have been heated to high temperatures in the process of dehydration, the wild yeast on those fruits may not have survived that process as well.

Wine yeasts are sold according to the type of wine being made—red, white, or sparkling; Beaujolais, Merlot, or Chardonnay, etc. There is also an all-purpose yeast that is designed for all wine types. I must confess that over the years I have tried many different yeasts and have not found one very different from another. I usually use white wine yeast for white wines, and red wine yeast for red wines, buying whatever is available at my local hardware store. Table 5.2 provides information about a number of available yeasts, and should help you choose the one that's best for your needs.

## DRIED FRUIT

Store-bought dried fruit may have been preserved with sulfites. If you want to avoid this chemical preservative, you can make your own dried fruit by using either an oven or a commercial dehydrator.

Dried fruit is used to add fullness to weak wines. As previously mentioned, dried fruit can also be used for the wild yeast found on their skins. Raisins are the most typical dried fruit added, but you can also use prunes, dried apricots, or other dried fruits. The darker the fruit, the more fullness it contributes to the finished wine. Lighter fruit contributes less body to wine.

Store-bought dried fruit may have sulfites added to prevent browning, so if you wish to avoid sulfites, be sure to read the label. "Organically grown" produce may be organic when it leaves the orchard, yet it can be manipulated with additives post-harvest. To make your own raisins and prunes, just follow the instructions for drying under "Preserving Plants for Future Use" in Chapter 4. (See page 45.) These dried fruits may be used interchangeably in equal weights in any of the wild wine recipes in this book.

## CITRUS FRUIT

Citrus fruits are added to wild wine to improve flavor and to add astringency to plants that are naturally low in acid. Each recipe that calls for citrus fruit lists a specific type of fruit, although you do not have to hold hard and fast to those instructions. I have used lemons, limes, grapefruits, and oranges interchangeably. If I need an orange, but I have a lemon, I will use the lemon but in a lesser amount because it is not as sweet as an orange. If I need a grapefruit but I have an orange, I will use the orange and slightly reduce the quantity of sugar. Winemaking need not be an exact science. Commercial vintners engage in a good deal of blending and adjusting to achieve the results they desire.

Lemons are my citrus fruit of choice, mainly because I nearly always have a lemon in my house. Just as bread and milk are common household staples for some folks, lemons are a household staple for me, and I can grow them myself! I use the

| TABLE 5.2. CHARACTERISTICS OF DIFFERENT TYPES OF YEAST | |
|---|---|
| **Red Wine Yeast** | **Characteristics** |
| Assmanshausen | Ferments slowly, somewhat spicy, intense fruity characteristics. Cold tolerant. |
| Beaujolais | Creates strong fermentation, fruity taste, nice for berries. |
| Cabernet Red | Initiates moderate fermentation, resulting in full-bodied flavor. |
| Flor Sherry | Good for sherry. Has a high alcohol tolerance. |
| Merlot Red | Produces very active fermentation, resulting in dryness. |
| Montrachet | Ferments fast and hot, occasionally "sticks" (stops fermentation). Used for dry red wines with a full-bodied, strong flavor. Does not work well with high levels of sugar. |
| Pasteur Red (also called French Red) | Ferments fast and strong, best for full-bodied red wines with complex aromas. Good for berry wine. |
| **White Wine Yeast** | **Characteristics** |
| Avize | Brings out some of the subtleties of white wine. |
| Champagne | Clean, neutral yeast. Good for champagne and dry wines. |
| Chardonnay | Dry wine yeast. Produces some esters (favorable fragrant compounds) and causes low sulfur dioxide production. |
| Cote des Blanc (also known as Eperney II) | Promotes fruity aroma and does not ferment too dry. Good for fruit wines (nongrape) and blush wines. Slow to medium fermenter, low foaming. Cold tolerant. |
| Pasteur White | Strongly ferments, making a lot of foam and creating a dry flavor. Good for all white wines, including champagne and sparkling wine. Creates a more acid than fruity flavor. Has a high alcohol tolerance. |
| Steinberg | Creates a nice bouquet, complex and fruity. Good for German-style wines. |
| **All-Purpose Yeast** | **Characteristics** |
| Premier Cuvee | Good for sparkling, red, white, and fruity wine. Fast and neutral, good for restarting "stuck" fermentations—fermentations that have started and then stopped. Can be used for champagne. |

Meyer lemon, which is thought to be a cross between a lemon and an orange, and is sweeter and less acidic than other lemons. It can be grown indoors as a house-plant, or outdoors as a small tree in milder climates. As a potted plant, the Meyer lemon tree will remain smaller; if grown outdoors, it can attain a height of eight to twelve feet with a horizontal crown. Check the Resources section under "Citrus Fruit Trees" for more information about the Meyer lemon. (See page 193.) Be aware, though, that you can use any type of lemon you have on hand.

Although each wild wine recipe specifies the type of citrus fruit that should be used, don't be afraid to add whatever you have on hand. Because some citrus fruits are tarter than others, though, you may have to adjust for sweetness, adding more or less citrus juice or sugar according to the fruit being used.

Each of the recipes that uses citrus fruit tells you what parts of the fruit to use and how you should add it to your wine. The colored part of the peel is filled with fragrant, flavorful citrus oils. To best release these oils, the peel can be grated or removed with a paring knife. The white rind just below the oily skin can be quite bitter and really does not make a positive contribution to the finished wine. Remove it if you wish, or just toss it in with the rest of the peel. The juicy "innards" contribute astringency to the wild wine. In some cases, you will be instructed to slice the fruit and add the whole slices to the wild wine—peel, rind, and pulp. Some recipes instruct you to squeeze out the juice and toss in the peels, or to add the juice alone. If you are constrained by time, add the citrus any way you like without changing the amount specified, and I'm sure you will not be disappointed by the results.

## GRAIN

Grain adds body to wine and increases the potency of the finished product. It is added uncooked and becomes damp, swollen, and soft after floating in the must for two weeks.

Wheat berries are used most often in my wild wines, and organic wheat can be purchased at bulk foods stores. Barley, a common ingredient in homemade soups, is sold in supermarkets. Organic barley can be found in bulk at whole foods stores.

Kibbled maize is really nothing more than dried kernels of corn. You can make kibbled maize at home by cutting the kernels from an organic corncob or by buying frozen organic corn kernels and dehydrating them. The dried maize can be stored in Mason jars indefinitely. As an alternative, coarsely ground cornmeal or dry polenta may be substituted in equal weights. The downside of using cornmeal or polenta is that it tends to soak up a bit more liquid than is desirable. The granules act like little corn sponges in the must.

When making wild wines, feel free to substitute foraged grains—wild oats or wild rice—for any grains called for in the recipe. If using wild rice, though, be sure to reduce the specified amount by half.

Two wild grains can be substituted for wheat, barley, or corn. Wild oats can be used interchangeably, measure for measure, in any of the wild wine recipes. Wild rice—which is quite strongly flavored—can be substituted at *half* the amount of grain called for, meaning that if a recipe calls for a cup of kibbled maize, wheat, or barley, you can substitute a half cup of wild rice. If used in larger amounts, the wild rice can overpower the primary plant flavor of the wine.

## TANNIN

Tannin is a natural component found in the seeds, skins, and stems of fruits. Some wild plants, though, are "tannin-challenged." Wine made from these tannin-lacking plants will benefit from this zesty wine component, which adds a pleasant astringency to the brew.

Tannin can be added in the form of raisins or other dried fruit, including apricots, crab apples, black currants, elderberries, figs, oranges, peaches, pears, and plums. It can also be added in the form of high-tannin plant matter such as nuts. Some easy-to-forage nuts high in tannin include acorns (from oak trees), chinquapins, hazelnuts, butternuts, wild pecans, hickory nuts, and black walnuts. Only a small amount of nuts is needed, as there is a fine line between the right amount of tannin and too much. An excess of this substance would make the product too astringent.

The most widely available tannin-bearing plant is the oak tree. As mentioned above, the nut from the oak—the acorn—provides a good means of adding tannin to wine. Oak leaves can also be added to wine for their tannin. Each recipe will instruct you as to what plant additions will give your wine the complexity and "bite" it needs, but if you feel a finished wine needs a bit more tannin, you can add a handful of oak leaves to your next batch.

You can probably see the pattern here—all-natural ingredients, clean water, pure additives, wholesome grains, and wild or home-grown fruits, leaves, and roots make up the contents of a bottle of wild wine. What about sulfites, fining agents, pectic enzymes, acid reducers, filters, decolorizing and defoaming agents, and other substances used in commercial products? I am happy to report that none of these additives is desired or necessary in creating a magnificent wild wine.

You've now learned about the food ingredients that make up homemade wine. In the next chapter, we'll explore the equipment needed to transform our native plants into intoxicating masterpieces.

# 6

—

# *Winemaking*
# *Supplies*

I f you flip through the catalogue of a winemaking supply company, the array of materials available to make wine may seem daunting. True, there are many items and devices sold for this purpose—ranging from testing kits to clearing solutions to all types of additives—but most are not necessary for creating wonderful wild wines. In fact, the goal of wild winemaking is to produce a natural libation whose liveliness is not depleted by the addition of unnatural ingredients.

The supplies you need to make your own wines are simple and few. Here's a list of these basic items presented in the order in which they are used:

- ❏ Large pot
- ❏ Plastic strainer
- ❏ Cheesecloth
- ❏ Large bucket
- ❏ Plastic tubing
- ❏ Suction device
- ❏ Large glass jars or carboy
- ❏ Pantyhose or airlock

- ❏ Long nonreactive spoon
- ❏ Long bottle brush
- ❏ Wine bottles
- ❏ Corks and optional heat shrink caps
- ❏ Extra-large roasting pan or boiling pot
- ❏ Canning lifter or tongs
- ❏ Bottle corker
- ❏ Screwdriver

Most likely, you already own some of the items just listed. If not, in certain cases, you may be able to substitute an item that you *do* have on hand. Many of the remaining supplies can probably be found in hardware stores, thrift shops, and garage sales. And if all else fails, restaurant supply stores and winemaking supply companies will have the equipment you want. Keep in mind that you don't need a matching set of cookware and tools to make wine. Both used and recycled supplies are perfectly suited to creating wild wine, and have the added benefit of being environmentally correct.

Winemaking doesn't have to put a strain on your budget. Don't hesitate to improvise and use items you already own— cooking pots, old condiment jars, and the like—to make your wild wine.

Table 6.1 provides an at-a-glance look at the items you need; lists possible substitutions, if any; and steers you away from tools that should *not* be employed in winemaking. Following the table, you will learn more about each of the supplies you'll be using.

## LARGE POT

A large nonreactive pot, with a 1$^1$/$_2$-gallon minimum capacity, will enable you to heat the typical gallon of water along with any amount of plant material that requires boiling. Good nonreactive cookware includes glass, stainless steel, and enamel-covered metal. (Make sure that the enamel isn't chipped.) Aluminum, copper, iron, and brass do not meet this criterion and should not be used. Reactive pots could interact negatively with the plant acids, resulting in dangerous metals leaching into your wine.

## PLASTIC STRAINER

Once the wild plants have been cooked or soaked in water, you will need to strain out the plant matter. Again, the strainer should be nonreactive. A good choice is a sieve made of plastic. Choose a strainer that is large enough to fit over the opening of your bucket. This will free you to use both your hands to pour the liquid from one container into another without worrying that the strainer might drop into the pail during the process. Two strainers are better than one, especially when working with finely particled plant matter that can easily clog the sieve. Having a second sieve on hand will save you time by allowing you to transfer your material from the clogged strainer to the clean one, rather than constantly stopping to clean your one sieve.

## CHEESECLOTH

After the combined water and plant material has been poured through a strainer, you will want to remove the finer particles from the liquid. To do this, you will restrain the same liquid through cheesecloth—a loosely woven cotton cloth originally designed to strain the curds from the whey in cheese making.

For best results, wet the cheesecloth first and wring out the excess water. Then line your strainer with a single layer of the wet fabric and start filtering. Again, having two straining cloths is better than having just one. Berry skins, in particular, will clog the fibers of your cheesecloth quickly. With two strainers and two pieces of cheesecloth, the liquid can be strained back and forth between the sieves, allowing you to rinse the cloth that is saturated with plant matter.

## TABLE 6.1. WINEMAKING SUPPLIES

| Supply | Substitutions | Do Not Use |
|---|---|---|
| Large pot made of glass or nonreactive metal | None. | Reactive metal pot, such as aluminum, copper, iron, or brass. |
| Plastic strainer | None. | Metal strainer. |
| Cheesecloth | Muslin, jelly bag, cotton bandana, or other natural fabric. | Not applicable. |
| Large bucket made of food-grade plastic with lid | If the bucket does not have a lid, one can be improvised by using a plate that is slightly larger than the diameter of the bucket. | Plastic that is not food grade. |
| Plastic tubing, 5 feet long, preferably in two different sizes ($1/4$ inch and $1/2$ inch) | J-tube. | Not applicable. |
| Bulb syringe, turkey baster, "needle-less" syringe, or other item to initiate suction. | None. | Avoid using your mouth to start suction. Although effective, it can introduce unwanted bacteria into your wine |
| One-gallon glass jars with lids | Smaller pickle jars will work if you can't find gallon-size jars. A carboy— a jar with a narrow opening—can also be used. | Avoid using plastic—it imparts odors and flavors absorbed from its previous contents. Also, clear glass is needed to observe fermentation and clearing. |
| Pantyhose | Tightly woven cloth secured with twine or large rubber bands can substitute for pantyhose. If using a carboy, a specially made airlock would work well. | Anything airtight that will not allow the carbon dioxide gases to escape. |
| Long nonreactive spoon | None. | Reactive metal or wooden spoon. |
| Long bottle brush | None. | Not applicable. |
| Wine bottles | Can be recycled bottles. | Not applicable. |
| Corks (must be new and nontapering) and optional heat shrinks (which also must be new) | None. | Tapered corks cannot be substituted. Wine corks cannot be reused. |
| Extra-large roasting pan or boiling pot | None. | No restriction on metal type for this pot; can be reactive or nonreactive. |
| Canning lifter | Tongs. | Not applicable. |
| Bottle corker | None. | Not applicable. |
| Screwdriver handle | Any object with a similar size and shape. | Hardware end of the screwdriver. |

Although cheesecloth does a good job of straining out plant matter, you can also use another natural material such as muslin, a jelly bag, or a cotton bandana.

## LARGE BUCKET

Having two strainers, two pieces of cheesecloth, and two food-grade buckets will speed the task of straining solid matter from the wild plant liquid.

A large plastic bucket is needed to catch the strained liquid and hold your soaking, heated, or fermenting wild plant liquid. Two buckets are better than one. If you have only one pail, that's fine, as you can always use your nonreactive pot as your second container. If you use a five-gallon commercial bucket, it is vital to ensure that it is food-grade plastic. You do not want to make wine in a container that once housed concrete mix or oil-based paint, as this could taint your finished product. If your bucket has a lid, that's a bonus. If it doesn't, a plate that is slightly larger than the diameter of the bucket can be used to cover the container.

## PLASTIC TUBING

Plastic tubing is needed to siphon your cleared wine from the lees (the wine sediment). Most fully stocked hardware stores have several tubing sizes to choose from at a minimal cost, so it wouldn't hurt to purchase two different sizes—quarter-inch and half-inch. When the lees are firm, cheeselike, and difficult to disturb, it is best to use the larger tubing. But when your wine has loose or floating lees, or you have simply made a smaller batch of wine, the smaller tubing will probably give you better results. Keep in mind that the larger the diameter of the tubing, the faster you can siphon the wine from one container to another. The downside of larger tubing is that its greater suction has a tendency to draw up some of the lees. Buy the tubing in five-foot lengths, as it must be long enough to reach from the inside of one elevated container to a second lowered container.

If possible, buy two sizes of plastic tubing—one that's a quarter-inch in diameter and one that's a half-inch in diameter. You will want to use the larger tubing for firmer lees, and the smaller tubing for loose or floating lees.

The J-tube, available through winemaking suppliers, is made specifically for siphoning wine. It is nothing more than a stiff plastic tube that is turned up at the bottom, suggesting the shape of the letter "J." Because of this turned-up end, you can siphon your wine at a height higher than the lees, reducing the chance of disturbing the lees and siphoning them up along with the liquid. Just keep in mind that J-tubing has a downside, as well. Made of molded plastic, a J-tube is quite stiff, and therefore more difficult to clean than flexible tubing. Because it is stiff, it also takes up a good deal more storage space than flexible tubing, which can be easily coiled and secured with a twist tie. For these reasons, I use flexible tubing in my own winemaking, and I find that it works well.

Regardless of the type of tubing you've chosen, it will have to be sterilized before each use. To do this, dip the tubing briefly in boiling hot water, and remove it with tongs. Make sure that the hot water fills the inside of the tube before you extract it and drain out the water.

# SUCTION DEVICE

When using your tubing to siphon wine from one container to another, you will need a device that creates suction and begins the liquid moving through the tubing. While many home winemakers simply suck on the free end of the tube with their mouth to start the wine flowing, this is not suggested because of the potential for introducing harmful bacteria to the brew. I also don't care for the suction devices sold especially for winemaking. The winemaking-specific tools I have tried were awkward to use, and required two hands to get them to work, which meant that I didn't have a free hand to hold the tubing.

I recommend that you use a bulb syringe sold in drugstores for use on infants; a turkey baster, sold in most supermarkets and household goods stores; or a "needle-less" syringe—the kind you use to refill the ink cartridges of printer and fax machines. Any of these devices can be inserted in the free end of the tube and used to start the wine moving. Once the flow of wine has been initiated, it will continue without further suction.

# LARGE GLASS JARS OR CARBOY

Once the wine has been strained, large glass jars are needed to hold it while it clears. You'll need a combination of glass containers equalling a little more than a gallon in capacity to provide enough "holding room" to clear each batch of wine. If, for instance, you secure a one-gallon glass jar and another glass jar between a pint and a quart in size, you will have what you need.

A one-gallon cider jug or glass jar can hold most of your wine during this phase of winemaking. Restaurants often buy bulk condiments, such as pickles, olives, ketchup, and mustard, in one-gallon jars, and may be willing to donate one to your winemaking endeavors. Glass condiment jars are becoming more rare as restaurateurs become far less willing to part with their "empties," and as packaging goes in the direction of lighter-weight plastic. However, these containers can still occasionally be found in thrift stores and garage sales. You may also want to check out oversized Mason jars, which, during the peak of canning season—from about June through October—become readily available in hardware stores, discount stores, supermarkets, and the like. And, of course, smaller glass condiment jars in one-pint or one-quart sizes can hold any excess wine that does not fit in the one-gallon container. These smaller jars can be secured from your own personal stock of empties. Just be sure to wash them thoroughly in hot, soapy water before use.

If you want to buy the "real McCoy," you can purchase a carboy, which is specifically designed for this purpose. (See Figure 6.1.) A carboy is a glass jug with a nar-

Figure 6.1. A Carboy

It's important to siphon the strained wild plant liquid into a *clear* container. This will allow you to determine when fermentation has stopped, to monitor the wine as it clears, and—ultimately—to siphon the wine without disturbing any remaining lees.

row opening, very similar in shape to the water bottles used in office water coolers. Carboys can be purchased at some hardware stores or wherever winemaking supplies are sold, and are available in half-gallon, one-gallon, two-gallon, and five-gallon sizes. If the carboy that you purchase is a larger capacity than the amount of wine you are making, this is fine, as the airlock system will protect the wine. But this tool—although designed for winemaking—has its negative aspects as well. Because the bottle has a small neck and a tall, wide body, carboys are difficult to clean, and require a long bottle brush plus an array of cleansers. This is why I use large glass jars when making my wild wines.

If you're tempted to use an opaque container for this stage of the winemaking process, realize that the advantages of a clear container are threefold. First, your wine may continue to ferment long past the usual two-week period, and a clear jar is ideal to ensure that fermentation has ceased before bottling begins. Second, during the phase of clarification, you can see what's going on within the jar, and monitor the pace at which your wine is clearing. You will see that the wine clears from the top to the bottom, meaning that the uppermost surface of the wine will appear to be the most transparent, while the wine toward the bottom of the jar will still appear cloudy. Third, when you rack the wine (siphon it) for the final bottling, a clear container will make it easy to see the lees so that you can keep your siphoning tube well above them.

## PANTYHOSE OR AIRLOCK

Believe it or not, pantyhose provide the perfect covering for your fermenting wine by allowing carbon dixoide gases to escape while keeping contaminants from entering the must. As an alternative, use a piece of cloth secured with twine or a large rubber band.

When your wine is left to ferment, you need to place a porous lid over your container to allow the carbon dioxide to escape. At the same time, you need a barrier to keep out fruit flies and other pests. Believe it or not, pantyhose accomplish both tasks—at very little cost. In the directions for the individual wine recipes, when it says to "cover with a porous lid," this means to cover your container with the stocking and loosely set the container's lid (or a slightly larger plate) on top. Do not seal the lid. If it has a snap-on top, do not snap it on. If it has a screw-top lid, do not screw it on. Doing so will prevent the gases from escaping. This will result in a buildup of pressure, and you could have a messy, potentially dangerous explosion on your hands.

To get a dual use from a single pair of pantyhose, cut off the legs of the stockings at about the knee level. Tie knots in the two cut ends of the part of the hose still connected to the panty, and use this part for covering the wider diameter of the bucket. Later in the winemaking instructions, you will be advised to cover your smaller jar opening with a stocking, and the cut-off leg portions will be just the right size to fit over the mouths of one-gallon glass jars. In lieu of pantyhose, you can secure a tightly woven cloth to the open top of the bucket with a large rubber band or twine.

If you are fermenting your wine in a carboy, rather than glass jars, you may want to invest in an airlock, which is specifically designed for this phase of winemaking. An airlock is a plastic or glass arrangement of tubes that fits into a specially designed rubber cork with a hole in the middle of it. (See Figure 6.2.) The cork then fits into the opening of the carboy, preventing unwanted contaminants such as fruit flies, bacteria, and undesirable yeast from getting into the wine, but allowing fermentation gases to escape.

Some people use balloons to allow carbon dioxide to escape while preventing "critters" from getting into the wine. The escaping gases inflate the balloon, which has to be periodically removed to deflate it, and then reaffixed to the jar. Balloons work only on cider jars with narrow openings and on carboys, as most other jars have mouths that are too wide to accommodate the balloon's opening. Although you may want to explore this option, my personal experience has shown that balloons are more trouble than they're worth. Even when tightly attached to the jars, they have a tendency to fly off as the pressure increases. And because the smell and taste of rubber lingers when the balloon is touched, I would not want to prepare a batch of wine that may have been accidentally dusted with the inner balloon powder. If you're looking for a low-cost but effective covering for your glass jar, pantyhose are a far better option.

Figure 6.2. An Airlock

## LONG NONREACTIVE SPOON

A long nonreactive spoon is needed to stir ingredients and dissolve the sugar into the heated water mixture. Because you will be mixing a large amount of liquid and plant matter in a tall bucket, the longer the spoon, the better. Do not use aluminum or copper, as they both are reactive. Although a wooden spoon is nonreactive, the flavor and odor of any other foods you have mixed with the spoon could be imparted to your wine. Imagine how your wine would taste if you stirred the must with a wooden spoon that had absorbed the flavor of onions or garlic. Additionally, the taste of the wood itself can be passed on to the wine. If a woody undertone is present in wine, it should be because you intentionally put it there, not because a pine spoon has imparted a pitch flavor to the brew.

Although glass spoons are sometimes available, and would work well in winemaking, stainless steel is really your best bet. It's nonreactive, durable, and inexpensive. If you don't already own a long-handled stainless steel spoon, check out your local discount or kitchen store, which probably offers suitable serving spoons in various sizes.

## LONG BOTTLE BRUSH

A long bottle brush is needed to thoroughly clean your wine bottles between uses.

Although hot, soapy water and a good shaking will remove the majority of debris within a wine bottle, a brush can do a better job. Sometimes there is a little residue in the bottom of a wine bottle that requires the attention of a bottle brush to coax it out. Bottle brushes can be found in the household section of department and hardware stores.

## WINE BOTTLES

Recycling wine bottles by filling them with your own homemade wild wine would make any environmentalist proud. Have your friends and neighbors save their "empties" for you as a no-cost alternative to purchasing new bottles. In the absence of used bottles, new wine bottles are inexpensive—about a dollar apiece—and are sold at some hardware stores and winemaking suppliers in cases of twelve. Keep in mind that whether you purchase new wine bottles or recycle old ones, you will always have to clean and sterilize them prior to refilling. (More about that later in the chapter.)

The typical wine bottle holds 750 milliliters, although larger bottles (1,500 milliliters) and half bottles (375 milliliters) are also available. You should get four to six glasses of wine from a 750-milliliter bottle. Using a larger bottle might com-

## My First Winemaking Experience

My earliest encounter with winemaking involved a balloon expansion system. After being introduced to winemaking by his young nephew, my dad grew excited at the prospect of making his own homemade wine. This seemed an unlikely endeavor since my parents rarely drank alcohol, and we didn't even own wineglasses.

In empty cider jugs, my father mixed store-bought Concord grape juice with sugar, yeast, and perhaps a bit of water. He then attached large-capacity balloons to the mouth of each jug with sturdy rubber bands. The attic of our suburban brick bungalow was always stiflingly hot in the summers, making the empty space between the rafters and the oak plank floor an excellent climate for fermentation. Those jugs foamed and frothed away, with their colorful balloons expanding to the point where they would pop off the lip of the

jug. Their haphazard flight beneath the wooden beams would make the sound of air being expelled from a giant whoopee cushion. Those balloons were no match for the fermentation forces of Nature, and the smell of fermenting wine permeated the attic for many months.

I don't know what happened to that curious batch of wine. I never saw my parents drink it; it just ceased to exist. It had been in the attic, and then it was no longer there. Perhaps the wine soured or fermented into vinegar as the vulnerable openings of the jugs were exposed to random yeast, bacteria, and rampant fruit flies. As the balloons freed themselves from the mouths of the bottles due to the mounting pressure of escaping gases, the lavender liquid may have fallen victim to any number of winemaking failures. Perhaps the best use for balloons is not as fermentation locks, but as birthday party decorations.

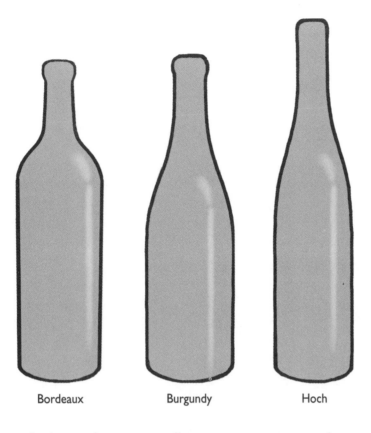

Bordeaux      Burgundy      Hoch

**Figure 6.3. Wine Bottles**

The most common bottle shapes are the Bordeaux bottle with its wide shoulder, the Burgundy bottle with its sloping shoulder, and the Hoch bottle with its more pronounced tapered shoulder.

pel you to drink more than you normally consume or necessitate refrigeration of the unused portion—a practice that could affect the flavor and aroma of the wine.

Red wine is generally sold in green glass bottles, and white wine, in clear glass bottles. Clear bottles are harder to find new, though, so if you're purchasing bottles, you'll probably have to use green glass for both reds and whites.

I asked several vintners why green glass is generally used for red wine, and while the answers varied, in sum, they said that green glass is used to prevent changes in flavor, color, and clarity due to oxidation. Because the answers varied, I wanted to conduct an experiment so I could observe firsthand the changes that occur in a red wine bottled in clear glass. I took a one-year-old huckleberry wine and put half of it in a green bottle in a dark place, and the other half in a clear bottle that was exposed to direct sunlight. After six months, the protected wine was virtually unchanged, but the wine exposed to light had not fared as well. The color had faded appreciably, the aroma had paled, and the wine was thin. It was as if the fullness and liveliness of the wine had evaporated. So my little experiment confirmed all of the vintners' responses.

Wine bottles made of green glass help protect the wine from losing flavor and color to oxidation. To further protect your wild wine, keep the bottles in a cool dark place.

## CORKS

Figure 6.4. A Wine Cork

*New wine corks are a must*—corks cannot be reused. This should not be a problem for even the most frugal of wild winemakers, as the average cork costs ten to fifteen cents. Corks are cylindrical without a tapering end, and an inch and a half long. They must be sterilized prior to use, which may be done by boiling them in the same water in which you sterilize your wine bottles. This process also helps to soften the cork so that it will slide more easily into the mouth of the wine bottle.

Cork comes from the inner layer of bark from a type of oak tree (*Quercus suber*) found mostly in Portugal or Spain. The tree must be at least twenty years old before it can yield a commercial cork. Stripping the bark for cork does not kill the tree, and additional cork can be harvested from the same oak tree every nine years.

## HEAT SHRINK CAPS

Heat shrink caps are cylinder-shaped paper, plastic, or foil caps that fit over the mouth of the bottle after your wine has been corked. They come in a variety of colors, and are a nice, inexpensive way to put the finishing touch on your wild wine creation. After the bottle has been corked, you place the heat shrink cap over the mouth of the bottle. It will be a very loose fit. You then invert the bottle and dip the capped end into boiling water, at which time the heat shrink reduces in size, conforming to the bottle's neck. Heat shrinks make your bottle more visually appealing, and cost only pennies apiece. Their value is purely aesthetic.

## EXTRA-LARGE ROASTING PAN OR BOILING POT

Always sterilize wine bottles and corks before bottling your wild wine. This will eliminate microorganisms such as wild yeast and bacteria, which could ruin your creation.

The large roasting pan or boiling pot differs from the large pot mentioned earlier in that it does not need to be nonreactive. It does, however, need to be very big, with a capacity of several gallons so that you can sterilize several wine bottles at a time, as well as corks. An oblong roasting pan with a two-gallon capacity, or a round boiling pot with a four-gallon capacity, will sterilize three wine bottles at a time.

To sterilize the bottles, fill the extra-large pot with tap water and add the bottles, making sure that each is filled with water to ensure its remaining submerged during sterilization. Cover the pot, and when the water reaches the boiling point, set your timer for fifteen minutes. Remove the bottles one at a time, inverting them to allow excess water to drain out. Fill them with wine while they are still hot.

## CANNING LIFTER OR TONGS

Either a canning lifter or a pair of tongs can be used to safely remove the hot, sterilized bottles and corks from the boiling water. A canning lifter is larger and sturdier than tongs, and fits the contours of the wine bottle a little better, as well. It also better grips the hot, wet bottles, making it a superior tool for the job.

Unfortunately, canning lifters are no longer easy to find in supermarkets and kitchen stores. But as canning becomes a lost art, and supplies for this craft are abandoned, lifters have become more readily available in thrift shops, antique stores, and garage sales—a plus for the frugal winemaker. If you can't find a canning lifter, though, a pair of sturdy tongs will do the job.

## BOTTLE CORKER

The average person is unable to insert a wine cork in a wine bottle without the assistance of a manual corker. At the cost of about twenty dollars, the corker will probably be your biggest investment when making wild wines. Corks are slightly wider than the lip of the wine bottle, so the wet, sterilized cork has to be squeezed to reduce its diameter while the plunger-type handle pushes the cork into the bottle. (See Figure 6.5.) Once you know what a corker looks like, you may be able to spot one secondhand. Otherwise, you will have to reach into your pockets and pay the full price.

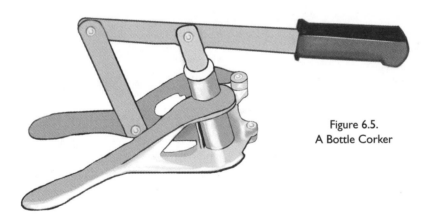

Figure 6.5.
A Bottle Corker

## SCREWDRIVER

Yes, it's true—the handyman's helpful tool is indeed an aid during the last phase of winemaking. Many times, even when the corker is used properly, a short stubble of stubborn cork will remain above the mouth of the bottle. The rounded butt of the screwdriver handle is ideal for pushing the cork down until it is flush with the top of the bottle's neck.

That just about covers the general supplies you will need to begin winemaking. As you can see, the items are quite basic and very inexpensive. With the exception of the plastic tubing, the corks, and the corker, you may already own most of the items that you'll need. In short order, you will have completed your inventory and secured any missing supplies. After venturing out and about, you will also have a basket, bag, or bucket brimming with Nature's good wild plants. Whenever you're ready to transform those wildings into wine, you'll want to turn to the next chapter, where the secrets for making wild wine are revealed.

# 7

## Following the Recipes

Now that you've read all about making wine, you're probably ready to dig in and create some of your own. Good for you! You're almost there. There are just a few more basics you need to learn before you're ready to use the wild plants you've collected.

Although winemaking steps vary slightly depending on the plant used, a basic procedure is followed whenever you create wild wine. In this chapter, you'll begin by learning about the extraction of the plant essence, and move through all the steps, up to and including the bottling and aging of your wine.

### EXTRACTING THE PLANT ESSENCE

In order to get maximum aroma, flavor, and spirit from a plant, you have to extract its essence before turning it into wine. This essence can be drawn out either by introducing the plant to cold water, or introducing it to hot water. Although there are exceptions, cold soaking is generally employed with fruits that contain seeds or pits, as the cold water softens the harsh tannins contained in the seeds. Heat soaking—which either steeps the plant in previously boiled water, or "cooks" the plant over heat for several minutes—is generally used with roots, flowers, and leaves. It is also used with some fruits.

### Cold Soaking

Cold soaking wild plants not only softens harsh tannins, but also extracts flavors and aromas, and adds body to the wine. When cold water is used, the recipe will tell you whether to keep the plant matter whole, or to crush or otherwise process it. Once this is done, combine the plant matter with the water in your bucket, and allow the mixture to soak for one to five days, as directed. Sometimes a recipe will instruct you to work the plant matter with your hands during cold soaking. Additional crushing or squeezing will ensure that you have released all of the plant's flavors and aromas.

Although the plant matter will not be fermenting at this point, you do want to keep away any fruit flies that may be attracted to your mixture. To do this, simply stretch pantyhose or fabric over the bucket opening, fastening with twine if needed, and cover with a plate or a loose-fitting lid. (Do not snap the lid in place; just let it rest on top of the bucket opening.) This will not only discourage unwanted insects, but will also keep away tiny particles of airborne household debris.

At this stage—and at every other stage of winemaking—it is a good idea to label your plant matter. The best way to do this is to write a note for yourself on a piece of masking tape and apply it to the container you are using. For example, if you are supposed to cold soak your plant for forty-eight hours, you may want to write, "Finish soaking on 7/15." This will give you a clear reminder of the day on which the next step of winemaking is expected to begin.

As you complete each step of the winemaking process, remember to label your concoction, clearly stating when the next stage should begin. This will give you an at-a-glance reminder of where your wild plants are in their journey to becoming wine.

## Heat Soaking

Heat soaking is used to extract essences from roots, leaves, flowers, and some fruits. As in cold soaking, each recipe will detail whether the plant matter should be left whole or processed through grating, slicing, or another means. You will then heat soak the plant either by steeping it in boiled water, or by actively boiling or simmering it in the water.

When steeping is used, place the plants in a bucket, pour the boiling water over them, and allow the plants to steep for the recommended amount of time, just as you would let tea leaves steep when brewing a pot of tea. This will release the flavors and aromas of the plant, while preventing undesirable bitter qualities from being liberated.

When boiling is used, combine the plants and cold water in a large nonreactive pot, and bring the mixture to a boil. Then, depending on the recipe, either boil or simmer the plants for the recommended number of minutes. Note that when plants are boiled, it is typical for a good deal of frothy scum to form on the surface of the water. Periodically skim off and discard the scum. If the scum is allowed to remain, or if you boil the plants longer than the stated time, your wine may end up cloudy. Although the mixture will eventually clear, the clearing process may take much longer than usual.

## STRAINING THE PLANT MATTER

After soaking, the plant matter must be strained from the liquid, and the liquid must be transferred to a second food-grade bucket or to your nonreactive pot before other ingredients are added and fermentation begins. Heat-soaked plants are strained while the liquid is still hot so that the sugar will have no trouble dissolving in it. Cold-soaked plants, however, must be heated after straining. This not only enables the sugar to dissolve, but also destroys any bacteria or wild yeasts that could ruin the wine. The liquid that results from brewing tea leaves should be reheated for the same reason.

When straining plant matter such as leaves, a single straining through cheesecloth is suitable for removing the solids from the liquid. When working with plants such as berries, the tiny seeds and plant pulp tend to clog the cheesecloth, so double-straining is used to ensure that all the plant matter has been removed. Pour the liquid and plant matter through an unlined plastic strainer first. Then re-strain by lining your strainer with a single layer of wet cheesecloth, and pouring the liquid through again to remove the finer solids. (Remember, the solids make excellent compost!) Unless the recipe instructs you to do so, do not squeeze or wring out the cheesecloth to extract every drop of liquid. When using certain plants, squeezing the pulp through cheesecloth could result in cloudiness. Just let the juice drain freely with the aid of gravity alone.

When working with fruit such as raspberries and blackberries, your cloth will become clogged, and the liquid will stop passing through. This is when a second strainer and a second piece of cheesecloth come in handy. Cradle the new strainer over your second bucket, and line it with another piece of wet cheesecloth. Then transfer the material into the new strainer. Rinse the old piece of cheesecloth, and keep transferring the material from one cheesecloth-lined strainer to another until all of the liquid has been extracted.

Although you may be tempted to squeeze out every last drop of plant essence from your cheesecloth, don't! Squeezing the pulp through the cloth may result in cloudiness, greatly increasing the time needed to clear the wine.

## ADDING OTHER INGREDIENTS

Ingredients such as grain, dried fruit, and citrus juice and peel are usually added to the strained liquid along with the sugar. If you have heat-soaked the plant matter, add these ingredients before the liquid has completely cooled. If you have cold-soaked the plant matter, do this after the room-temperature liquid has been brought to a boil in your nonreactive pot.

Once your additional ingredients have been poured into the liquid, use your nonreactive spoon to stir the juice until the sugar has dissolved. If the sugar is not thoroughly blended with the liquid, it may settle to the bottom of your vessel, creating a sunken syrup. Rather than working with the wine and enabling fermentation, this overly sweetened bottom layer could end up being discarded with your lees, making the siphoned wine unpalatably dry. So be sure that your sugar has fully dissolved before moving on to the next step of winemaking.

## ADDING THE YEAST

Yeast should be added to the bucket when the liquid is lukewarm. If the liquid is too hot, the yeast will be destroyed and fermentation will not take place. If the liquid is too cool, the yeast will eventually begin to work, but it may be slow to start. When the temperature of the liquid has cooled to slightly warmer than your own body temperature, it is just right for adding the yeast.

The yeast can be floated on top of your warmed liquid; it does not need to be stirred in to start working. At this point, as directed in the recipe, you'll want to add a porous cover to your bucket—pantyhose topped with a loose-fitting lid, for instance—to protect the wine during the next fourteen days of fermentation. Keep your container in a warm, dark place that is not likely to be disturbed during the fermentation period. A quiet, out-of-the-way corner of your kitchen is probably a good spot.

Remember to label your fermentation container with a note indicating the date when fermentation will stop. For example, your tape might read, "Finish fermenting 7/29."

## MONITORING FERMENTATION

Fermentation may occur as a wild frothing of the must, as occasional bubbles rising to the surface and popping, or as almost indiscernible bubbles moving upwards through the liquid. However it occurs, it is a good sign.

Within the first few days of adding the yeast and putting your brew in a warm place, you will observe the initial signs that it is indeed fermenting. Very active fermentation is seen as a bubbling, frothing mass of active liquid, often rising well up the sides of your container. Moderate fermentation is seen as occasional bubbles rising to the surface and popping when they reach the top. Slow fermentation, which can be seen only under close inspection, appears as the tiniest of air bubbles rolling up the inside wall of your container to the surface of the liquid, where they become almost invisible. All types of fermentation, from the most active to the least active, are welcome signs that the winemaking process is proceeding as it should.

During fermentation, you may notice an increase in the fruit fly population in the area around your container. These annoying little creatures are attracted to the smell of the fermentation gases, and will appear out of thin air no matter what type of wine you're making. As long as the nylon stocking is without holes, these little creatures cannot get into your wine vat. Additionally, fruit fly traps, sold at most local hardware stores, can lessen the annoyance of Nature's hovering creatures. A source for this handy contraption is listed in the Resources section at the end of this book. (See page 193.)

Sometimes, the wine does not finish fizzing during the usual fourteen-day period of fermentation. Do not proceed with straining and clearing until the wine has decided it's ready to do so—until the mixture becomes "still." Sometimes the must will take as long as one month to finish fermenting.

## STRAINING THE WINE

Once your mixture has stopped fermenting, you will need to remove as much of the solids as possible to ready your wine for clearing. Remember that wild wine recipes often call for the addition of ingredients such as raisins, citrus peel, and grains before fermentation begins. It is these solids, as well as the dead yeast cells, that you will be removing.

The quickest way to remove this organic material is to line your strainer with wet cheesecloth and pour the whole lot through the lined strainer, into your large glass jar. This activity will stir up the lees (sediment), which means that your strained liquid may look cloudier after you strain it than it was before you strained it. The lees will then settle, returning your wine to the clear libation it is intended to be.

## CLEARING THE WINE

Once your wine has been strained into your clear glass container, cover it with pantyhose or—if you are using a carboy—with an airlock. As long as you are certain that fermentation has ceased, you may screw the lid on the jar. If you are not certain that fermentation has ceased, it's a good idea to merely set the lid on top of the jar or to loosely screw it on with only a partial twist. You don't want to run the risk of the jar's exploding due to a buildup of fermentation gases.

The typical recipe in this book yields about a gallon of wine, so the liquid should fit into a one-gallon jar, leaving almost no dead air space between the surface of the wine and the lid of the jar. This is ideal, because air can be detrimental to your wine. Moreover, the greater the space, the more likely that bacteria, wild yeast, or other unwanted airborne matter will come in contact with your wine, possibly altering flavor, aroma, and composition. If the jar you're using is too large for the amount of wine you're making, leaving a sizable air space, you may choose to fill it with another complementary wine. This process is called "topping off." If you'd prefer not to introduce a new flavor to your wine, you can simply transfer the liquid to smaller jars that can be filled to the brim. Quart-sized Mason jars and clean recycled pickle jars are great for this purpose.

If you've chosen to use a carboy for this stage of the winemaking process, it is best to choose a size that's suitable for the volume of the wine—a one-gallon carboy, in other words. As long as you're using an airlock to seal the carboy, though, even a large air space shouldn't be a problem, because the airlock creates a "closed" system.

Although wine is drinkable any time after fermentation ceases—or even during fermentation, if you so desire—the flavor is best after it has aged a bit. Just as important, wine is much smoother on the tongue and palate after it has been cleared of dead yeast and other tiny particles.

Wine begins to clear as soon as fermentation has ceased, but while some wines start looking pretty good after about two weeks of clearing, other wines remain cloudy for months and months. Squeezing the plant matter during straining, over-boiling roots, using more plant matter than called for in the recipe, or using flowers rich in pollen can slow the clearing process.

During the clearing phase, leave your wine in a dark, undisturbed area for at least six months, and—if you can—for as long as twelve months. Remember to label the container or containers with tape that shows the type of wine you're making, as well as the date the clarification process should be complete. For instance, your masking tape might say something like, "Finish clearing 1/29." During this time, the lees will completely settle, and the wine will clear from top to bottom, meaning that the wine at the top of the containers will appear the least hazy, while the wine at the bottom will remain hazy for a longer period of time.

## RACKING THE WINE

The term *racking* refers to the practice of siphoning the wine off the lees—the sediment—to aid in clarification and stabilization. During the six-to-twelve-month period when the wine is clearing, it is a good practice to rack it at least once every three months. In other words, if clearing takes six months, you would rack it once, three months into the clarification process. If clearing takes longer, you would rack it a second time, six months into the process. Allowing the lees to remain in contact with the clearing wine for too long can result in "off" flavors. Each time you siphon off the cleared wine, you lessen the chance of negative flavor components remaining in contact with your wine. On the downside, the more frequently the wine is racked, the greater the risk of introducing unwanted microorganisms by exposing the wine to air. Wait until the wine looks very clear and there is a defined line of demarcation between the transparent liquid and the settled lees.

The greater the variation in height between the two containers, the greater the flow of siphoned wine will be. The diameter of the tubing used also affects the rate of wine flow. The larger the diameter, the faster the wine will move into the second container.

Your first step in racking the wine is to place the container that is currently holding your brew higher than the container that will be receiving it. For example, you can place the "old" container on your kitchen counter, and the new clean container in the basin of your kitchen sink or on a chair beside the countertop. This will enable the wine to flow freely from the first container to the second.

Your next step is to sterilize your siphoning device by dipping your plastic tubing in boiling water, making sure to fill the inside of the tube with the hot water. This will not only eliminate any unwanted bacteria that may be clinging to the tube, but will also make the tubing more pliable and easy to use. You will also want to sterilize your suction device—your bulb syringe, turkey baster, or needle-less syringe. (See page 61.)

Once the tubing has been sterilized, and while it is still hot, place one end in the wine, holding it above the lees so that they are not drawn into the tubing. As an alternative, use a J-tube, which automatically holds the tip of the tube above the level of the lees. (See the discussion on page 60.)

To create suction, place your suction device in the nonsubmerged end of the tubing, and use it as approriate to start the wine flowing. Once you've generated sufficient suction, place that end of the tube in the empty container, and the wine should begin moving from the higher container into the lower one. (See Figure 7.1.) If you need to stop the flow for any reason, pinch the tubing, bend it in half, or remove the tubing from the liquid in the uppermost container.

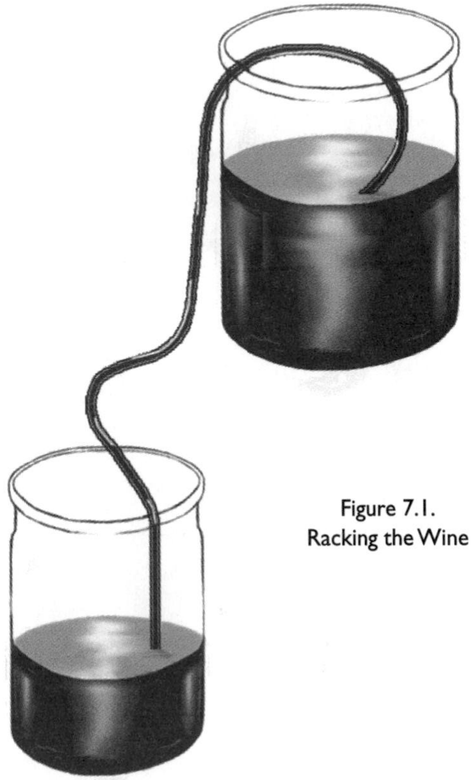

Be aware that you will always lose a little bit of liquid in the siphoning process. Because your tubing must be held above the level of the lees, the shallowest drops of wine will remain unsiphoned. The untransferred amount is usually quite small, though—perhaps a quarter cup to a half cup. If this loss concerns you, try using tubing of smaller diameter. Because narrower tubing creates less suction, there is a lesser chance of the lees being drawn up into the tubing, allowing you to safely siphon out more of the wine. Just keep in mind that the racking process takes more time when narrower tubing is used.

Figure 7.1.
Racking the Wine

Once the racked wine is in the clean glass jar, reapply the nylon stocking and the lid. Once again, do not screw the lid on tightly unless you are absolutely certain that fermentation has completely ceased. It's always better to apply the cap of the jar loosely. Return your wine to a cool, dark place, and leave it alone until the six-to-twelve-month period of time has passed.

## BOTTLING AND CORKING

After your wine has cleared for six months to a year, examine it carefully and conduct a taste test to make sure that it is properly aged, cleared, and ready to be bottled. On rare occasions, you may produce a wine of lesser quality, and decide to discard it. It's far better to determine this now, before you go through the steps of preparing and bottling an undesirable end product. Before you pour your brew down the drain, though, be sure to read the problem-solving discussion on page 80. As you will learn, many disappointing wines can be saved.

When your wine is ready to be bottled, it is imperative to sterilize all the equipment you'll be using, including the siphoning tube, tongs, wine bottles, and corks. Simply fill your extra-large roasting or boiling pot with water and bring it to a boil. First, sterilize the tubing as described on page 60, and dip the tongs into the boiling water. Then immerse the bottles and corks in the water for at least fifteen minutes, working in batches as required by the capacity of your pot.

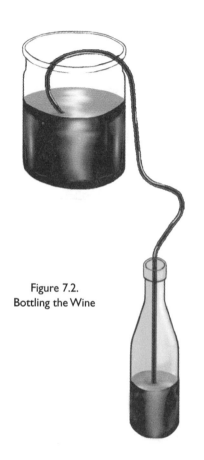

**Figure 7.2.
Bottling the Wine**

When your first batch of bottles and corks has been sterilized, remove one bottle at a time from the hot water and, holding it inverted with the tongs, allow the water to drain out. The bottle does not need to be towel-dried; just make sure that the water has completely dripped out. Place your glass jar of cleared wine in a higher position, such as on the kitchen counter, and your hot, empty wine bottle in a lower position, such as in the basin of the sink. Then place one end of your hot siphoning tube in the wine, create suction in the non-immersed end, and quickly place that end into the empty wine bottle. (See Figure 7.2.) The wine should begin flowing into the waiting bottle.

While you're bottling the wine, you'll have to monitor two things. First, you'll have to watch the large glass jar with the cleared wine, making sure you do not dip the end of your siphoning tube too deeply and disturb the lees that have settled so nicely to the bottom of the jar. (Note that even "cleared" wine will have some lees.) Second, you'll have to watch the level of the wine as it rises in the wine bottle. You want enough wine in the bottle to accommodate the cork, but no more than one inch of air space between the surface of the wine and the bottom of the fully inserted cork. (So if a $1^{3}/_{4}$-inch cork is used, the wine should be poured until it's about $2^{3}/_{4}$ inches below the mouth of the bottle.) The wine will be higher than the shoulder of the bottle and partially within the neck. If the bottle is underfilled, there should be no ill effects, as the bottle will be stored on its side, allowing the wine to keep the cork moist. If the bottle is overfilled, though, the cork will not remain inserted, but will immediately start easing out as steam from the still-hot bottle pushes it upwards. Once the wine has reached the cor-

Don't be tempted to pressure-cook your wine as a means of preserving it. The heat used in pressure cooking will actually cause the alcohol to evaporate, turning your creation into a nonalcoholic beverage. Remember that the alcohol in the wine will act as a natural preservative.

rect level, pinch off or bend the tubing to stop the flow of liquid, and insert the sterilized cork.

Because the cork is wet, it will be more pliable, and will work with the efforts of your wine bottle corker. Place the cork in the corker and squeeze the two handles together to make the cork small enough to fit inside the neck of the wine bottle. Then put the cork over the mouth of the bottle and push the plunger down on the handle of the corker. (See Figure 7.3.) If the top of the inserted cork is not flush with the top of the wine bottle, take the handle of a screwdriver and push the cork down the rest of the way. If the wine level is too high, and the cork starts easing out, remove the cork, empty a small amount of wine from the botttle, and recork it.

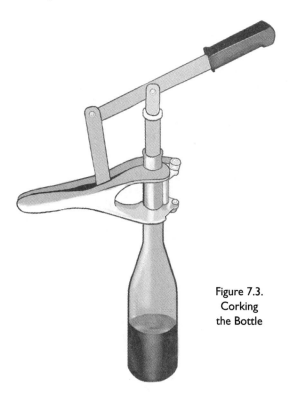

Figure 7.3.
Corking
the Bottle

## FINISHING TOUCHES

If the wine you've made is for your personal enjoyment, you may not want to further embellish the bottles. However, labeling is recommended. Minimally, take a piece of masking tape, record the year and the type of wine you have made, and stick it to the bottom of the bottle. This will enable you to avoid any unpleasant surprises down the road.

If you want to make your bottled wine truly your own—and especially if you intend to give it as a gift—you'll probably want to add some finishing touches. Colored shrink wraps, first discussed on page 66, are always attractive. Simply fit the shrink wrap sleeve over the neck of the wine bottle like a cap, and invert it into boiling water for just a few seconds. It will shrink tightly, conforming to the bottle. You can even choose shrink wraps in colors that complement or match the hue of your wine—blue for blueberry wine, maroon for cranberry wine, and gold for dandelion wine.

Additional labeling and decorative enhancements are limited only by your imagination. I like to tie a color picture of the plant used to create the wine around the neck of the bottle with a color-coordinated satin ribbon. Dried flowers or fruit can also be used to decorate the bottle and indicate the origin of its contents. And, of course, you can easily design beautiful labels on your computer and affix them to the bottles with glue. Your local craft store will provide you with more ideas, as well as a range of materials that you can use to to dress up your wines.

Don't feel pressured to decorate your wine bottles as soon as they've been filled. You can always wait until a gift-giving occasion arises to add a shrink wrap or an attractive label.

## STORING YOUR WINE

Always store your bottled wine on its side to keep the cork moist and prevent it from shrinking. Dry, shrunken corks can allow wine to escape and unwanted microorganisms to enter the bottle.

Once your wine has been bottled, unless you plan to drink it immediately, be certain to store it on its side to keep the corks moist. A cork that remains dry for an extended period of time will shrink, allowing the contents of the bottle to slowly evaporate or fall prey to unwanted bacteria. Be aware, too, that if you keep the bottles upright for some time, and then decide to correctly place them on their side, any cork that's shrunk will not fit snugly within the neck of the bottle, letting your lovely wine seep out over time.

Wine connoisseurs generally advise people to keep wine within a very specific temperature range, but I have not found this to be necessary with wild wine. It's true that I try not to expose my finished wine to extreme shifts in temperature, but with the changing of the seasons, it may enjoy a slightly cooler climate in the winter or endure a warmer one in the summer. I store my wine in green glass bottles on an open, metal wine rack on the north side of my kitchen. This location is farthest from any sources of heat from the fireplace, living room heater, and kitchen stove.

## AGING YOUR WINE

Commercial vintners barrel-age their wines, and the chemical changes that take place in the wine during its contact with the oak continue to age the product even after it has been transferred to other containers. Your wine will be fermented in glass containers, though, so unless you add oak wood chips during fermentation, the aging process may occur more slowly after the wine has been bottled. Nevertheless, it, too, will continue to age after bottling.

Wild wine—and especially root wine—may taste "green" when it is first bottled. This does not mean that the wine tastes leafy or grass-like, but just that it is very new and very raw. You may like your wine just fine at this point, only to be pleasantly surprised by the results of aging months or years later. This is another reason to label your wine with the bottling date. It will enable you to determine when your homemade wine is at its best—suitable for drinking, for gift-giving, or even as an entry in a wine contest. Over time, you will learn how long you want to age each of your favorite wild wines, if at all.

Aged wine has a smoother, richer, more complex flavor than newly made wine. I have aged wild wine for as long as ten years, and have always been pleased by the results.

After wine has aged for a period of time, it will "peak," meaning that it will reach its full potential. It may then begin to diminish in flavor as acidity and astringency fade. I can honestly say that I have enjoyed wild wines as much as ten years after bottling, and have never had one "go bad." Just the same, you want to make sure to enjoy your wild wines while they are in their prime. Don't be afraid to drink them! You can always make more.

# CREATING YOUR OWN WINE RECIPES AND BLENDS

You may wish to try your hand at creating your own wild wine recipes. This can be done either by using a new and different plant, or by blending several finished wines together.

If you decide to make your wine out of a new plant, first try to find a recipe in this book that uses a similar fruit, leaf, or root. For example, let's say that you've picked a quantity of mayapples—a wild plant with a juicy yet pulpy fruit and a strong, tart flavor. Since wild apples are also juicy and pulpy with a strong, tart flavor, I would use the recipe for Wild Apple Wine (see page 86), and substitute the mayapple for the apple. I think mayapples would blend nicely with the raisins called for in the Wild Apple Wine recipe, and that the amount of water and sugar needed would be similar.

When you use a new plant to make a wild wine, try to analyze the flavor of the plant so that you can determine the ancillary ingredients that would best complement it. For instance, if the plant does not seem acidic enough, try adding citrus fruit. If acid is not exactly what the plant is missing, try tossing in a few oak leaves or nuts to increase the tannin and add an astringent "bite." If the plant lacks intensity of flavor and fullness, the addition of dried fruit might solve the problem. If the plant has a thin flavor and aroma, add some grain, slowly increasing the amount until you achieve the flavor and alcohol content you want. (The addition of grain will boost the alcohol content.) If you're not sure which ancillary ingredients would amplify the flavor, body, and aroma of your wine, it's best to make the wine without changing the recipe. Once you have the finished product, you should be able to determine the ingredients that would best improve future batches. (See the discussion on page 80 for help in fixing disappointing wines.)

This is a good time to suggest that when you create your own recipe using a new plant, you make a reduced quantity of wine. Why waste hours of time collecting wild plant matter—not to mention pounds of organic sugar and other ingredients—when the outcome of the process is a mystery? If you quarter the typical wild wine recipe, you will end up with about a quart of finished wine—slightly more than one full bottle. Then, if the wine is not drinkable and you are unable to correct the problem, you will have used only a quarter of the ingredients, as well as far less of your valuable time.

As you create wild wines, you may discover that flavors of certain finished wines combine very well with one another. One of my favorite blends, for instance, is chokecherry wine mixed with wild plum wine. It is perfectly fine to combine wines after they have cleared and are ready to bottle. In fact, this is what commercial wineries do. They sometimes go through a complex system of blending a variety of fruits and/or wines to produce a product that satisfies their standards of

Delicious, beautifully balanced wines can be made by blending two or more different wild wines together. Over the years, you may develop your own signature blend that has just the right levels of sweetness, acidity, and body.

sweetness, acidity, and flavor—and that remains consistent from year to year, regardless of crop variations.

If you are feeling especially daring during a year in which you make multiple types of wine, there's another way to create a totally original wild wine. Start by sterilizing a one-gallon cider jug and its cap or tapered cork. Then every time you have a little leftover wine, or a less-than-perfect wine, pour it into the jug. By the time winemaking season has ended, the combination of all of the wines you have created—wines that individually may have been too sweet, too dry, too strong, or too weak—should make a good quantity of wine that has a pleasing balance of sweetness, acidity, and fullness. If the end result is satisfactory, go ahead and bottle it, and don't forget to add a label that identifies the blend.

## SOLVING PROBLEM OUTCOMES

Through the process of making many batches of wine, you will no doubt experience many successes. You will also likely be disappointed by the occasional failure. I can honestly say, though, that only rarely have I needed to pour a batch of wine down the drain. This is because in most cases, steps can be taken to correct any problem.

## What if Your Wine Turns Into Vinegar?

It's certainly no fun to discover that your carefully nurtured wild wine has turned into vinegar, but occasionally this does happen to the wild winemaker. If and when it happens to you, there's no need to fret, because there are a number of fine uses for homemade vinegar.

As mentioned on page 82, the vinegar can be saved and simply used in recipes calling for vinegar—salad dressings, sauces, etc. Keep the large bottle of vinegar in your basement or some other out-of-the-way place, and refill your kitchen vinegar bottle as needed. You couldn't ask for a purer product.

If you preserve food by pickling, your homemade vinegar can be used for home brining. Just make sure to test the acidity level of the vinegar to ensure that it meets the criteria established by the United States Department of Agriculture.

An interesting and refreshing beverage can be made by combining equal amounts of vinegar and sugar, and then diluting with water to taste. This concoction is quite a bit like freshly squeezed lemonade, minus the pulp.

Vinegar makes a great all-natural glass cleaner. Fill a spray bottle with the product and use it to clean your windows and mirrors.

Finally, if you've made a light-colored batch of vinegar, consider using it as a hair rinse. To prevent your hair from having a vinegary smell, heat your vinegar to the boiling point, take it off the heat, and add a generous bunch of your favorite fresh or dried herbs. (French tarragon is my favorite.) Allow this to soak overnight, strain out the herbs, and pour the scented vinegar into bottles for hair-care use. The vinegar will strip off any soapy residue or shampoo buildup, leaving your hair shiny, clean, and healthy.

| TABLE 7.1 TROUBLESHOOTING CHART | | |
|---|---|---|
| **Problem** | **Cause** | **Solution** |
| Exploding wine bottle or popped cork | Wine is fermenting in a corked and sealed bottle—carbon dioxide is continuing to form, yet it cannot escape. | Clean up the mess, reopen all bottles from that batch of wine, and pour the wine into a clean glass jar covered with pantyhose and loose-fitting lid. When fermentation has truly ceased, rebottle in sterilized bottles using new sterilized corks. Or refrigerate the wine to slow the process of fermentation, and drink your sparkling wine as soon as possible. |
| Wine is too dry | Not enough sugar was used or a secondary fermentation has taken place. | Combine wine with another wine that is too sweet or make sugar syrup by combining one part sugar with three parts heated water, and add to overly dry wine. Make note on recipe to increase amount of sugar. |
| Wine is too sweet | Too much sugar was used. | Combine with another wine that is too dry. Make note on recipe to decrease amount of sugar. |
| Fermentation will not start | Too much sugar was used, or not enough yeast nutrient was used, or temperature of must was too hot or too cold. | Dilute must with water, or add handful of wheat berries, or heat a cup of must to lukewarm and add new yeast. If must begins to ferment, add yeast/warm must back into liquid to ferment. If needed, place must in warm spot to allow yeast to start working. |
| Wine has turned to vinegar | Acetic bacteria has entered wine. | There is no way to correct this problem. Make use of the vinegar you have created. (See page 80.) |
| Wine will not clear | Plant matter was boiled too long, or foam was not removed from boiling water, or plant matter was squeezed during straining, or flower pollen is slowing clarification. | Time will clear the wine, but it may take longer than expected. Make note on recipe to reduce amount of time plant matter is boiled, to be certain to skim froth during boiling, and to avoid squeezing plant matter during straining. |
| Wine has too much acid | Natural acid in plant was high or too much citrus was used. | Add sugar syrup to wine. If this does not correct acid balance, combine wine with a too-little-acid wine. Make note on recipe to reduce amount of citrus added. |
| Wine has too little acid | Natural acid in plant was low or too little citrus was used. | Add strained citrus juice to wine to achieve desired acid balance or combine with a too-much-acid wine. Make note on recipe to increase amount of citrus added. |
| Wine is too strong | Too much grain was used. | Dilute with water and add sugar syrup or combine with a too-weak wine. Make note on recipe to decrease amount of grain. |
| Wine is too weak | Not enough grain was used. | Combine with a too-strong wine and increase amount of grain on recipe. |
| Wine is lacking body or fullness | Not enough dried fruit was used. | Combine with a full-bodied wine and increase amount of dried fruit in recipe. |

Table 7.1 provides solutions for wines that are too dry or too sweet, wines that have failed to clear, and other unsatisfactory results. As you'll learn, by combining several different wines, adding ingredients such as sugar syrup or citrus juice to your brew, or making other adjustments, you can often turn an undrinkable wine into a delicious libation.

In commercial wine-making, malolactic fermentation is sometimes intentionally used to create rounder, softer-tasting wine.

A fairly common mistake of the home winemaker is to bottle wine prematurely, before it has finished fermenting. Similar to this is the problem of malolactic fermentation (fermentation caused by lactic acid bacteria), which causes the wine to undergo a secondary fermentation after it has been bottled. Regardless of the reason for the in-bottle fermentation, the resulting gases will have nowhere to go, and can result in a forceful expulsion of the cork or, worse, an exploding bottle.

To avoid in-bottle fermentation, always wait at least six months before bottling your wine. Then keep your eye on your creation. If the wine is being properly stored on its side, and fermentation has continued or restarted, the mounting pressure inside the bottle will cause a few droplets of wine to leak out around the edges of cork. At the same time, tiny bubbles of carbon dioxide will be seen within the bottle. Don't wait for the bottles to explode or pop their corks on their own! Instead, open all the bottles, dump the contents into a clean glass jar, and allow fermentation to be completed before again bottling the wine. Or, if you prefer, refrigerate any unopened bottles to slow fermentation, and consume as soon as possible. You may be wonderfully surprised by the delicious sparkling wine you have created!

Of course, not every bottle of wine can be saved—at least, not as a wine. Sometimes, despite your efforts to prevent unwanted microorganisms from entering the wine mixture, bacteria will turn your creation into vinegar. While this is certainly disappointing, there's no need to throw your gallon or so of brew out the window. Instead, you can simply use it to sauté mushrooms or to stand in for store-bought vinegar in salad dressings and such. The inset on page 80 provides more creative ways to use that unintentional gallon of homemade vinegar.

Over the past two decades or so, I have probably made every winemaking mistake possible, and I am embarrassed to admit I have made some blunders more than once. These flawed results, although frustrating, have led me to perfect the wild wines that I create and relish today. You, too, can embrace any "surprise" results as a learning experience, and constantly improve your winemaking abilities.

If you have finished reading Part One, you know how to forage for wild plants; process the plants you collect; set up a winemaking "kitchen" of pots, jars, and other supplies; choose appropriate ancillary ingredients; and complete the winemaking process. All you need now are the recipes. Part Two provides detailed instructions that will allow you to take your wildings and transform them into terrific wild wine.

# PART TWO

---

# The Recipes

Welcome to the wild winemaking recipes! I hope that the road here has been an eye-opening and enlightening journey. Remember that although the instructions for each recipe may vary slightly, very detailed instructions for each step of winemaking can be found in Chapter 7, "Following the Recipes." There is also a handy Glossary in the back of this book (see page 189), which can refresh your memory regarding any terminology that has been introduced in the pages of this book.

Wild plants grow in various habitats and at different times of the year. To make your collection less difficult, in the pages that follow, I have listed where and when each plant can be found, have guided you in collecting edible plant matter, and have stated the plant's botanical name. Hopefully, this brief synopsis will prevent you from trying to find plants that are not indigenous to your geographical location, or from trying to harvest a plant in the spring when it will not be ready for collection until autumn. As mentioned earlier in the book (see page 40), it is extremely important to use detailed plant identification books to ensure that you are collecting the correct plant. The botanical plant name is the only way to do this with certainty, as the common name used on the West Coast may be quite different from that used on the East Coast.

Not all wild plants are suited to the taste buds of all people. If you attempt a wild wine and find it to be unpalatable, perhaps you could try making your next wine with a plant that is more familiar to you. If you find a wine to be too sweet or too dry, next time adjust the sugar so that the sweetness is more to your liking. These recipes have been created to my liking, which may be very different from your own. After trying any new recipe, you may decide to omit or add certain ingredients when making future batches.

Just remember that in many recipes, some ingredients are necessary to add acid, tannin, water, or other important components to the wine. Nevertheless, the possibilities for your own creations are limitless!

The wines are divided into five sections based upon the part of the plant that is used. We move from recipes for fruit wine, to root wine, flower wine, leaf wine, and wine made from other plant parts.

The recipe for each individual plant entry is prefaced by special collection instructions, as well as cautions about thorns or other concerns, when applicable. You will also learn specific techniques that can make plant retrieval easier. This information is followed by detailed recipe instructions for making wild wine with that plant.

In some cases, you may choose to prepare your wine with produce purchased at a fruit stand or supermarket, rather than plants gathered in the wild. While you can certainly make delicious wine with cultivated plants, be aware that the recipes presented in Part Two were created specifically for wild plants, which in many cases are different from their cultivated counterparts. Wild cherries, for instance, have a distinctive taste that is quite different from that of cultivated cherries, while wild strawberries are actually sweeter than supermarket strawberries. This is not meant to discourage you from creating wine with purchased produce, but to make you aware that should you choose to use cultivated plants, you will have to experiment, adjusting sweetness and tartness as needed until you get the results you want. In those cases in which the cultivated plant is very different from or very similar to the wild plant, I have noted this in the wild plant collection tip.

While we're on the subject of wild plants versus cultivated plants, I'd like to explain why in the following chapters, the headings that begin the discussion of each plant sometimes include the word "wild" (as in "Wild Apple") and sometimes don't (as in "Gooseberry"). The plants without the "wild" designation do not have cultivated counterparts. For this reason, you will never have to wonder whether to use wild gooseberries or cultivated gooseberries; cultivated gooseberries are simply not available. On the other hand, the plants described as "wild" do indeed have cultivated cousins, so I have included the wild designation to eliminate any possible confusion regarding which plant I'm recommending for use in the recipe.

If you do decide to make your wines truly "wild" by foraging for your plants, your efforts will be lavishly rewarded. You can collect dandelions in the spring, and a year later when the golden petals again splash color on your lawn, you can enjoy a fine glass of long-awaited dandelion wine! The beautiful blackberries collected amidst the briars on a hot summer day will become the sweetest, richest nectar imaginable. The leaves from tea plants can be enjoyed as a refreshment on a slow-moving summer's day. Apple wine can be mulled and sipped in winter while enjoying the warm, glowing flames dancing within a cozy fireplace. All of this satisfying pleasure can begin right here. Just turn the page to begin your wild winemaking adventure!

# 8

## Fruit Wines

The most commonly known and accepted winemaking plant part is fleshy fruit, and many wild fruits have cultivated counterparts that can be purchased in stores. So if you like the idea of making your own wine, but not the foraging part where you have to venture out and collect the raw materials, this is a good place for you to begin. Produce found at your local grocers can be substituted for the wild fruit in many of the following fruit wine recipes, including apples, blackberries, blueberries, cherries, cranberries, grapes, plums, raspberries, and strawberries. Just remember that the fruit you get in the supermarket has been cultivated to increase its size, color, etc., and both looks and tastes somewhat different from its wild counterparts. For that reason, you will probably have to experiment to get the results you want, adjusting the levels of sweetness and tartness as desired.

## Wild Apple

**When to Collect.** October and November.

**Where to Collect.** Forest fringes and grassy clearings throughout most of the United States.

**Wine Color.** Cider-colored.

**Wine Flavor.** Sweet and smooth.

**Wine Aroma.** Fruity.

### Wild Plant Collection Tip

Wild Apple

The quality and size of wild apples varies greatly from tree to tree. Although any *Malus* species can be collected for this recipe, the best results are achieved with apples that are both tart and sweet. Varieties of apples from different trees can be blended for this wine to achieve the right balance of tanginess and sweetness. Look for fruit that has unblemished skins and, of course, is worm-free.

The red and/or green fruit can be identified by its apple aroma or by cutting a cross-section to observe the five-point-star seed pattern. The apples will range from shooter-marble-sized to store-bought-apple-sized, and are ripe when you see an abundance of fallen fruit beneath the tree. Sometimes, fruit that is not yet ripe will fall from the branches due to weather or disease. If you cut into one of these fruits and find green seeds, the apples are not yet ripe and should not be used.

Fallen fruit that has not been lying on the ground for any length of time is fine to collect, and hanging fruit can be plucked from the lower, easy-to-reach branches. If you are physically able and willing to climb an apple tree, you may do so and loosen the fruits by shaking the limbs from your perch. Crabapples are a fine substitute for wild apples in this recipe, although they contain less natural sweetness so that a larger amount of sugar may be needed to produce a palatable wine. The seeds of all apples contain cyanide-producing compounds, and should not be eaten or used in your wine. This is also true for cultivated apples found at the grocers.

Can you use cultivated apples to make apple wine? Of course you can. Just keep in mind that wild apples are tarter than their cultivated cousins, so you'll want to reduce the amount of sugar when substituting cultivated fruit.

## WILD APPLE WINE

6 pounds unpeeled wild apples,
wiped clean of debris

1 gallon cold water

8 cups sugar

3 cups raisins

¼ teaspoon wine yeast

1. Grate the apples using a cheese grater or finely chop the fruit with a kitchen knife, and place in a large food-grade bucket. Pour the cold water over the grated wild apples, cover with a porous lid, and allow to soak for forty-eight hours, periodically stirring the fruit with a long nonreactive spoon.

2. Strain the liquid, first through a strainer and then through cheesecloth, into a large nonreactive pot. Bring the liquid to a boil, reduce the heat to low, and let simmer for five minutes. Skim off any scum that rises to the surface.

3. Return the heated juice to the bucket and add the sugar and raisins, stirring until the sugar is dissolved. When cooled to lukewarm, sprinkle the yeast on top. Cover the bucket with a nylon stocking and a loose-fitting lid, and allow to ferment for at least fourteen days.

4. Strain the liquid into a clean glass container and cover as appropriate. (See page 73.) In six to twelve months, the wine will be ready for bottling. During this time frame the wine will be clearing, and should be siphoned from the lees into another clean glass jar about once every three months. When sufficiently clear, the wine may be siphoned into sterilized wine bottles and corked. Enjoy immediately, or store your wine on its side for later consumption.

# *Blackberry*

**When to Collect.** July and August.

**Where to Collect.** Fields and clearings throughout most of the United States.

**Wine Color.** Deep purple with red undertones.

**Wine Flavor.** Full and fruity.

**Wine Aroma.** Fruity.

## Wild Plant Collection Tip

Wild blackberries (*Rubus allegheniensis*) are shiny, dark-purple, seedy fruits that grow in clusters, which can be easily separated from their prickly canes. Blackberry brambles can attain a height of eight feet, and the thorns are pointed downward. Usually the fruit is pretty easy to reach, although sometimes blackberry masses must be wrestled to get to the luscious fruits. Because these plants are relentlessly thorny and the juice will temporarily stain your fingers and clothes dark purple, wear something tattered that you don't mind tearing or staining, and use rubber gloves if you want to reduce the discoloration of your hands.

Blackberry

If you are not "wild" about the idea of foraging for berries, but still want to make your own fruit wine, you'll be happy to know that cultivated blackberries are not all that different in flavor from their wild counterpart. For this reason, you should feel free to use the wild blackberry's cultivated cousin to make this deliciously fruity wine.

## WILD BLACKBERRY WINE

4½ pounds (about 16 cups) blackberries,
rinsed with cold water

1 gallon boiling water

8 cups sugar

¼ teaspoon wine yeast

1. In a large food-grade bucket, crush the fruit with your hands or a potato masher to break the berries. Pour the boiling water over the fruit, and while the pulp is still hot, strain it first through a colander and then through cheesecloth.

2. Return the heated liquid to the bucket and add the sugar. Using a long nonreactive spoon, stir until the sugar is dissolved.

3. When the mixture has cooled to lukewarm, sprinkle the yeast on top. Cover the bucket with a nylon stocking and a loose-fitting lid, and allow to ferment for at least fourteen days.

4. Strain the liquid into a clean glass container and cover as appropriate. (See page 73.) In six to twelve months, the wine will be ready for bottling. During this time frame the wine will be clearing, and should be siphoned from the lees into another clean glass jar about once every three months. When sufficiently clear, the wine may be siphoned into sterilized wine bottles and corked. Enjoy immediately, or store your wine on its side for later consumption.

# *Wild Blueberry*

Wild Blueberry

**When to Collect.** July and August.

**Where to Collect.** Wet or dry areas including sandy soil throughout most of the United States.

**Wine Color.** Rich purple.

**Wine Flavor.** Mild and fruity.

**Wine Aroma.** Full-bodied and fruity.

## Wild Plant Collection Tip

Wild blueberries (*Vaccinium augustifolium* and various related *Vaccinium* species) grow as thornless shrubs up to fifteen feet tall. When berries are fully ripe, they are about one-half inch in diameter and dark blue with a whitish bloom on them. The fruits contain numerous small, soft seeds, and the berries will easily separate from their stems into your collection container. Cultivated blueberries may be substituted for wild blueberries in this recipe.

## WILD BLUEBERRY WINE

4½ pounds (about 16 cups) wild blueberries,
rinsed with cold water

1 gallon boiling water

8 cups sugar

¼ teaspoon wine yeast

1. In a large food-grade bucket, crush the fruit with your hands or a potato masher. Add the boiling water and stir with a long nonreactive spoon to extract the maximum amount of juice.

2. While the liquid is still hot, strain it through cheesecloth into a large nonreactive pot. Reheat the juice and allow it to simmer for two minutes; then remove from the heat immediately.

3. Return the liquid to the bucket and add the sugar, stirring until the sugar is dissolved.

4. When the mixture has cooled to lukewarm, sprinkle the yeast on top. Cover with a nylon stocking and a loose-fitting lid, and allow to ferment for at least fourteen days.

5. Strain the liquid into a clean glass container and cover as appropriate. (See page 73.) In six to twelve months, the wine will be ready for bottling. During this time frame the wine will be clearing, and should be siphoned from the lees into another clean glass jar about once every three months. When sufficiently clear, the wine may be siphoned into sterilized wine bottles and corked. Enjoy immediately, or store your wine on its side for later consumption.

# Wild Cherry

Mazzard Cherry

**When to Collect.** June and July for mazzard cherry; August and September for rum cherry.

**Where to Collect.** Clearings and forest fringes. Rum cherry grows in the eastern half of the United States; mazzard cherry grows on the northwest coast.

**Wine Color.** Deep maroon.

**Wine Flavor.** Fruity and reminiscent of the flavor of old-time cherry cough syrup.

**Wine Aroma.** Sweet and full.

## Wild Plant Collection Tip

The rum cherry (*Prunus serotina*) is also known as the black cherry because it is so deeply maroon in color that it is nearly black. Each fruit contains one round, slightly flattened pit that is almost as large as the pea-sized fruit. These trees bear their fruit in *racemes:* fruiting clusters on which individual fruits are connected to a common central stem by smaller stalks—much like the strands of a mop are connected to the handle—with each stalk bearing one piece of fruit. These cherries can be easily tickled from their branches by stripping them with a cupped hand. This fruit stains the fingers brown (although it washes off over time), so you may wish to don a pair of rubber gloves during collection. The rum cherry is a naturally sweet fruit and has been used to flavor cherry cough syrup.

The mazzard cherry (*Prunus avium*) is a cultivated variety of cherry that is grown in the western states, and often transplants itself in open areas, resulting in a West Coast version of the wild cherry. The fruit ripens earlier than the rum cherry, and grows as a slightly larger solitary cherry, rather than in racemes like its eastern counterpart. The fruit is also sweet and deeply maroon when ripe. It easily separates from the branches of the tree, and can be used interchangeably with the wild cherry discussed above.

If you choose to buy cherries in a store rather than foraging for them, keep in mind that cultivated cherries taste very different from their wild counterparts. Cultivated cherries can, of course, be used to make wine, but the resulting brew will not have the same flavor as wine made from wild cherries.

## WILD CHERRY WINE

6 pounds (about 16 cups) rum cherries (wild cherries)
or mazzard cherries, rinsed with cold water

1 gallon boiling water

8 cups sugar

¼ teaspoon wine yeast

1. In a large food-grade bucket, crush the cherries with your hands or a potato masher. The pits do not need to be removed, but be careful not to crack them open, as they are toxic.

2. Pour the boiling water over the fruit, and cover with a porous lid. Allow to soak for forty-eight hours.

3. Strain the liquid first through a strainer, and then through cheesecloth to remove the finer particles. Place in a large nonreactive pot, and bring to a boil; then remove from the heat immediately.

4. Return the heated liquid to the bucket. Add the sugar and, using a long nonreactive spoon, stir until the sugar is dissolved.

5. When the liquid has cooled to lukewarm, sprinkle the yeast on top. Cover with a nylon stocking and a loose-fitting lid, and allow to ferment for at least fourteen days.

6. Strain the liquid into a clean glass container and cover as appropriate. (See page 73.) In six to twelve months, the wine will be ready for bottling. During this time frame the wine will be clearing, and should be siphoned from the lees into another

clean glass jar about once every three months. When sufficiently clear, the wine may be siphoned into sterilized wine bottles and corked. Enjoy immediately, or store your wine on its side for later consumption.

# *Chokecherry*

Chokecherry

**When to Collect.** August through November.

**Where to Collect.** Along roadsides and forest edges throughout most of the United States.

**Wine Color.** Dark maroon.

**Wine Flavor.** Resembles cherry cough syrup with a tangy undertone.

**Wine Aroma.** Fruity and pleasant.

## Wild Plant Collection Tip

Chokecherries (*Prunus virginiana*) grow as shrubs that can attain a height of twenty-five feet, although most plants are shorter. The bright red cherries can be easily stripped from their racemes by grasping the fruiting stem with a cupped hand and gently pulling away from the plant. Chokecherries are very different from sweet wild cherries, as the fruit is extremely astringent. If you taste the raw fruit, you will surely agree that this fruit was aptly named. Additional sugar must be added to chokecherry wine to balance out the natural tartness. If your chokecherry wine is too tart for your liking, blend it half and half with a sweeter wine. Chokecherry wine melds especially well with wild plum wine.

## CHOKECHERRY WINE

6 pounds (about 16 cups) chokecherries,
rinsed with cold water

1 gallon cold water

9 cups sugar

3 cups raisins

2 cups wheat berries

¼ teaspoon wine yeast

1. Crush the fruit in a large food-grade bucket with your hands or a potato masher. The pits do not need to be removed, but be careful not to break them as they contain cyanogenic compounds. Add the cold water and cover the bucket with a porous lid. Allow this mixture to soak for forty-eight hours.

2.  Strain the liquid first through a colander to remove the fruit skins and cherry pits, and then through a layer of cheesecloth to remove the finer sediment. Pour into a large nonreactive pot and bring the liquid to a boil. Turn the heat to low and allow to simmer for seven minutes, skimming the scum that bubbles up to the top.

3.  Return the heated liquid to the bucket. Add the sugar, raisins, and wheat berries, and use a long nonreactive spoon to stir until the sugar is dissolved.

4.  When the sweetened chokecherry juice has cooled to lukewarm, sprinkle the yeast on top. Cover with a nylon stocking and a loose-fitting lid, and allow to ferment for at least fourteen days.

5.  Strain the liquid into a clean glass container and cover as appropriate. (See page 73.) In six to twelve months, the wine will be ready for bottling. During this time frame the wine will be clearing, and should be siphoned from the lees into another clean glass jar about once every three months. When sufficiently clear, the wine may be siphoned into sterilized wine bottles and corked. Enjoy immediately, or store your wine on its side for later consumption.

# *Wild Cranberry*

Wild Cranberry

**When to Collect.** Wild or bog cranberries ripen in October and November. Lowbush or mountain cranberries ripen from August through September.

**Where to Collect.** Wild or bog cranberries can be found on sphagnum moss and in lowland lakes of the Pacific Northwest (Washington, Oregon, and northern Idaho). Lowbush or mountain cranberries can be found in drier areas of the Great Lake region and the Atlantic coast.

**Wine Color.** Vivid red.

**Wine Flavor.** Rich, cranberry taste.

**Wine Aroma.** Sweet, not fruity.

## Wild Plant Collection Tip

Wild or bog cranberries (*Vaccinium occycoccos*) and lowbush or mountain cranberries (*Vaccinium vitus-idaea*) can be used interchangeably in this recipe. The bright red fruit from this herbaceous plant is better after it has been touched by frost. Wild cranberries are either matting plants (meaning they grow close to the ground, overlapping and intertwining with one another, forming a carpet or "mat"), as with lowbush or mountain cranberries; or they grow to a height of twelve to twenty inches, as with wild or bog cranberries. With either type, the fruit is easily collected from beneath its dense foliage.

Note that highbush cranberries (*Viburnum trilobum*) are unrelated to the lowbush varieties. Although they can be made into wine, highbush cranberries are bitter and should not be used as a substitute in the following recipe. On the other hand, cultivated cranberries are indiscernible from their wild counterpart, so if you're thinking of buying your cranberries rather than foraging for them, you can feel confident that your wine will not suffer from the substitution.

## WILD CRANBERRY WINE

4 pounds (about 16 cups) wild (bog)
or lowbush (mountain) cranberries, rinsed in cold water

1 gallon cold water

9 cups sugar

1½ cups raisins

2 cups wheat berries

¼ teaspoon wine yeast

1. To release the flavors of the fruit, the cranberries will need to be crushed. Although they may be chopped on a cutting board, it is easier to place two to four cups of fruit in a blender, adding enough of the cold water to cover the fruit. Turn the blender on until the fruit is broken—about a minute or less. Repeat this step with the remaining fruit.

2. In a large food-grade bucket, combine the puréed wild cranberry mixture with the rest of the cold water. Cover the bucket with a porous lid, and allow to soak for twenty-four hours, stirring occasionally with a long nonreactive spoon.

3. Strain the liquid through cheesecloth into a large nonreactive pot. Bring the liquid to a boil over high heat. Lower the heat and simmer for three minutes, removing any scum that forms on top of the bubbling liquid.

4. Return the liquid to the bucket. Add the sugar, raisins, and wheat berries, and stir until the sugar is dissolved.

5. When the juice has cooled to lukewarm, sprinkle the yeast on top. Cover with a nylon stocking and a loose-fitting lid, and allow to ferment for at least fourteen days.

6. Strain the liquid into a clean glass container and cover as appropriate. (See page 73.) In six to twelve months, the wine will be ready for bottling. During this time frame the wine will be clearing, and should be siphoned from the lees into another clean glass jar about once every three months. When sufficiently clear, the wine

may be siphoned into sterilized wine bottles and corked. Enjoy immediately, or store your wine on its side for later consumption.

# *Wild Currant*

Wild Currant

**When to Collect.** July and August.

**Where to Collect.** Sunny borders throughout most of the United States.

**Wine Color.** Bluish berries (commonly known as black currants) produce a mauve wine, red fruit produces a richer red wine, and green berries produce an amber wine.

**Wine Flavor.** Potent.

**Wine Aroma.** Full-bodied.

## Wild Plant Collection Tip

Currants (*Ribes* species) are waist-high shrubs that may or may not be thorny. The plants that do have prickles, though, are not very intimidating. You may wish to wear leather gloves when collecting, although this decreases the dexterity of your hands when retrieving the berries. Currant fruits are a quarter- to a half-inch in size, and grow individually like dangling holiday ornaments. They greatly range in color from green to reddish-mauve to deep purple, and are sometimes round and sometimes slightly oval in shape. Due to the fact that the fruits do not grow clustered, and need to be plucked one at a time, collection can be slow going. Once you've tried this wine, I think you'll agree that this libation is worth the effort. But if you decide to buy your currants in the store, rather than foraging for them, your wine should still turn out well, as cultivated currants are not very different from their wild cousins.

## WILD CURRANT WINE

3 pounds (about 12 cups) currants,
rinsed with cold water

1 gallon water (use boiling water if fruit is juicy
and cold water if fruit is dry)

6 cups sugar

¼ teaspoon wine yeast

1. Test the juiciness of the fruit by pinching it between your fingers. If the juice bursts from the currants, the currants are juicy. If very little pulp comes out, as if the fruit had been dried, the currants are dry.

2. *For juicy fruit:* In a large food-grade bucket, crush the fruit with your hands or a potato masher to break the skins, and cover with boiling water. *For dry fruit:* Place two to four cups of fruit in a blender at a time. Add enough cold water to cover the fruit and blend it until it is puréed. Boil the remaining water, and place the puréed fruit and boiling water in a large food-grade bucket.

3. Cover the bucket with a porous lid, and allow to soak for forty-eight hours.

4. Crush or stir the fruit once more to release the fruit flavors; then strain through cheesecloth into a large nonreactive pot. Bring to a boil over high heat; then remove from the heat immediately.

5. Return the heated liquid to the bucket. Add the sugar and, using a long nonreactive spoon, stir until the sugar is dissolved.

6. When the juice has cooled to lukewarm, sprinkle the yeast on top. Cover with a nylon stocking and a loose-fitting lid, and allow to ferment for at least fourteen days.

7. Strain the liquid into a clean glass container and cover as appropriate. (See page 73.) In six to twelve months, the wine will be ready for bottling. During this time frame the wine will be clearing, and should be siphoned from the lees into another clean glass jar about once every three months. When sufficiently clear, the wine may be siphoned into sterilized wine bottles and corked. Enjoy immediately, or store your wine on its side for later consumption.

## *Blue Elderberry*

**Blue Elderberry**

**When to Collect.** August and September.

**Where to Collect.** Sunny locations throughout most of the United States.

**Wine Color.** Deep purple.

**Wine Flavor.** Strong and musty.

**Wine Aroma.** Fruity, musty.

### Wild Plant Collection Tip

The fruit of the common elder (*Sambucus canadensis*) and blue-berried elder (*Sambucus glauca*) is pea-sized or smaller. It grows in *umbels*—fruiting clusters in which the individual fruit stalks radiate from the same point, like the ribs of an umbrella. Each fruit contains three to five rough seeds. Depending on the species, the fruit may be either shiny and nearly black or blue, and is covered with a whitish bloom. Although the raw fruit is somewhat bland in flavor, it can be transformed into a wonderful wine.

While you can pick the individual berries in the field, it might be preferable to snap off the entire fruiting umbel and separate the fruit from the little branches when you get home, as the fruit seems to retain its shape better when the entire fruiting head is collected rather than the individual berries. Remove the small stems attached to the fruit as soon as possible, as the twigs will impart a rank odor and flavor to the wine. Incidentally, only the flowers and fruit of this plant are edible—all other plant parts are poisonous.

Red elderberry (*Sambucus racemosa*) is a rank-smelling, brushy shrub that grows in moist woods throughout the Pacific coast range. It is a questionably edible wild plant that would result in an unpalatably bitter finished wine. It should not be used in this recipe.

## BLUE ELDERBERRY WINE

4 pounds (about 16 cups) blue elderberries, stems removed,
rinsed with cold water (seeds do not need to be removed)

1 gallon cold water

8 cups sugar

2 cups wheat berries

1½ cups raisins

¼ teaspoon wine yeast

1.  In a large food-grade bucket, crush the fruit with your hands or a potato masher until the skins are broken. Pour the cold water over the crushed berries, cover with a porous lid, and allow to soak for twenty-four hours. During this soaking time, crush and stir the mixture several times.

2.  Strain the liquid through cheesecloth into a large nonreactive pot. Place over high heat and bring the liquid to a boil. Lower the heat and allow to simmer for four minutes, removing any scum that rises to the surface.

3.  Return the heated liquid to the bucket. Add the sugar, wheat berries, and raisins, and use a long nonreactive spoon to stir until the sugar is dissolved.

4.  When the liquid has cooled to lukewarm, sprinkle the yeast on top. Cover with a nylon stocking and a loose-fitting lid, and allow to ferment for at least fourteen days.

5.  Strain the liquid into a clean glass container and cover as appropriate. (See page 73.) In six to twelve months, the wine will be ready for bottling. During this time

frame the wine will be clearing, and should be siphoned from the lees into another clean glass jar about once every three months. When sufficiently clear, the wine may be siphoned into sterilized wine bottles and corked. Enjoy immediately, or store your wine on its side for later consumption.

# *Gooseberry*

Gooseberry

**When to Collect.** July and August.

**Where to Collect.** Rich woods and sunny borders throughout most of the United States.

**Wine Color.** Bluish berries produce a mauve wine, red fruit produces a richer red wine, and green berries produce an amber wine.

**Wine Flavor.** Potent.

**Wine Aroma.** Full-bodied.

## Wild Plant Collection Tip

Gooseberries (*Ribes* species) are waist-high shrubs that may or may not be thorny. The plants that do have prickles, though, are not very intimidating. You may wish to wear leather gloves when collecting, although this decreases the dexterity of your hands when retrieving the berries. Gooseberries are a quarter- to a half-inch in size, and grow individually like dangling holiday ornaments. They are typically green fruits, although their color range also includes red and purple. They are sometimes round, and sometimes slightly oval in shape. Due to the fact that the fruits do not grow clustered, and need to be plucked one at a time, collection can be slow going. Once you've tried gooseberry wine, I think you'll agree that this libation is worth the extra effort.

## GOOSEBERRY WINE

3 pounds (about 12 cups) gooseberries, rinsed with cold water

1 gallon boiling water

6 cups sugar

¼ teaspoon wine yeast

1.  In a large food-grade bucket, crush the fruit with your hands or a potato masher until the skins are broken. Pour the boiling water over the fruit, cover with a porous lid, and allow to soak for forty-eight hours.

2. Crush or stir the fruit once more, and strain through cheesecloth into a large non-reactive pot. Bring to a boil over high heat; then remove from the heat immediately.

3. Return the heated juice to the bucket. Add the sugar and, using a long nonreactive spoon, stir until the sugar is dissolved.

4. When the juice has cooled to lukewarm, sprinkle the yeast on top. Cover with a nylon stocking and a loose-fitting lid, and allow to ferment for at least fourteen days.

5. Strain the liquid into a clean glass container and cover as appropriate. (See page 73.) In six to twelve months, the wine will be ready for bottling. During this time frame the wine will be clearing, and should be siphoned from the lees into another clean glass jar about once every three months. When sufficiently clear, the wine may be siphoned into sterilized wine bottles and corked. Enjoy immediately, or store your wine on its side for later consumption.

Wild Grape

# *Wild Grape*

**When to Collect.** August and September.

**Where to Collect.** Sunny locations throughout the United States.

**Wine Color.** Rich, deep purple with red undertones.

**Wine Flavor.** Sweet, full-bodied, fruity.

**Wine Aroma.** Full and rich.

## Wild Plant Collection Tip

Many types of wild grapes (*Vitis* species) are found as tendrilled vines with shreddy bark, growing over, around, and entwined with any other plants that are flourishing nearby. Wild grapes are much smaller than store-bought fruit, and quarter-inch grapes are typical, with each bearing several teardrop-shaped seeds. Many times, wild grapes will look like a mound of green leaves, but a quick peek beneath the greenery will reveal the lavender fruit covered by a whitish bloom. Snip off the whole fruit clusters while you are in the field, and separate the fruits from their stems when you get home in preparation for winemaking. The flavor of wild grapes can vary from year to year, depending on the amount of rainfall and whether the grapes are fully ripe and at their peak of sweetness when collected. You may find variations in flavor and quality that makes each year's wild grape wine a unique taste encounter. Sugar should be adjusted accordingly.

If you choose to buy your wine grapes in a store rather than foraging for them, keep in mind that compared with cultivated grapes, wild grapes are more sour with thicker skins and more seeds—and, therefore, more tannin. So while you can use cultivated grapes, you'll have to tinker with the recipe a bit, decreasing the sugar until you end up with the level of sweetness you like.

## WILD GRAPE WINE

4 pounds (about 16 cups) wild grapes, removed from stems, rinsed with cold water (seeds do not have to be removed)

1 gallon boiling water

8 cups sugar

¼ teaspoon wine yeast

1. In a large food-grade bucket, crush the fruit with your hands or a potato masher until the skins are broken. Pour the boiling water over the fruit, cover with a porous lid, and allow to soak for forty-eight hours.

2. Strain the mixture first through a colander to remove the bulkier fruit skins and grape seeds, then through a layer of cheesecloth to remove the finer sediment. Pour into a large nonreactive pot and bring to a boil over high heat; then remove from the heat immediately.

3. Return the liquid to the bucket. Add the sugar and use a long nonreactive spoon to stir until the sugar is dissolved.

4. When the juice has cooled to lukewarm, sprinkle the yeast on top. Cover with a nylon stocking and a loose-fitting lid, and allow to ferment for at least fourteen days.

5. Strain the liquid into a clean glass container and cover as appropriate. (See page 73.) In six to twelve months, the wine will be ready for bottling. During this time frame the wine will be clearing, and should be siphoned from the lees into another clean glass jar about once every three months. When sufficiently clear, the wine may be siphoned into sterilized wine bottles and corked. Enjoy immediately, or store your wine on its side for later consumption.

## *Red Hawthorn Berry*

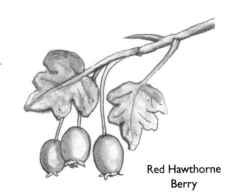

**When to Collect.** August through December. Although the fruits ripen in the summer, the berries can often be found still clinging to the branches in winter.

**Where to Collect.** Meadows, hillsides, and areas near streams throughout most of the United States.

**Wine Color.** Dark amber.

Red Hawthorne Berry

# Making Wild Raisin Wine

Once you've been able to locate and gather wild grapes as described on page 98, you'll have the makings of not just Wild Grape Wine, but also Wild Raisin Wine. This delicious wine is amber in color and full and fruity in flavor, with a sweet aroma.

Your first step, of course, is to turn your foraged grapes into raisins. To dry your wild grapes, puncture the skin with a fork, nut pick, or needle, depending on the size of the fruit. Typically, wild grapes will be no larger than the size of a small pea. Dry in a commercial dehydrator or in the oven on the lowest temperature setting. (This will take several hours or overnight, depending on the size and water content of the fruit.) Store the dried wild grapes in glass jars until they are ready to use. Then, when you have the time, use the following recipe to make your Wild Raisin Wine.

## WILD RAISIN WINE

9 cups wild raisins
4½ quarts boiling water
Juice from 2 oranges
Juice from 2 lemons
5 cups sugar
¼ teaspoon wine yeast

1. Place the raisins in a large food-grade bucket, and pour the boiling water over them. Cover with a porous lid, and allow to soak for twenty-four hours.

2. Squeeze the raisins well with your hands to release the fruit flavors, and strain the liquid through cheesecloth into a large nonreactive pot. Add the citrus juices.

3. Bring the liquid to a boil over high heat; then remove from the heat immediately.

4. Return the heated liquid to the bucket. Add the sugar and use a long nonreactive spoon to stir until the sugar is dissolved.

5. When the liquid has cooled to lukewarm, sprinkle the yeast on top. Cover with a nylon stocking and a loose-fitting lid, and allow to ferment for at least fourteen days.

6. Strain the liquid into a clean glass container and cover as appropriate. (See page 73.) In six to twelve months, the wine will be ready for bottling. During this time frame the wine will be clearing, and should be siphoned from the lees into another clean glass jar about once every three months. When sufficiently clear, the wine may be siphoned into sterilized wine bottles and corked. Enjoy immediately, or store your wine on its side for later consumption.

***Wine Flavor.*** Strong, sweet, and reminiscent of the deeply intense flavor of buckwheat honey.

***Wine Aroma.*** Powerful, but pleasant.

## Wild Plant Collection Tip

The shiny, oval, bright red berries of Red hawthorn (*Crataegus mongyna*) grow on small, shrub-like trees. The inner pulp is yellow, and there are one to five seeds in each fruit. The berries do not separate easily from their stems, and you must work around some rather long thorns to retrieve the berries, so wear protective clothing. The fruit can be plucked with a good, solid pull.

## RED HAWTHORN BERRY WINE

6 pounds (about 16 cups) red hawthorn berries,
rinsed with cold water

1 gallon cold water

8 cups sugar

3 cups raisins

¼ teaspoon wine yeast

1. Purée the fruit by placing two to four cups of berries into a blender at a time. Add enough of the cold water to cover the fruit, and blend to a puréed consistency. Repeat with the remaining berries.

2. In a large food-grade bucket, combine the puréed hawthorn berries with the rest of the cold water. Cover with a porous lid and allow to soak for forty-eight hours, periodically stirring the fruit with a long nonreactive spoon. The crushed fruit may emit a sour smell during this initial two-day period, but this odor will not carry through to the finished wine.

3. Strain this mixture first through a strainer, and then through cheesecloth to remove the finer particles. Place the liquid in a large nonreactive pot.

4. Bring the liquid to a boil over high heat; then reduce the heat to low and simmer for five minutes. Skim off any scum that rises to the surface.

5. Return the liquid to the bucket. Add the sugar and raisins, and stir until the sugar is dissolved.

6. When the liquid has cooled to lukewarm, sprinkle the yeast on top. Cover with a nylon stocking and a loose-fitting lid, and allow to ferment for at least fourteen days

7. Strain the liquid into a clean glass container and cover as appropriate. (See page 73.) In six to twelve months, the wine will be ready for bottling. During this time

frame the wine will be clearing, and should be siphoned from the lees into another clean glass jar about once every three months. When sufficiently clear, the wine may be siphoned into sterilized wine bottles and corked. Enjoy immediately, or store your wine on its side for later consumption.

# *Evergreen Huckleberry*

**Evergreen Huckleberry**

**When to Collect.** July through December. The fruits ripen in the summer but can often be collected through early winter as they continue to cling to their branches.

**Where to Collect.** Shaded areas and thickets, including sand dunes, from Washington to northern California.

**Wine Color.** Rich purple.

**Wine Flavor.** Mild and fruity.

**Wine Aroma.** Rich, full-bodied, fruity.

## Wild Plant Collection Tip

Evergreen huckleberries (*Vaccinium ovatum*) grow as ten-foot-tall multi-branching shrubs. Look for the taller bushes, as the lower, easier-to-reach berries may have been stripped off by other foraging animals in the area. When the berries are fully ripe, they are shiny, smaller than peas, and dark purple—nearly black. The seeds are tiny and indiscernible just as they are in their relative, the blueberry. The fruits can be easily tickled from their branches into a collection container.

## EVERGREEN HUCKLEBERRY WINE

4½ pounds (about 16 cups) evergreen huckleberries, rinsed with cold water

1 gallon boiling water

1 cup wheat berries

8 cups sugar

¼ teaspoon wine yeast

1. In a large food-grade bucket, crush the fruit with your hands or a potato masher to break the skins. Add the boiling water, and stir for a few minutes to extract the maximum amount of juice.

2. While the liquid is still hot, strain the fruit through cheesecloth into a large nonreactive pot. Bring the juice to a boil over high heat; then reduce the heat to low, and allow it to simmer for two minutes.

3. Return the heated liquid to the bucket. Add the wheat berries and sugar, and use a long nonreactive spoon to stir until the sugar is dissolved.

4. When the juice has cooled to lukewarm, sprinkle the yeast on top. Cover with a nylon stocking and a loose-fitting lid, and allow to ferment for at least fourteen days. If fermentation does not begin after five days, add another half cup of wheat berries to activate the yeast.

5. Strain the liquid into a clean glass container and cover as appropriate. (See page 73.) In six to twelve months, the wine will be ready for bottling. During this time frame the wine will be clearing, and should be siphoned from the lees into another clean glass jar about once every three months. When sufficiently clear, the wine may be siphoned into sterilized wine bottles and corked. Enjoy immediately, or store your wine on its side for later consumption.

# *Red Huckleberry*

Red Huckleberry

**When to Collect.** July and August.

**Where to Collect.** Lowland wet forests, sunny hillsides, and on decaying tree stumps west of the Cascade Mountains.

**Wine Color.** Pink, like pink lemonade.

**Wine Flavor.** Mild, with an aftertaste of fruit-flavored gum.

**Wine Aroma.** Sweet and fruity.

## Wild Plant Collection Tip

Red huckleberry (*Vaccinium parvifolium*) grows as a delicate, square-stemmed, lacy shrub with lime green foliage and bright red berries that are smaller than peas. The seeds are small and inconsequential as they are in their relative, the blueberry. Because of the staggered flowering and fruiting season, you will notice that at the same time ripe fruits are ready to be picked, you can also find some pinkish, bell-shaped flowers (which are the future fruit) growing on the same plant. If you return to the same plant each week, you should be able to collect more ripened fruit.

## RED HUCKLEBERRY WINE

4½ pounds (about 16 cups) red huckleberries,
rinsed with cold water

1 gallon boiling water

8 cups sugar

¼ teaspoon wine yeast

1.  In a large food-grade bucket, crush the fruit with your hands or a potato masher to break the skins. Add the boiling water and stir with a long nonreactive spoon for a minute or two to extract the maximum amount of juice.

2.  While still hot, strain the mixture through cheesecloth into a large nonreactive pot. Bring the liquid to a boil over high heat; then reduce the heat and simmer for two minutes.

3.  Return the heated liquid to the bucket. Add the sugar, and stir until the sugar is dissolved.

4.  When the liquid has cooled to lukewarm, sprinkle the yeast on top. Cover with a nylon stocking and a loose-fitting lid, and allow to ferment for at least fourteen days.

5.  Strain the liquid into a clean glass container and cover as appropriate. (See page 73.) In six to twelve months, the wine will be ready for bottling. During this time frame the wine will be clearing, and should be siphoned from the lees into another clean glass jar about once every three months. When sufficiently clear, the wine may be siphoned into sterilized wine bottles and corked. Enjoy immediately, or store your wine on its side for later consumption.

# *Kinnikinnick Berry*

Kinnikinnick Berry

**When to Collect.** August through October.

**Where to Collect.** Sandy clearings and sunny, well-drained soil in the northern third of the United States.

**Wine Color.** Dark amber.

**Wine Flavor.** Sweet and fruity.

**Wine Aroma.** Medicine-like.

## Wild Plant Collection Tip

Kinnikinnick (*Arctostaphylos uva-ursi*) is an evergreen matting plant that grows in dense patches, bearing dull red, quarter- to half-inch fruit. Each berry contains a single hard seed that does not need to be removed prior to puréeing. Because these are ground-hugging plants, much bending and stooping is required to collect the needed amount of fruit.

## KINNIKINNICK WINE

1 gallon (about 16 cups) kinnikinnick berries,
rinsed with cold water (seeds do not need to be removed)

1 gallon cold water

7 cups sugar

3 cups raisins

¼ teaspoon wine yeast

1.  Purée the fruit by placing two to four cups of fruit into a blender. Add enough of the cold water to cover, and blend to a puréed consistency. Repeat with the remaining fruit.

2.  Place the pulp in a large food-grade bucket, and add any remaining water. Cover with a porous lid, and allow to soak for forty-eight hours.

3.  Strain the mixture through cheesecloth into a large nonreactive pot. Bring to a boil over high heat, reduce the heat to low, and simmer for five minutes.

4.  Return the liquid to the bucket. Add the sugar and raisins, and use a long nonreactive spoon to stir until the sugar has dissolved.

5.  When the liquid has cooled to lukewarm, sprinkle the yeast on top. Cover with a nylon stocking and a loose-fitting lid, and ferment for at least fourteen days.

6.  Strain the liquid into a clean glass container and cover as appropriate. (See page 73.) In six to twelve months, the wine will be ready for bottling. During this time frame the wine will be clearing, and should be siphoned from the lees into another clean glass jar about once every three months. When sufficiently clear, the wine may be siphoned into sterilized wine bottles and corked. Enjoy immediately, or store your wine on its side for later consumption.

## *Manzanita Berry*

**When to Collect.** July through September.

**Where to Collect.** Dry, rocky slopes west of the Cascade Mountains.

**Wine Color.** Rust-colored.

**Wine Flavor.** Slightly nutty.

**Wine Aroma.** Sweet.

Manzanita Berry

## Wild Plant Collection Tip

Manzanita (*Arctostaphylos columbiana*) fruit is half red, half green, and blueberry-sized, resembling miniature apples with a drier but still pulpy flesh. Until they are fully ripe, the berries cling tightly to the cinnamon-colored branches, which are three to six feet high, sometimes gnarled, loosely arranged, and peeling. When ripe, the manzanita berries can be easily plucked from their small, irregularly shaped fruiting clusters.

## MANZANITA BERRY WINE

6 pounds (about 16 cups) manzanita fruit,
rinsed with cold water

1 gallon cold water

8 cups sugar

3 cups raisins

¼ teaspoon wine yeast

1. Purée the fruit by placing two to four cups of fruit into a blender. Add enough of the cold water to cover, and blend to a puréed consistency. Repeat with the remaining fruit. The resulting pulp will resemble a very thick pea soup.

2. Place the pulp in a large food-grade bucket, and add any remaining water. Cover with a porous lid, and allow to soak for forty-eight hours.

3. Strain the mixture first through a strainer, and then through cheesecloth into a large nonreactive pot. The plant matter will tend to plug up the cheesecloth, so you'll have to rinse the mush out of your cloth periodically to complete the straining.

4. Place the pot over high heat, and boil for five minutes. Return the heated liquid to the bucket, and add the sugar and raisins. Using a long nonreactive spoon, stir until the sugar is dissolved.

5. When the liquid has cooled to lukewarm, sprinkle the yeast on top. Cover with a nylon stocking and a loose-fitting lid, and allow to ferment for at least fourteen days.

6. Strain the liquid into a clean glass container and cover as appropriate. (See page 73.) In six to twelve months, the wine will be ready for bottling. During this time frame the wine will be clearing, and should be siphoned from the lees into another clean glass jar about once every three months. When sufficiently clear, the wine may be siphoned into sterilized wine bottles and corked. Enjoy immediately, or store your wine on its side for later consumption.

# *Mountain Ash Berry*

**When to Collect.** September and October.

**Where to Collect.** In rocky terrain from Alaska to northern California.

**Wine Color.** Pink, like pink lemonade.

**Wine Flavor.** Bitter.

**Wine Aroma.** Bitter.

Mountain Ash Berry

## Wild Plant Collection Tip

Mountain ash (*Pyrus americana* or *Sorbus americana*) is a small tree or large shrub that grows more compactly in poor soils. The berries form in dense clusters of orange to red fruit that are slightly larger than pea-sized. Each fruit has one to two elliptical, sharply pointed seeds. Separating the individual berries from their clusters requires a little tugging, as they seem to not want to part from their fruiting umbels. Mountain ash berries are bitter and somewhat hard, not juicy like most berries. Although these berries make a bitter wine, they were much-used by the American pioneers, who prepared a jelly from the tart fruit.

## MOUNTAIN ASH BERRY WINE

1 gallon (about 16 cups) mountain ash berries,
rinsed with cold water

1 gallon boiling water

Sugar, 2 cups for each quart of
strained berry mixture (6–8 cups)

¼ teaspoon wine yeast

1. Place the fruit in a large food-grade bucket, and pour the boiling water over it. Cover with a porous lid, and allow to soak for forty-eight hours.

2. Using a colander, strain out the solids from the berry mixture. Measure the liquid, and pour it into a large nonreactive pot. Bring to a boil; then remove from the heat immediately.

3. For each quart of measured liquid, put two cups of sugar in the bucket, and pour the hot juice over it. Using a long nonreactive spoon, stir to dissolve the sugar.

4. When the liquid has cooled to lukewarm, sprinkle the yeast on top. Cover with a nylon stocking and a loose-fitting lid, and allow to ferment for at least fourteen days.

5. Strain the liquid into a clean glass container and cover as appropriate. (See page 73.) In six to twelve months, the wine will be ready for bottling. During this time frame the wine will be clearing, and should be siphoned from the lees into another clean glass jar about once every three months. When sufficiently clear, the wine may be siphoned into sterilized wine bottles and corked. Enjoy immediately, or store your wine on its side for later consumption.

**Black Mulberry**

# *Black Mulberry*

**When to Collect.** May through July.

**Where to Collect.** Valleys, flood plains, and in rich, moist soil throughout most of the United States, except the dry Southwest.

**Wine Color.** Deep purple.

**Wine Flavor.** Strong and full-bodied.

**Wine Aroma.** Lightly fruity.

## Wild Plant Collection Tip

Black mulberries (*Morus nigra*) are dark purple to black, half-inch to one-inch-long cylinder-shaped fruits. During mulberry fruiting season, the berries can be found lying beneath the tree, as they fall from their branches with the slightest touch. Make sure the fruit you collect is ripe, as unripe berries contain hallucinogens. Mulberry trees are small to medium-sized with a broad, rounded crown.

This fruit stains the hands, so rather than picking mulberries individually, you may wish to spread an old sheet or tarp beneath the branches of the tree, give the limbs a good solid shake, and then pour the fallen fruit from the cloth into a bucket. This gathering technique is also a fast and effective way to collect the fragile fruit. Do not be concerned if a short piece of stem remains attached to the fruit when the berries separate from the branches, as the stem can remain on the fruit when you make the wine.

Red mulberries (*Morus rubra*) and white mulberries (*Morus alba*) may be used interchangeably in the following recipe, although the color of the finished wine will vary, depending on the color of the fruit used.

## BLACK MULBERRY WINE

4 pounds (about 16 cups) mulberries, gently rinsed
1 gallon boiling water
Juice from 4 lemons
8 cups sugar
¼ teaspoon wine yeast

1. Place the fruit in a large food-grade bucket, and pour the boiling water over it. Add the lemon juice, cover with a porous lid, and allow to soak for twenty-four hours.

2. Strain the liquid first through a colander, and then through cheesecloth into a large nonreactive pot. Bring to a boil; then remove from the heat immediately.

3. Place the sugar in the bucket, and pour the heated liquid over it. Using a long nonreactive spoon, stir until the sugar is dissolved.

4. When the juice has cooled to lukewarm, sprinkle the yeast on top. Cover with a nylon stocking and a loose-fitting lid, and allow to ferment for at least fourteen days.

5. Strain the liquid into a clean glass container and cover as appropriate. (See page 73.) In six to twelve months, the wine will be ready for bottling. During this time frame the wine will be clearing, and should be siphoned from the lees into another clean glass jar about once every three months. When sufficiently clear, the wine may be siphoned into sterilized wine bottles and corked. Enjoy immediately, or store your wine on its side for later consumption.

## *Oregon Grape Berry*

**When to Collect.** July through October.

**Where to Collect.** Forest fringes west of the Cascade Mountains from Washington to California. Those plants found growing beneath a heavy tree canopy, with little exposure to the sun, may not be fruiting. Look for plants with greater exposure to the sun.

**Wine Color.** Rust-colored.

**Wine Flavor.** Strong but pleasant.

**Wine Aroma.** Strong but pleasant.

Oregon Grape Berry

## Wild Plant Collection Tip

When fully ripe, the Oregon grape berry (*Mahonia nervosa* or *Berberis nervosa*) is pea-sized, with an exterior that is purple with a whitish bloom, and pulp that is greenish-yellow, tart, and juicy. At this stage, the woody knee-high stems of the plant are turning red, and the fruit separates easily from its stem. If you succeed in finding a large patch of Oregon grape plants growing in at least partial sunlight, you can collect the amount needed for this recipe in short order. Oregon grape leaves are shiny and holly-like with pointed tips. Wear gloves if desired when collecting.

## OREGON GRAPE WINE

4½ pounds (about 16 cups) Oregon grapes, rinsed with cold water

1 gallon boiling water

8 cups sugar

¼ teaspoon wine yeast

1. In a large food-grade bucket, crush the fruit with your hands or a potato masher to break the skins. Add the boiling water and stir with a long nonreactive spoon to extract the juice.

2. While the pulp is still hot, strain it first through a colander and then through cheesecloth into a bucket. Add the sugar, and stir to dissolve.

3. When the mixture has cooled to lukewarm, sprinkle the yeast on top. Cover with a nylon stocking and a loose-fitting lid, and allow to ferment for at least fourteen days.

4. Strain the liquid into a clean glass container and cover as appropriate. (See page 73.) In six to twelve months, the wine will be ready for bottling. During this time frame the wine will be clearing, and should be siphoned from the lees into another clean glass jar about once every three months. When sufficiently clear, the wine may be siphoned into sterilized wine bottles and corked. Enjoy immediately, or store your wine on its side for later consumption.

Wild Plum

## *Wild Plum*

**When to Collect.** August and September.

**Where to Collect.** Thickets and moist soil throughout most of the United States.

**Wine Color.** Varies, depending on color of fruit skin. Usually tea-colored with slightly lighter or darker variations.

**Wine Flavor.** Full and Fruity.

**Wine Aroma.** Full and fruity.

## Wild Plant Collection Tip

The wild plum (*Prunus americana*) can be found growing as shrubs or small trees with fruit that can range from purple to red to golden yellow. All fruits have an apparent whitish bloom. Wild plums can be as small as marbles and as large as store-bought plums, with each fruit containing a single almond-shaped pit, just like the orchard fruit. Plums can be collected by picking individual fruits, or can be shaken from the limbs onto the ground. If a large sheet or tarp is placed beneath the tree, this will help ensure that the fruit you collect has not been lying on the ground too long and is insect-free. Thanks to their ability to reproduce rapidly—and thanks to our furry, fruit-eating, four-legged friends— many wild plums are the offspring of cultivated or orchard fruit, and all are suitable for winemaking. Cultivated plums may be substituted for wild plums in this recipe.

## WILD PLUM WINE

6 pounds (about 16 cups) wild plums,
rinsed with cold water

1 gallon boiling water

7 cups sugar

¼ teaspoon wine yeast

1. In a large food-grade bucket, crush the plums with your hands or a potato masher to break the skins. The pits do not need to be removed, but make certain you do not break them open. Add the boiling water, cover with a loose-fitting lid, and allow to soak for four hours.

2. Strain the liquid first through a colander, and then through cheesecloth into a large nonreactive pot. Bring the juice to a boil; then remove from the heat immediately.

3. Return the heated liquid to the bucket. Add the sugar and, using a long nonreactive spoon, stir to dissolve.

4. When the mixture has cooled to lukewarm, sprinkle the yeast on top. Cover with a nylon stocking and a loose-fitting lid, and allow to ferment for at least fourteen days.

# Making Wild Prune Wine

Like wild grapes, wild plums can be used to create two different wines—Wild Plum Wine and, when dried, Wild Prune Wine. Homemade wild prunes make a wonderful tea-colored beverage that is sweet in flavor, with a robust aroma.

Once you've gathered the plums as described on page 111, your next step will be to dry the fruit. First, make a slit through the skin of each plum, or puncture the skin with a fork to allow the liquid to escape during the drying process. The pits do not need to be removed. Then dry the fruit in a commercial dehydrator or in your oven on the lowest temperature setting. Depending on the size and juiciness of the fruit, drying may take several days, so you will need to be patient. Store your wild prunes in glass jars until you are ready to follow the recipe below.

## WILD PRUNE WINE

3 pounds (about 12 cups) wild prunes, not pitted
4½ quarts boiling water
Juice from 1 grapefruit
6 cups sugar
1½ cups raisins
¼ teaspoon wine yeast

1. Place the whole prunes in a large food-grade bucket, and pour the boiling water over them. Cover with a porous lid, and allow to soak for twenty-four hours.

2. Squeeze the fruit well with your hands, and strain the liquid through cheesecloth into a large nonreactive pot. Add the grapefruit juice, and bring to a boil over high heat. Reduce the heat to low and simmer for three minutes.

3. Return the heated liquid to the bucket. Add the sugar and raisins, and use a long nonreactive spoon to stir until the sugar is dissolved.

4. When the liquid has cooled to lukewarm, sprinkle the yeast on top. Cover with a nylon stocking and a loose-fitting lid, and allow to ferment for at least fourteen days.

5. Strain the liquid into a clean glass container and cover as appropriate. (See page 73.) In six to twelve months, the wine will be ready for bottling. During this time frame the wine will be clearing, and should be siphoned from the lees into another clean glass jar about once every three months. When sufficiently clear, the wine may be siphoned into sterilized wine bottles and corked. Enjoy immediately, or store your wine on its side for later consumption.

5. Strain the liquid into a clean glass container and cover as appropriate. (See page 73.) In six to twelve months, the wine will be ready for bottling. During this time frame the wine will be clearing, and should be siphoned from the lees into another clean glass jar about once every three months. When sufficiently clear, the wine may be siphoned into sterilized wine bottles and corked. Enjoy immediately, or store your wine on its side for later consumption.

# *Wild Raspberry*

**When to Collect.** July and August.

**Where to Collect.** Sunny locations and forest fringes throughout most of the United States.

**Wine Color.** Deep pinkish-red.

**Wine Flavor.** Tangy and fruity.

**Wine Aroma.** Sweet and fruity.

Wild Raspberry

## Wild Plant Collection Tip

Black (*Rubus occidentalis*) and red wild raspberries (*Rubus strigosus*) grow on thorny upright canes that are several feet high. Their prickles are less intimidating than those of wild blackberries; however, the risk remains of damaging clothing during the collection process. Wild raspberries range from red to dark purple with a whitish bloom, and are indistinguishable from their cultivated counterparts. The fruits can be rolled off their cone-shaped cap, leaving you with a hollow multi-seeded berry.

If you're wild about raspberries but not about foraging, you may be thinking of using cultivated raspberries in your wine. If so, be aware that wild raspberries have a unique flavor that is unlike that of their cultivated cousins. Although you can make wine out of cultivated raspberries, it will taste quite different from wild raspberry wine.

## WILD RASPBERRY WINE

5 pounds (about 16 cups) wild raspberries,
gently rinsed with cold water

1 gallon cold water

8 cups sugar

Juice and rind of 1 large grapefruit,
halved and squeezed (or 2 oranges and 2 lemons)

¼ teaspoon wine yeast

1.  In a large food-grade bucket, crush the fruit with your hands or a potato masher to break it up. Pour the cold water over the fruit, cover with a porous lid, and allow to soak for forty-eight hours, stirring and crushing the fruit occasionally.

2. Strain the liquid first through a colander and then through cheesecloth into a large nonreactive pot. Bring the liquid to a boil over high heat, reduce the heat to low, and simmer for three minutes, skimming any scum that forms.

3.  Return the heated liquid to the bucket. Add the sugar, citrus juice, and rinds, and use a long nonreactive spoon to stir until the sugar is dissolved.

4.  When the liquid has cooled to lukewarm, sprinkle the yeast on top. Cover with a nylon stocking and a loose-fitting lid, and allow to ferment for at least fourteen days.

5.  Strain the liquid into a clean glass container and cover as appropriate. (See page 73.) In six to twelve months, the wine will be ready for bottling. During this time frame the wine will be clearing, and should be siphoned from the lees into another clean glass jar about once every three months. When sufficiently clear, the wine may be siphoned into sterilized wine bottles and corked. Enjoy immediately, or store your wine on its side for later consumption.

# *Rose Hips*

**When to Collect.** November, and throughout winter in some locations.

**Where to Collect.** Grows in nearly any habitat, including rich woods, full sun, near lakes and streams, and in the high desert.

**Wine Color.** Dark amber.

**Wine Flavor.** Mild.

**Wine Aroma.** Slightly fruity.

Rose Hips

## Wild Plant Collection Tip

Rose hips are the swollen fruiting body of the wild rose (*Rosa* species) flower. Wherever you see a wild rose growing, look for the hips on the same plant later in the year. The fruiting body grows at the tips of this shrub's thorny branches, so you don't have to reach into a caning mass of prickles to collect them. Just snap them off at the tips of the branches. Rose hips are between pea-sized and one inch in diameter. They loosely resemble small, elongated crab apples and are comprised of a thin, red covering filled with many seeds and hairs. The dried hips can be stored in glass jars for use later in the year. The seeds do not need to be removed prior to grinding. If this were done, very little plant matter would be left to be transformed into wine.

## ROSE HIP WINE

1 pound (about 5 cups) rose hips, rinsed with cold water
(seeds should not be removed)

1 gallon hot water

6 cups sugar

1½ cups raisins

¼ teaspoon wine yeast

1. Grind the rose hips using a coffee grinder or other food processing implement.

2. In a large food-grade bucket, combine the ground rose hips, hot water, sugar, and raisins. Using a long nonreactive spoon, stir until the sugar is dissolved.

3. When the liquid has cooled to lukewarm, sprinkle the yeast on top. Cover with a nylon stocking and a loose-fitting lid, and allow to ferment for at least fourteen days.

4. Strain the liquid into a clean glass container and cover as appropriate. (See page 73.) In six to twelve months, the wine will be ready for bottling. During this time frame the wine will be clearing, and should be siphoned from the lees into another clean glass jar about once every three months. When sufficiently clear, the wine may be siphoned into sterilized wine bottles and corked. Enjoy immediately, or store your wine on its side for later consumption.

## *Salal Berry*

**Salal Berry**

**When to Collect.** August.

**Where to Collect.** In woods and areas of partial sunlight in the Pacific Northwest.

**Wine Color.** Rich, dark purple.

**Wine Flavor.** Strong, full-bodied.

**Wine Aroma.** Fruity with hints of musk.

## Wild Plant Collection Tip

Salal (*Gaultheria shallon*) is a three-foot-tall evergreen shrub that bears an oval, dull, dark purple fruit. The berries do not readily fall from its red, zigzagging branches, but can be removed with a good tug. Sometimes when you pull the fruit, you will find nothing more than salal skin between your fingers, and the juicy fruit "innards" still attached to the stem of the plant. Salal exudes a sticky substance that causes airborne extraneous matter to adhere to the fruits.

## SALAL BERRY WINE

6 pounds (about 16 cups) salal berries,
rinsed with cold water

1 gallon boiling water

½ cup wheat berries

8 cups sugar

¼ teaspoon wine yeast

1.  In a large food-grade bucket, crush the fruit with your hands or a potato masher to break the skins. Pour the boiling water over the crushed fruit. Then, while the liquid is still hot, strain the mixture first through a colander and then through cheesecloth to remove the finer particles.

2.  Add the wheat berries and the sugar to the juice. Using a long nonreactive spoon, stir until the sugar is dissolved.

3.  When the liquid has cooled to lukewarm, sprinkle the yeast on top. Cover with a nylon stocking and a loose-fitting lid, and allow to ferment for at least fourteen days. If fermentation has not begun after five days, add a half cup more wheat berries to activate the yeast.

4.  Strain the liquid into a clean glass container and cover as appropriate. (See page 73.) In six to twelve months, the wine will be ready for bottling. During this time frame the wine will be clearing, and should be siphoned from the lees into another clean glass jar about once every three months. When sufficiently clear, the wine may be siphoned into sterilized wine bottles and corked. Enjoy immediately, or store your wine on its side for later consumption.

Salmonberry

# *Salmonberry*

**When to Collect.** May through August.

**Where to Collect.** Streams and wet areas of lower elevations along the Pacific coast.

**Wine Color.** Coral.

**Wine Flavor.** Strong, with a hint of salmonberry.

**Wine Aroma.** Strong, but not fruity.

## Wild Plant Collection Tip

Salmonberries (*Rubus spectabilis*) are ripe when they are plump, salmon colored, and easily separated from their stem. Less often, you will find red salmonberries, which can be used interchangeably. Salmonberries are a close relative of the raspberry; however, they are much less flavorful. From March through June, you will see the vivid fuchsia salmonberry flower, which transforms into fruit later in the year. The berries do not grow in clusters, although they are easy to collect in bulk as each individual six- to twelve-foot-tall shrub fruits fairly prolifically, and the shrubs grow in dense patches. The branches of this shrub are mildly prickly, but do not pose a hazard when you are collecting the fruits. Although fresh salmonberries are somewhat lacking in flavor, they make a good, strong wine.

## SALMONBERRY WINE

4 pounds (about 16 cups) salmonberries,
rinsed gently in cold water

1 gallon boiling water

10 cups sugar

¼ teaspoon wine yeast

1. In a large food-grade bucket, crush the fruit with your hands or a potato masher to break the berries. Pour the boiling water on top, and use a long nonreactive spoon to stir for a minute or two.

2. While the mixture is hot, strain it through cheesecloth. Add the sugar, and stir until the sugar is dissolved.

3. When the liquid has cooled to lukewarm, sprinkle the yeast on top. Cover with a nylon stocking and a loose-fitting lid, and allow to ferment for at least fourteen days.

4. Strain the liquid into a clean glass container and cover as appropriate. (See page 73.) In six to twelve months, the wine will be ready for bottling. During this time frame the wine will be clearing, and should be siphoned from the lees into another clean glass jar about once every three months. When sufficiently clear, the wine may be siphoned into sterilized wine bottles and corked. Enjoy immediately, or store your wine on its side for later consumption.

## *Serviceberry*

**When to Collect.** July through September.

**Where to Collect.** Dry or open pine woods, slopes, and canyons from Nebraska to Oregon.

**Wine Color.** Rust-colored.

**Wine Flavor.** Full-bodied.

**Wine Aroma.** Dried fruit-like.

Serviceberry

## Wild Plant Collection Tip

Serviceberries (*Amelanchier alnifolia*)—also called juneberries—are half-inch, dark purple, oval fruits that grow on shrubs. Although the shrubs grow up to four-teen feet in height, the fruit can be easily picked off the lower branches. Once the shrub is fruiting, it is less showy and more difficult to spot. For this reason it's best to "scope out" these densely clumped shrubs when they are flowering—sometime between April and July. The five-petal serviceberry blossoms are hard to miss, making spring and early summer a good time to locate the bushes. Some years, although the raggedy white flowers have bloomed prolifically, the serviceberries themselves are somewhat sparse. This fruit is well liked by wildlife, and may be difficult to collect in abundance before it is eaten by various birds, deer, rabbits, and other animals.

## SERVICEBERRY WINE

4½ pounds (about 16 cups) serviceberries,
rinsed with cold water

1 gallon boiling water

8 cups sugar

¼ teaspoon wine yeast

1. In a large food-grade bucket, crush the fruit with your hands or a potato masher to break the skins. Be aware that serviceberries are drier than most fruits, and that mashing will not produce the anticipated wet, pulpy mush.

2. Pour the boiling water over the fruit, and stir with a long nonreactive spoon, crushing well to extract as much juice as possible. While the liquid is still hot, strain the liquid first through a colander and then through cheesecloth.

3. Return the liquid to the bucket. Add the sugar, and stir to dissolve.

4. When the mixture has cooled to lukewarm, sprinkle the yeast on top. Cover with a nylon stocking and a loose-fitting lid, and allow to ferment for at least fourteen days.

5. Strain the liquid into a clean glass container and cover as appropriate. (See page 73.) In six to twelve months, the wine will be ready for bottling. During this time frame the wine will be clearing, and should be siphoned from the lees into another clean glass jar about once every three months. When sufficiently clear, the wine may be siphoned into sterilized wine bottles and corked. Enjoy immediately, or store your wine on its side for later consumption.

# Wild Strawberry

**When to Collect.** June and July.

**Where to Collect.** Shaded woods or open paths throughout most of the United States.

**Wine Color.** Pink, like pink lemonade.

**Wine Flavor.** Like strawberries.

**Wine Aroma.** Like strawberries.

**Wild Strawberry**

## Wild Plant Collection Tip

Wild strawberry (*Fragaria virginiana*) grows as a creeping plant with runners. The bright red berries are much smaller than cultivated strawberries, and are well hidden beneath the greenery of this herbaceous plant. For this reason, it's best to look for the shape of the leaf rather than the redness of the fruit. Once you find a patch, you can return there year after year, because wild strawberry grows as a perennial plant. These are tiny ground-hugging berries, and much bending and stooping is required to collect the needed amount of fruit.

If you are tempted to use store-bought strawberries in place of wild strawberries, be aware that wild strawberries are both sweeter and more flavorful than anything you're likely to find in a store. Although you can make wine with cultivated strawberries, you'll have to increase the sugar, experimenting until you find the level of sweetness you prefer.

## WILD STRAWBERRY WINE

4½ pounds (about 16 cups) wild strawberries,
rinsed gently with cold water

1 gallon boiling water

8 cups sugar

¼ teaspoon wine yeast

1. In a large food-grade bucket, crush the fruit with your hands or a potato masher to break the berries. Pour the boiling water on top, and use a long nonreactive spoon to stir for a minute or two.

2. While the mixture is hot, strain it first through a colander and then through cheesecloth into a large nonreactive pot. Bring to a boil over high heat, reduce the heat to low, and simmer for two minutes.

3. Return the hot liquid to the bucket. Add the sugar, and stir until the sugar is dissolved.

4. When the liquid has cooled to lukewarm, sprinkle the yeast on top. Cover with a nylon stocking and a loose-fitting lid, and allow to ferment for at least fourteen days.

5. Strain the liquid into a clean glass container and cover as appropriate. (See page 73.) In six to twelve months, the wine will be ready for bottling. During this time frame the wine will be clearing, and should be siphoned from the lees into another clean glass jar about once every three months. When sufficiently clear, the wine may be siphoned into sterilized wine bottles and corked. Enjoy immediately, or store your wine on its side for later consumption.

# *Sumac Berry*

**Sumac Berry**

**When to Collect.** July through winter.

**Where to Collect.** Sunny locations throughout most of the United States.

**Wine Color.** Dark tea-colored.

**Wine Flavor.** Like tart Kool-Aid.

**Wine Aroma.** Familiar, yet indescribable.

## Wild Plant Collection Tip

Staghorn sumac (*Rhus typhina*) and smooth sumac (*Rhus glabra*) may be used interchangeably in this recipe, although staghorn sumac is more flavorful than smooth sumac. Both plants grow as tropical-looking large shrubs or small trees, and can be found in colonies or patches bearing nonfleshy fruits. The flame-shaped red berry clusters measure up to eight inches long, and are composed of hundreds of tiny, sixteenth-inch, hard, round seeds. Staghorn sumac berries have a fuzzy appearance. They are covered by short hairs that give this fruit its tartness. Smooth sumac is less hairy, and therefore is lacking some of the tanginess found in its fuzzier counterpart. *Caution:* Poison sumac (*Rhus vernix*) has white berries, and, as the name implies, it is a toxic plant. Due to the color of the fruit, the edible versus the nonedible plants are easy to distinguish from one another.

## SUMAC BERRY WINE

12–15 sumac berry clusters, intact, shaken or dusted off
(do not remove berries from branchlets and do not rinse)
1 gallon cold water, divided
6 cups sugar
¼ teaspoon wine yeast

1. In a large food-grade bucket, cover the sumac berry clusters with two quarts of the cold water. Sumac should not come in direct contact with hot water because an undesirable bitter property would be released. Squeeze the berries in the water to release the flavor, and loosen the fruit from its branches. It is not necessary to remove the small branches. Cover with a porous lid and allow to soak overnight.

2. The following day, strain the plant matter first through a strainer and then through cheesecloth into the bucket. Set this pinkish liquid aside.

3. Place the remaining two quarts of water in a large nonreactive pot, and bring to a boil. Add the sugar, and stir to dissolve.

4. Add the hot sugar water to the cold sumac-flavored water, and use a long non-reactive spoon to combine. Because the fruiting cluster has been removed, the risk of releasing the plant's bitterness no longer exists.

5. When the liquid has cooled to lukewarm, sprinkle the yeast on top. Cover with a nylon stocking and a loose-fitting lid, and allow to ferment for at least fourteen days.

6. After the bubbling of fermentation has ceased, the surface of the wine may sport a very thin, almost blackish "skin." Remove the skin, strain the liquid into a clean glass container, and cover as appropriate. (See page 73.) In six to twelve months, the wine will be ready for bottling. During this time frame the wine will be clearing, and should be siphoned from the lees into another clean glass jar about once every three months. When sufficiently clear, the wine may be siphoned into sterilized wine bottles and corked. Enjoy immediately, or store your wine on its side for later consumption.

# *Thimbleberry*

**When to Collect.** June and July.

**Where to Collect.** Damp borders from Washington to California and east to the Great Lakes.

**Wine Color.** Fire-engine red.

**Wine Flavor.** Full-bodied.

**Wine Aroma.** Pleasantly sweet.

Thimbleberry

## Wild Plant Collection Tip

Thimbleberries (*Rubus parviflorus*) grow on three- to eight-foot-tall thornless shrubs. The fragile, bright red berry deteriorates quickly, so it's best to use the fruit soon after it is collected. It is nearly impossible to collect these fruits without ending up with red, sticky hands, but the stains wash off effortlessly. Thimbleberries can be pulled or tickled from their branches and dropped into a collection container. Another name for this fruit is "bottle cap," and you will see the resemblance when you gather these berries. Their delicate cap pulls away from a rounded, whitish "hub," leaving a fruit with a hollow core. Select only clean fruit, free of cobwebs or other debris, as you cannot rinse these berries. Due to their fragile constitution, doing so would rinse away the fruit as well.

## THIMBLEBERRY WINE

4½ pounds (about 16 cups) thimbleberries,
unrinsed, largest debris removed by hand

1 gallon boiling water

8 cups sugar

¼ teaspoon wine yeast

1. In a large food-grade bucket, crush the fruit with your hands or a potato masher to break it up. Pour the boiling water on top.

2. While the mixture is still hot, strain it through cheesecloth. (The holes of a strainer are too large to catch the tiny thimbleberry seeds.) Add the sugar, and use a nonreactive spoon to stir until the sugar is dissolved.

3. When the mixture has cooled to lukewarm, sprinkle the yeast on top. Cover with a nylon stocking and a loose-fitting lid, and allow to ferment for at least fourteen days.

4. Strain the liquid into a clean glass container and cover as appropriate. (See page 73.) In six to twelve months, the wine will be ready for bottling. During this time frame the wine will be clearing, and should be siphoned from the lees into another clean glass jar about once every three months. When sufficiently clear, the wine may be siphoned into sterilized wine bottles and corked. Enjoy immediately, or store your wine on its side for later consumption.

# 9

## Root Wines

In this chapter you'll find recipes for wine made from a lesser-known winemaking plant part—roots. The advantage of making root wine is that fresh, beautiful taproots do not need to be used. If you have some shriveled-up carrots in your fridge, you can begin a batch of root wine today. Just be aware that if those root vegetables were bought in the store rather than being found in the wild, the resulting wine may be a little different from the wine I make, as cultivated plants are often different from their wild counterparts. This is especially true of cultivated carrots, as the wild versions are white instead of orange, and have a stronger flavor than store-bought carrots.

Many readers are familiar with "hooch," which was distilled from potatoes during prohibition. Wine made from wild roots is a bit more refined than that, although many root wines ferment into potent, almost whiskey-like concoctions with a high alcohol level. If these qualities are desirable to you, this chapter is a good place to begin your winemaking adventures.

### Aniseroot

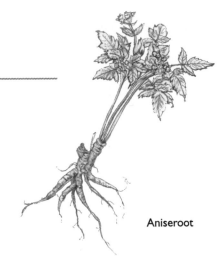

**When to Collect.** April through October.

**Where to Collect.** Shady woods throughout most of the United States, but not in the arid Southwest.

**Wine Color.** Amber.

**Wine Flavor.** Sweet and delicate.

**Wine Aroma.** Hints of anise.

Aniseroot

## Wild Plant Collection Tip

Aniseroot (*Osmorhiza longistylis*) can be collected whenever positive identification can be made, which is easiest when the plant is flowering in May and June. However, the leaves—which possess a distinctive anise aroma when bruised—are visible from April through October, and as early as February in some climates. The stems are grooved and maroon to purplish in color. The roots of this herbaceous plant are easy to retrieve with a small hand shovel. They are close to the surface of the soil and resemble very small, white carrots, sometimes branching and shaped like a jester's hat. Fresh aniseroot may be used, or the roots can be sliced, dried on a screen or dehydrator until brittle, and stored in a glass jar for future winemaking.

# ANISEROOT WINE

4 cups fresh aniseroot, scrubbed with a vegetable brush to remove dirt,
*or* 1 cup dried aniseroot, scrubbed, sliced, and dried

1 gallon boiling water

6 cups sugar

3 cups raisins

1 orange, juiced, rind reserved

1 lemon, juiced, rind reserved

¼ teaspoon wine yeast

1. In a large food-grade bucket, combine the aniseroot and boiling water. Cover with a porous lid, and allow to soak for twenty-four hours.

2. Strain the liquid through cheesecloth into a large nonreactive pot. Bring to a boil over high heat; then remove from the heat immediately.

3. Return the heated liquid to the bucket, and add the sugar, raisins, citrus juices, and rind. Using a long nonreactive spoon, stir until the sugar has dissolved.

4. When the liquid has cooled to lukewarm, sprinkle the yeast on top. Cover with a nylon stocking and a loose-fitting lid, and allow to ferment for at least fourteen days.

5. Strain the liquid into a clean glass container and cover as appropriate. (See page 73.) In six to twelve months, the wine will be ready for bottling. During this time frame the wine will be clearing, and should be siphoned from the lees into another clean glass jar about once every three months. When sufficiently clear, the wine may be siphoned into sterilized wine bottles and corked. Enjoy immediately, or store your wine on its side for later consumption.

# *Arrowleaf Balsamroot*

**When to Collect.** April through September.

**Where to Collect.** Sagebrush plains, open hillsides, flat grasslands, and open pine forests in Northwestern United States.

**Wine Color.** Amber.

**Wine Flavor.** Strong, whiskey-like.

**Wine Aroma.** Potent.

Arrowleaf
Balsamroot

## Wild Plant Collection Tip

Arrowleaf balsamroot (*Balsamorhiza sagittata*) is a one-and-a-half-foot-tall herbaceous plant with completely yellow, daisy-like flowers that bloom from April through July. Collection, though, can continue through September once identification is made. A full-sized digging shovel will be needed to unearth these furrowed taproots, which are thick, deep, and often growing in dense, dry ground. Be aware that this plant contains inulin, a sugar that may be difficult for some people to digest.

## ARROWLEAF BALSAMROOT WINE

5 pounds (about 10 cups) arrowleaf balsamroot

4½ quarts cold water

8½ cups sugar

1½ cups raisins

1½ cups kibbled maize, dried corn kernels,
or coarsely ground cornmeal

Juice from 2 oranges

Juice from 2 lemons

¼ teaspoon wine yeast

1. Scrub the arrowleaf balsamroot with a vegetable brush to remove the dirt. Pound the roots with a meat mallet to remove the outer skin and finer rootlets attached to the taproot. Discard the removed skins and rootlets, and grate or grind the inner root with a cheese grater or coffee grinder.

2. In a large nonreactive pot, combine the grated or ground arrowleaf balsamroot with the cold water, and bring to a boil over high heat. Reduce the heat to low and simmer for fifteen minutes, skimming any scum that forms.

3.  Strain the liquid through cheesecloth into a large food-grade bucket. Add the sugar, raisins, kibbled maize, and citrus juices. Using a long nonreactive spoon, stir until the sugar is dissolved.

4.  When the mixture has cooled to lukewarm, sprinkle the yeast on top. Cover with a nylon stocking and a loose-fitting lid, and allow to ferment for at least fourteen days.

5.  Strain the liquid into a clean glass container and cover as appropriate. (See page 73.) In six to twelve months, the wine will be ready for bottling. During this time frame the wine will be clearing, and should be siphoned from the lees into another clean glass jar about once every three months. When sufficiently clear, the wine may be siphoned into sterilized wine bottles and corked. Enjoy immediately, or store your wine on its side for later consumption.

# *Burdock*

Burdock

**When to Collect.** June through November.

**Where to Collect.** Open fields in the upper two-thirds of the United States.

**Wine Color.** Dark amber.

**Wine Flavor.** Strong, whiskey-like.

**Wine Aroma.** Potent.

## Wild Plant Collection Tip

Burdock (*Arctium minus*, *Arctium lappa*, and *Arctium tomentosum*) roots can be collected from June to November once positive identification has been made. The flowers bloom atop five-foot-high stems from July through October, and appear as tubular, prickly, purple florets. These flowers transform into the marble-sized burrs that stick to your clothing when you brush against them, hence the plant's name. The leaves are large and wooly, the lower leaves are heart-shaped and the upper leaves are nearly oval—a little wider at their base.

This herbaceous plant is a biennial, which means that it grows over the course of two years. The first year, the seeds grow into a root with a green plant top. The second year, the root toughens and the greenery sends forth a flower, which goes to seed. During this second year, the root is less desirable, although it can still be used for wine. It is best to collect either the early burdock roots from the second year growth, or the mature roots from the first year's growth. You want the roots to be large enough to be worth the effort to dig up, yet tender enough to grate. When the root is mature, it will be twelve to twenty-four inches long and about the size of a quarter or a half dollar in diameter. Unless you are digging the roots up from recently loosened soil, a shovel will be necessary.

If you like the idea of burdock root wine, but not the idea of foraging for the roots, be aware that burdock is available in some specialty stores, sometimes under the Asian name of *gobo*. The store-bought root can be substituted for the wild root with good results.

## BURDOCK ROOT WINE

5 pounds (about 10 cups) burdock roots, scrubbed with a vegetable brush to remove dirt, then grated or ground

4½ quarts cold water

8 cups sugar

1½ cups raisins

1½ cups kibbled maize, dried corn kernels, or coarsely ground cornmeal

Juice from 2 oranges

Juice from 2 lemons

¼ teaspoon wine yeast

1. In a large nonreactive pot, combine the grated or ground burdock roots with the cold water, and bring to a boil over high heat. Reduce the heat to low and simmer for fifteen minutes, skimming any scum that forms.

2. Strain the liquid through cheesecloth into a large food-grade bucket. Add the sugar, raisins, kibbled maize, and citrus juices. Using a long nonreactive spoon, stir until the sugar is dissolved.

3. When the mixture has cooled to lukewarm, sprinkle the yeast on top. Cover with a nylon stocking and a loose-fitting lid, and allow to ferment for at least fourteen days.

4. Strain the liquid into a clean glass container and cover as appropriate. (See page 73.) In six to twelve months, the wine will be ready for bottling. During this time frame the wine will be clearing, and should be siphoned from the lees into another clean glass jar about once every three months. When sufficiently clear, the wine may be siphoned into sterilized wine bottles and corked. Enjoy immediately, or store your wine on its side for later consumption.

# *Wild Carrot*

**Wild Carrot**

**When to Collect.** May through August.

**Where to Collect.** Grassy clearings throughout most of the United States.

**Wine Color.** Orange—even though the roots are white.

**Wine Flavor.** Strong.

**Wine Aroma.** Full-bodied.

## Wild Plant Collection Tip

Wild carrot plants (*Daucus carota*) are commonly known as Queen Anne's lace. Their white taproots can be collected whenever proper identification can be made, usually between May and August when the white, lacy flower cluster is in bloom. The foliage is lacy as well, nearly identical to the greenery of the cultivated carrot, with a similar smell. This plant is one to three feet tall and a biennial, which means that the plant grows over the course of two years. The first year, the seeds grow into a root with a green plant top, just like a store-bought carrot. The second year, the greenery sends forth a flower that goes to seed and the root toughens, although it can still be used for making wine. It is best to collect either the early roots from the second year's growth, or the mature roots from the first year's growth. You want the roots large enough to be worth the effort, yet tender enough to grate. When the root is mature but not yet spent, it will be a little smaller in length and diameter than a cultivated carrot. Most wild carrot roots can be retrieved with a hand shovel.

If you choose to buy carrots in a store rather than foraging for them, keep in mind that cultivated carrots are very different from their wild counterpart. The wild version is white instead of orange, and has a much stronger flavor. Cultivated carrots can, of course, be used to make wine, but the resulting brew will both look and taste different from wine made with wild carrots.

## WILD CARROT WINE

5 pounds (about 10 cups) wild carrots,
scrubbed with a vegetable brush to remove dirt,
then grated or ground

4½ quarts cold water

8 cups sugar

1½ cups raisins

1½ cups kibbled maize, dried corn kernels,
or coarsely ground cornmeal

Juice from 2 oranges

Juice from 2 lemons

¼ teaspoon wine yeast

1. In a large nonreactive pot, combine the grated or ground wild carrots with the cold water, and bring to a boil over high heat. Reduce the heat to low and simmer for fifteen minutes, skimming any scum that forms.

2. Strain the liquid through cheesecloth into a large food-grade bucket. Add the sugar, raisins, kibbled maize, and citrus juices. Using a long nonreactive spoon, stir until the sugar is dissolved.

3. When the mixture has cooled to lukewarm, sprinkle the yeast on top. Cover with a nylon stocking and a loose-fitting lid, and allow to ferment for at least fourteen days.

4. Strain the liquid into a clean glass container and cover as appropriate. (See page 73.) In six to twelve months, the wine will be ready for bottling. During this time frame the wine will be clearing, and should be siphoned from the lees into another clean glass jar about once every three months. When sufficiently clear, the wine may be siphoned into sterilized wine bottles and corked. Enjoy immediately, or store your wine on its side for later consumption.

# *Coltsfoot*

Coltsfoot

**When to Collect.** February through September.

**Where to Collect.** Wet areas, cut banks, and seeping ground from Massachusetts to California.

**Wine Color.** Amber.

**Wine Flavor.** Coltsfoot flavor with citrus undertones.

**Wine Aroma.** Citrusy.

## Wild Plant Collection Tip

Coltsfoot (*Petasites palmatus* or *Petasites frigidus*) can be collected as soon as the plant emerges from the ground and proper identification can be made. This can be as early as February at lower elevations in moderate climates. The flowers are barely pink, raggedly daisy-like, and about nickel-sized, growing in spherical clusters. The flowers bloom briefly, and then become floating tufts of fluff, like dandelion fuzz, to be carried off in the wind. All plant parts give off the distinctive aroma of coltsfoot. The coltsfoot plant attains a height of about eighteen inches with large, palmate leaves. The roots are maroon and white, about a quarter inch in diameter, with fine white rootlets. This easy-to-collect underground plant part grows matted just beneath the surface of the soil. When you get a grip on a root and pull on it, usually a network of adjacent roots can be procured at the same time. Coltsfoot also has medicinal properties, making the wine a soothing remedy for adult colds.

## COLTSFOOT ROOT WINE

1 quart (about 4 cups) sliced coltsfoot root,
swished in a bucket of cold water to remove major debris,
then scrubbed with a vegetable brush

1 gallon boiling water

8 cups sugar

Juice from 1 lemon

Juice from 1 orange

¼ teaspoon wine yeast

1. Place the sliced root in a large food-grade bucket, and pour the boiling water over it. Cover with a porous lid, and allow to soak for three days.

2. Strain the liquid through cheesecloth into a large nonreactive pot. Bring to a boil over high heat; then remove from the heat immediately.

3. Return the heated liquid to the bucket and add the sugar and citrus juices. Using a long nonreactive spoon, stir to dissolve the sugar.

4. When the liquid has cooled to lukewarm, sprinkle the yeast on top. Cover with a nylon stocking and a loose-fitting lid, and allow to ferment for at least fourteen days.

5. Strain the liquid into a clean glass container and cover as appropriate. (See page 73.) In six to twelve months, the wine will be ready for bottling. During this time frame the wine will be clearing, and should be siphoned from the lees into another clean glass jar about once every three months. When sufficiently clear, the wine may be siphoned into sterilized wine bottles and corked. Enjoy immediately, or store your wine on its side for later consumption.

Day Lily

# *Day Lily*

**When to Collect.** May through July, or whenever proper identification can be made.

**Where to Collect.** In meadows and along roadsides throughout most of the United States.

**Wine Color.** Cider-colored.

**Wine Flavor.** Strong with undertones of day lily roots.

**Wine Aroma.** Strong, full-bodied.

## Wild Plant Collection Tip

Day lilies (*Hemerocallis fulva*) are easier to identify when they are flowering, which is from May through July, although the roots can be collected any time the ground is not frozen. The orange or yellow flowers are lily-like, and grow up to four feet tall. These herbaceous plants grow in patches amidst their cattail-like leaves, which are nearly as tall as the flowers. Some of the roots are spaghetti-like, and others are swollen like tiny one-inch potatoes with tapering ends. The latter are the ones you want to use. The new-growth roots are bright white after the dirt is removed, and the older roots are covered by a thin brown skin that does not need to be peeled prior to chopping or grinding. Both types of roots are suitable for winemaking, although the older roots with the brown peel have a much stronger flavor. Many roots are clustered together underground at the base of the plant, and digging up a single plant will yield about a dozen or more small tubers. *Caution:* Do not confuse day lilies, which are edible, with "true" lilies, which can be toxic.

## DAY LILY ROOT WINE

1 pound (about 2 cups) ground or chopped day lily roots,
swished in a bucket of cold water to remove the large debris,
then scrubbed with a vegetable brush to remove finer dirt

4½ quarts water

8 cups sugar

1½ cups raisins

1 cup wheat berries

Juice from ½ lemon

Juice from ½ orange

¼ teaspoon wine yeast

1. In a large nonreactive pot, combine the roots with the water. Bring to a boil over high heat, and boil for ten minutes. Then skim off any scum that rises to the surface.

2. Strain the liquid through cheesecloth into a food-grade bucket. Add the sugar, raisins, wheatberries, and citrus juices. Using a long nonreactive spoon, stir until the sugar is dissolved.

3. When the mixture has cooled to lukewarm, sprinkle the yeast on top. Cover with a nylon stocking and a loose-fitting lid, and allow to ferment for at least fourteen days.

4. Strain the liquid into a clean glass container and cover as appropriate. (See page 73.) In six to twelve months, the wine will be ready for bottling. During this time frame the wine will be clearing, and should be siphoned from the lees into another clean glass jar about once every three months. When sufficiently clear, the wine may be siphoned into sterilized wine bottles and corked. Enjoy immediately, or store your wine on its side for later consumption.

Wild Ginger

# *Wild Ginger*

**When to Collect.** April and May, or whenever the foliage is visible for proper identification.

**Where to Collect.** Rich, shaded woods of the northern United States.

**Wine Color.** Tea-colored.

**Wine Flavor.** Mildly "gingery," unique, and very good.

**Wine Aroma.** Scented of wild ginger, but not overpoweringly so.

## Wild Plant Collection Tip

Wild ginger (*Asarum canadense*) is a perennial herbaceous plant that flowers from April through May. The blossoms aid in identification, although the roots can be collected any time the ground is not frozen. The flowers are a deep maroon and are usually hidden beneath the ground-hugging, deeply notched, heart-shaped, velvety leaves. The jointed roots lie just below the surface of the ground in a matted network that can be easily lifted from the ground with a hand trowel.

If you're thinking of buying your ginger root in the store rather than foraging for it, be aware that wild ginger is completely unrelated to the Asian ginger that's found in supermarkets and produce stores. You simply can't use Asian ginger to make Wild Ginger Wine.

## WILD GINGER WINE

2 quarts (about 8 cups) wild ginger root,
scrubbed with a vegetable brush to remove dirt,
then cut into one-inch sections

1 gallon boiling water

8 cups sugar

2 cups prunes

Juice from 4 oranges

Juice from 4 lemons

¼ teaspoon wine yeast

1. Place the sliced roots in a large food-grade bucket, and pour the boiling water over them. Cover with a porous lid, and allow to soak for three days.

2. Strain the liquid through cheesecloth into a large nonreactive pot. Bring to a boil over high heat; then remove from the heat immediately.

3 Return the heated liquid to the bucket, and add the sugar, prunes, and citrus juices. Using a large nonreactive spoon, stir until the sugar is dissolved.

4. When the liquid has cooled to lukewarm, sprinkle the yeast on top. Cover with a nylon stocking and a loose-fitting lid, and allow to ferment for at least fourteen days.

5. Strain the liquid into a clean glass container and cover as appropriate. (See page 73.) In six to twelve months, the wine will be ready for bottling. During this time frame the wine will be clearing, and should be siphoned from the lees into another clean glass jar about once every three months. When sufficiently clear, the wine may be siphoned into sterilized wine bottles and corked. Enjoy immediately, or store your wine on its side for later consumption.

# *Thistle*

Thistle

**When to Collect.** May through October, or whenever proper identification can be made.

**Where to Collect.** Grassy clearings throughout most of the United States.

**Wine Color.** Dark amber.

**Wine Flavor.** Strong, whiskey-like.

**Wine Aroma.** Full-bodied.

## Wild Plant Collection Tip

Thistle (*Cirsium vulgare*) roots can be collected whenever proper identification can be made. Once you become familiar with this six-foot-tall herbaceous, prickly plant, you will be able to identify young plants growing as early as late January in mild climates, and later elsewhere. The baby thistle plants grow in a rosette, and appear silvery in color due to the fine, hairy prickles that appear to coat the surface of the leaves, like down. At this stage, the roots are quite slender and very tender, so you may want to wait until later in the year to collect them, at which point they will be larger in size. For ease in identification, thistle shows its lavender, brush-like flowers surrounded by spiny-tipped bracts from June through September.

This plant is a biennial, which means it grows over the course of two years. The first year, the seeds grow into a root with a green plant top. The second year, the greenery sends forth a flower that goes to seed and the root toughens, although it can still be used for winemaking. It is best to collect either the early roots from the second year's growth or the mature roots from the first year's growth. You want them to be large enough to be worth the effort to dig up, yet tender enough to grate. When the root is mature but not yet spent, it will be up to twelve inches long and white in color, but turning brown when cooked. Young thistle roots can be retrieved with a hand shovel, although older roots, or those growing in dry or rocky soil, may need to be procured using a full-sized gardening shovel. Wearing gloves is recommended.

## THISTLE WINE

5 pounds (about 10 cups) unpeeled thistle roots, scrubbed clean with a vegetable brush, then grated or ground

4½ quarts cold water

8 cups sugar

1½ cups raisins

1½ cups kibbled maize, dried corn kernels, or coarsely ground cornmeal

Juice from 2 oranges

Juice from 2 lemons

¼ teaspoon wine yeast

1. In a large nonreactive pot, combine the thistle roots with the cold water. Bring to a boil over high heat, reduce the heat to low, and simmer for fifteen minutes, skimming any scum that forms.

2. Strain the liquid through cheesecloth into a large food-grade bucket. Add the sugar, raisins, kibbled maize, and citrus juices. Using a long nonreactive spoon, stir until the sugar is dissolved.

3. When the mixture has cooled to lukewarm, sprinkle the yeast on top. Cover with a nylon stocking and a loose-fitting lid, and allow to ferment for at least fourteen days.

4.  Strain the liquid into a clean glass container and cover as appropriate. (See page 73.) In six to twelve months, the wine will be ready for bottling. During this time frame the wine will be clearing, and should be siphoned from the lees into another clean glass jar about once every three months. When sufficiently clear, the wine may be siphoned into sterilized wine bottles and corked. Enjoy immediately, or store your wine on its side for later consumption.

# 10

---

# *Flower Wines*

This chapter is blooming with flower wine recipes. When foraging for flowers, keep in mind that many are delicate and must be collected midday, after the dew has evaporated. Haste should be made to return home quickly with your petals, as they are fragile and should be readied for winemaking as soon as possible. Many wildflowers lose their unique color and fragrance through the process of winemaking; however, some plants retain the scent of their blooms. Since flowers are a fragile plant part with delicate flavor and aroma, you should not rinse them with water. Collect only debris-free petals so that cleaning is unnecessary.

A word should be said about the importance of foraging for flowers rather than using flowers from your local flower shop—or, for that matter, from your garden. Wild flowers can be quite different from their cultivated counterparts. Wild roses, for instance, are more delicately scented and colored than cultivated roses, and wild violets are a unique plant, very different from the African violets you may enjoy as a houseplant. For that reason, you'll want to use only foraged wild flowers when making your wild wines.

## *Apple Blossom*

**When to Collect.** February through June.

**Where to Collect.** Areas of full sun throughout the United States.

**Wine Color.** Cider-colored.

**Wine Flavor.** Pleasantly unique, no hint of apple.

**Wine Aroma.** Sweet and spicy, almost cinnamon-like.

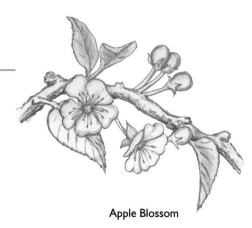

**Apple Blossom**

## Wild Plant Collection Tip

Wild apple (*Malus* species) blossoms are fragrant, white or pink, five-petaled, and roselike, although smaller in size than roses. The petals can be tickled from the lower, easy-to-reach branches of the tree, and the quantity of flowers required for winemaking can be collected with little time or effort. If you collect the petals only, rather than the entire flower, the fruiting part of the bloom can develop to maturity on the tree, and you will then be able to collect apples from those same branches in the fall.

# APPLE BLOSSOM WINE

1 gallon (about 16 cups) wild apple blossoms, unrinsed

1 gallon boiling water

7½ cups sugar

2 cups raisins

¼ teaspoon wine yeast

1. Place the flowers in a large food-grade bucket, and pour the boiling water over them. Using a long nonreactive spoon, stir for a minute or two. Then cover with a porous lid, and allow to soak for forty-eight hours.

2. Strain the liquid through cheesecloth into a large nonreactive pot. Bring to a boil over high heat; then remove from the heat immediately.

3. Return the hot liquid to the bucket. Add the sugar and raisins, and stir until the sugar is dissolved.

4. When the mixture has cooled to lukewarm, sprinkle the yeast on top. Cover with a nylon stocking and a loose-fitting lid, and allow to ferment for at least fourteen days.

5. Strain the liquid into a clean glass container and cover as appropriate. (See page 73.) In six to twelve months, the wine will be ready for bottling. During this time frame the wine will be clearing, and should be siphoned from the lees into another clean glass jar about once every three months. When sufficiently clear, the wine may be siphoned into sterilized wine bottles and corked. Enjoy immediately, or store your wine on its side for later consumption.

# Black Locust

**Black Locust**

**When to Collect.** May through June.

**Where to Collect.** Rich woods throughout most of the United States.

**Wine Color.** Cider-colored.

**Wine Flavor.** Strong and sweet.

**Wine Aroma.** Hearty.

## Wild Plant Collection Tip

The hefty white, pea-like blossoms of the black locust tree (*Robinia pseudoacacia*) are highly fragrant, almost overpoweringly so. They grow on large flower heads, which are easily stripped from their drooping racemes. Collect black locust flowers when in full bloom, before they start to fade. The black locust is a large tree, but there should be some lower-hanging branches where the flowers are easier to reach, enabling you to collect the needed quantity of flowers in a short amount of time.

## BLACK LOCUST FLOWER WINE

1 gallon (about 16 cups) black locust flowers, unrinsed

4½ quarts boiling water

6¼ cups sugar

2¼ cups raisins

¼ teaspoon wine yeast

1. Place the flowers in a large food-grade bucket, and pour the boiling water over them. Cover with a porous lid, and allow to soak for five days, stirring the mixture with a long nonreactive spoon daily.

2. Strain the liquid through cheesecloth into a large nonreactive pot. Bring to a boil over high heat; then remove from the heat immediately.

3. Return the heated liquid to the bucket. Add the sugar and raisins, and use a long nonreactive spoon to stir until the sugar is dissolved.

4. When the mixture has cooled to lukewarm, sprinkle the yeast on top. Cover with a nylon stocking and a loose-fitting lid, and allow to ferment for at least fourteen days.

5. Strain the liquid into a clean glass container and cover as appropriate. (See page 73.) In six to twelve months, the wine will be ready for bottling. During this time frame the wine will be clearing, and should be siphoned from the lees into another clean glass jar about once every three months. When sufficiently clear, the wine may be siphoned into sterilized wine bottles and corked. Enjoy immediately, or store your wine on its side for later consumption.

California Poppy

# *California Poppy*

**When to Collect.** February through September.

**Where to Collect.** Open areas from Washington to southern California.

**Wine Color.** Yellowish-orange.

**Wine Flavor.** Strong tasting.

**Wine Aroma.** Without fragrance.

## Wild Plant Collection Tip

The flowers of the California poppy (*Eschscholzia californica*) are the brightest orange imaginable, and are papery thin, bearing a resemblance to crepe paper. The petals separate easily from their greenery, and can be plucked from the plant while leaving the reproductive parts intact. Even though you can often find large patches of this one- to two-foot-tall annual herbaceous plant, it is difficult to collect these blooms in bulk due to their fragility. You may want to reduce the quantity of this recipe to accommodate a lesser amount of flower petals.

If you live in California, note that the poppy is your state flower, and is a protected plant in your state. Be certain that you are not collecting petals from restricted lands.

## CALIFORNIA POPPY FLOWER WINE

1 gallon (about 16 cups) California poppy flower petals, unrinsed

1 gallon boiling water

6 cups sugar

Juice and rind from ½ lemon

Juice and rind from ½ orange

¼ teaspoon wine yeast

1. Place the flowers in a large food-grade bucket, and pour the boiling water over them. Cover with a porous lid, and allow to soak for forty-eight hours.

2. Strain the liquid through cheesecloth into a large nonreactive pot. Bring to a boil over high heat; then remove from the heat immediately.

3. Return the heated liquid to the bucket. Add the sugar, citrus juices, and rinds, and use a long nonreactive spoon to stir until the sugar is dissolved.

4. When the liquid has cooled to lukewarm, sprinkle the yeast on top. Cover with a nylon stocking and a loose-fitting lid, and allow to ferment for at least fourteen days.

5. Strain the liquid into a clean glass container and cover as appropriate. (See page 73.) In six to twelve months, the wine will be ready for bottling. During this time frame the wine will be clearing, and should be siphoned from the lees into another clean glass jar about once every three months. When sufficiently clear, the wine may be siphoned into sterilized wine bottles and corked. Enjoy immediately, or store your wine on its side for later consumption.

## *Red Clover*

Red Clover

**When to Collect.** May through October.
**Where to Collect.** In open fields throughout the United States.
**Wine Color.** Amber.
**Wine Flavor.** Like sweet clover tea, reminiscent of clover honey.
**Wine Aroma.** Sweet.

### Wild Plant Collection Tip

Growing from six to sixteen inches in height, red clover (*Trifolium pratense*) bears flowers that are dark pink in color. The blooms should be collected after the dew has evaporated from the plants—usually after 11:00 AM—and can be easily removed by pinching them off between two fingers. Red clover and white clover (*Trifolium repens*) often grow together in similar habitats, and can be used interchangeably in this recipe. Red clover flowers are larger and sweeter than those of the white clover plant, though, making it easier to collect the needed amount of blooms.

It is very important to remove any and all plant greenery from the flower head and tubelike flower petals. The green plant parts of clover contain the blood-thinning substance coumarin, which can prevent blood from clotting. By grasping the greenery in one hand and the tubular flower petals in the other, the flower parts can be easily separated from the nonflowering parts.

## RED CLOVER WINE

3 quarts (about 12 cups) red clover blossoms,
unrinsed and completely cleaned of greenery

1 gallon boiling water

6 cups sugar

½ cup wheat berries

⅓ cup raisins

¼ teaspoon wine yeast

1. Place the flower heads in a large food-grade bucket, and pour the boiling water over them. Cover with a porous lid, and allow to soak for four days.

2. Strain the liquid into a large nonreactive pot. Bring to a boil over high heat; then remove from the heat immediately.

3. Return the heated liquid to the bucket. Add the sugar, wheat berries, and raisins, and use a long nonreactive spoon to stir until the sugar is dissolved.

4. When the liquid has cooled to lukewarm, sprinkle the yeast on top. Cover with a nylon stocking and a loose-fitting lid, and allow to ferment for at least fourteen days.

5. Strain the liquid into a clean glass container and cover as appropriate. (See page 73.) In six to twelve months, the wine will be ready for bottling. During this time frame the wine will be clearing, and should be siphoned from the lees into another clean glass jar about once every three months. When sufficiently clear, the wine may be siphoned into sterilized wine bottles and corked. Enjoy immediately, or store your wine on its side for later consumption.

Coltsfoot

## *Coltsfoot*

**When to Collect.** February through June.

**Where to Collect.** Cool, moist areas along mountain roadsides from Massachusetts to California.

**Wine Color.** Dark tea-colored.

**Wine Flavor.** Potent.

**Wine Aroma.** Faintly sweet.

### Wild Plant Collection Tip

The flower heads of the perennial coltsfoot plant (*Petasites palmatus* and *Petasites frigidus*) are whitish-pink, and raggedly daisy-like. These blooms emerge atop sturdy stalks, with the lower-lying, flannel-like, palm-shaped foliage not breaking ground until later in the season. Coltsfoot flowers are floppy, and grow in spherical umbels that quickly turn into airborne dandelion-like fuzz. Remove them by plucking them off the stalks. If you find that the flowers have already become fluffy seed balls, drive to a higher elevation in the same area, where the plants might be in an earlier stage of development. The small amount of greenery that holds the petals together does not need to be removed.

## COLTSFOOT FLOWER WINE

2 quarts (about 8 cups) coltsfoot flowers, unrinsed

1 gallon boiling water

6 cups sugar

3 cups raisins

¼ teaspoon wine yeast

1.  Place the flowers in a large food-grade bucket, and pour the boiling water over them. Cover with a loose-fitting lid, and allow to soak for forty-eight hours.

2.  Strain the liquid through cheesecloth into a large nonreactive pot. Bring to a boil over high heat; then remove from the heat immediately.

3.  Return the heated liquid to the bucket. Add the sugar and raisins, and use a long nonreactive spoon to stir until the sugar is dissolved.

4.  When the liquid has cooled to lukewarm, sprinkle the yeast on top. Cover with a nylon stocking and a loose-fitting lid, and allow to ferment for at least fourteen days.

5.  Strain the liquid into a clean glass container and cover as appropriate. (See page 73.) In six to twelve months, the wine will be ready for bottling. During this time frame the wine will be clearing, and should be siphoned from the lees into another clean glass jar about once every three months. When sufficiently clear, the wine may be siphoned into sterilized wine bottles and corked. Enjoy immediately, or store your wine on its side for later consumption.

## *Dandelion*

**When to Collect.** June through October.

**Where to Collect.** Grassy meadows throughout most of the United States.

**Wine Color.** Yellow.

**Wine Flavor.** Substantial and distinct, yet difficult to describe.

**Wine Aroma.** Mousy, but improves with age. In spite of its unfavorable aroma, the taste of the wine is good.

Dandelion

## Wild Plant Collection Tip

The distinctive yellow-rayed flower of the dandelion (*Taraxacum officinale*) blooms from June through October. Collect dandelions by snapping the flowers off their stems. The yellow petals can be easily pulled from their green collar by grasping the yellow portion with one hand and pulling it out of the greenery in your other hand. This herbaceous plant will exude a milky liquid (latex) at the point where the flower has been severed. Dandelions are best collected midday after the dew has had a chance to evaporate from the blooms. You do not need to meticulously remove every bit of greenery that holds the petals together, but the more greenery you remove, the better tasting your wine will be.

## DANDELION WINE

1 gallon (about 16 cups) dandelion flowers,
unrinsed, with most of the green base removed

1 gallon boiling water

12 whole cloves

3 oranges, sliced, with rinds on

1 lemon, sliced, with rinds on

7 cups sugar

¼ teaspoon wine yeast

1. In a large food-grade bucket, combine the dandelion flowers and the boiling water. Cover with a porous lid, and allow to steep for five days.

2. Strain the liquid through cheesecloth into a large nonreactive pot, squeezing the liquid from the flowers. Add the cloves, oranges, and lemon.

3. Bring the mixture to a boil, and boil gently for twenty minutes. Return the heated mixture to the bucket and add the sugar. Using a long nonreactive spoon, stir until the sugar is dissolved.

4. When the mixture has cooled to lukewarm, sprinkle the yeast on top. Cover with a nylon stocking and a loose-fitting lid, and allow to ferment for at least fourteen days.

5. Strain the liquid into a clean glass container and cover as appropriate. (See page 73.) In six to twelve months, the wine will be ready for bottling. During this time frame the wine will be clearing, and should be siphoned from the lees into another clean glass jar about once every three months. When sufficiently clear—a process that can take several months—the wine may be siphoned into sterilized wine bottles and corked. Enjoy immediately, or store your wine on its side for later consumption.

# Day Lily

**When to Collect.** April through July.

**Where to Collect.** In meadows and along roadsides throughout most of the United States.

**Wine Color.** Orange.

**Wine Flavor.** Strong, pleasant.

**Wine Aroma.** Citrusy.

Day Lily

## Wild Plant Collection Tip

The orange or yellow flowers of the herbaceous day lily (*Hemerocallis fulva*) are lily-like, and grow up to four feet tall. The flowers can be easily snapped off the plant with a little twist of the wrist. The leaves of this plant are sword-like—long and narrow. Unopened flower buds may be collected along with the flowering portions of the plant, and any combination of the flowers and buds can be used in this recipe. These flowers are easy to collect in the large quantities needed for winemaking. *Caution:* Do not confuse day lilies, which are edible, with "true" lilies, which can be toxic.

## DAY LILY FLOWER WINE

1 gallon (about 16 cups) day lily flowers and/or flower buds, unrinsed

1 gallon boiling water

7 cups sugar

Juice and rind from ½ lemon

Juice and rind from ½ orange

¼ teaspoon wine yeast

1. Place the flowers in a large food-grade bucket, and pour the boiling water over them. Cover with a porous lid, and allow to soak for forty-eight hours.

2. Strain the liquid through cheesecloth into a large nonreactive pot. Bring to a boil over high heat; then remove from the heat immediately.

3. Return the heated liquid to the bucket. Add the sugar, citrus juice, and citrus rind, and use a long nonreactive spoon to stir until the sugar is dissolved.

4. When the liquid has cooled to lukewarm, sprinkle the yeast on top. Cover with a nylon stocking and a loose-fitting lid, and ferment for at least fourteen days.

5. Strain the liquid into a clean glass container and cover as appropriate. (See page 73.) In six to twelve months, the wine will be ready for bottling. During this time

frame the wine will be clearing, and should be siphoned from the lees into another clean glass jar about once every three months. When sufficiently clear, the wine may be siphoned into sterilized wine bottles and corked. Enjoy immediately, or store your wine on its side for later consumption.

**Blue Elderberry**

# *Blue Elderberry*

**When to Collect.** June through July.

**Where to Collect.** Sunny locations throughout most of the United States.

**Wine Color.** Root beer-colored.

**Wine Flavor.** Robust and excellent.

**Wine Aroma.** Resembles anise.

## Wild Plant Collection Tip

The flowers of the common elder (*Sambucus canadensis*) and blue-berried elder (*Sambucus glauca*) are small, fragrant, cream-colored, and shaped like five-pointed stars. They grow in flat-topped umbels on branching shrubs. You can either pluck the individual flowers in the field, or you can snap off the entire flowering umbel and separate the flowers from the little branches when you get home. I prefer the latter method, as the flowers wilt more rapidly after they have been removed from their clustering heads. Just rub the flowers between two fingers or both hands, and the blossoms will fall like cream-colored snowflakes into your collection container. Tiny insects like to hide in these flowers, so be sure to shake the flower umbel lightly to dislodge them.

Red elderberry (*Sambucus racemosa*) is a rank-smelling, brushy shrub that grows in moist woods throughout the Pacific coast range. It is a questionably edible wild plant that would result in an unpalatably bitter finished wine. The flowers from this plant should not be used in this recipe.

## ELDER FLOWER WINE

1 gallon (about 16 cups) fresh elder flowers,
unrinsed and removed from umbel

1 gallon boiling water

8 cups sugar

3 cups raisins

¼ teaspoon wine yeast

1.  Place the flowers in a large food-grade bucket, and pour the boiling water over them. Cover with a porous lid, and allow to soak for four days.

2.  Strain the liquid through cheesecloth into a large nonreactive pot. Bring to a boil over high heat; then remove from the heat immediately.

3.  Return the heated liquid to the bucket. Add the sugar and raisins, and use a long nonreactive spoon to stir until the sugar is dissolved.

4.  When the liquid has cooled to lukewarm, sprinkle the yeast on top. Cover with a nylon stocking and a loose-fitting lid, and allow to ferment for at least fourteen days.

5.  Strain the liquid into a clean glass container and cover as appropriate. (See page 73.) In six to twelve months, the wine will be ready for bottling. During this time frame the wine will be clearing, and should be siphoned from the lees into another clean glass jar about once every three months. When sufficiently clear, the wine may be siphoned into sterilized wine bottles and corked. Enjoy immediately, or store your wine on its side for later consumption.

# *Fennel*

Fennel

**When to Collect.** May through September.

**Where to Collect.** Along roadsides and in fields west of the Sierra Nevada and Cascade Mountains.

**Wine Color.** Golden orange.

**Wine Flavor.** Tastes of fennel.

**Wine Aroma.** Herbal and sweet.

## Wild Plant Collection Tip

Wild fennel (*Foeniculum vulgare*) is an herbaceous plant that grows up to seven feet tall. All parts of this plant, including the flowers, possess the distinctive fennel aroma. The tiny, yellow, five-petaled flowers grow on flat-topped umbels, and the floral portion can be easily removed from the feathery greens. The blooms can then be used fresh, or dried on a screen or in a dehydrator until they are brittle, and then crumbled for more compact storage. Because the greenery of this plant can also be transformed into wine, it is not necessary to meticulously remove all greens from the flower heads. Note that because of fennel's potent flavor and aroma, a smaller-than-usual amount of flowers is needed to make this wine.

## FENNEL FLOWER WINE

½ cup dried fennel flowers, *or* 2 cups fresh fennel flowers, unrinsed

1 gallon boiling water

6 cups sugar

3 cups raisins

¼ teaspoon wine yeast

1.  In a large food-grade bucket, combine the flowers and the boiling water. Cover with a porous lid, and allow to soak for twenty-four hours.

2.  Strain the liquid through cheesecloth into a large nonreactive pot. Bring to a boil over high heat; then remove from the heat immediately.

3.  Return the heated liquid to the bucket. Add the sugar and raisins, and use a long nonreactive spoon to stir until the sugar is dissolved.

4.  When the liquid has cooled to lukewarm, sprinkle the yeast on top. Cover with a nylon stocking and a loose-fitting lid, and allow to ferment for at least fourteen days.

5.  Strain the liquid into a clean glass container and cover as appropriate. (See page 73.) In six to twelve months, the wine will be ready for bottling. During this time frame the wine will be clearing, and should be siphoned from the lees into another clean glass jar about once every three months. When sufficiently clear, the wine may be siphoned into sterilized wine bottles and corked. Enjoy immediately, or store your wine on its side for later consumption.

# *Goldenrod*

**When to Collect.** July through September.

**Where to Collect.** Dry fields and open woods throughout most of the United States, but not in the arid Southwest.

**Wine Color.** Yellow.

**Wine Flavor.** Full-bodied.

**Wine Aroma.** Floral-citrus.

**Goldenrod**

## Wild Plant Collection Tip

The tiny yellow flowers of goldenrod (*Solidago odora*) grow in clusters that weigh down the tip of the three-foot-tall plant, causing it to arch. Because the flowering head is so dense, it is an easy task to collect the amount of plant material needed for this recipe. Before you separate the flowers from their mother plant, it's best to shake the flower head to dislodge any little insects that may be inside. The entire flower cluster is used to make this wine, so the individual blooms do not need to be separated from the floral head. Be aware that if you are allergic to goldenrod pollen, it is recommended that you avoid consuming this wine.

## GOLDENROD FLOWER WINE

1 gallon (about 16 cups) goldenrod flower clusters, unrinsed

1 gallon boiling water

8 cups sugar

3 cups raisins

¼ teaspoon wine yeast

1. In a large food-grade bucket, combine the flower clusters with the boiling water. Cover with a porous lid, and allow to soak for forty-eight hours.

2. Strain the liquid through cheesecloth into a large nonreactive pot. Bring to a boil over high heat; then remove from the heat immediately.

3. Return the heated liquid to the bucket. Add the sugar and raisins, and use a long nonreactive spoon to stir until the sugar is dissolved.

4. When the liquid has cooled to lukewarm, sprinkle the yeast on top. Cover with a nylon stocking and a loose-fitting lid, and allow to ferment for at least fourteen days.

5. Strain the liquid into a clean glass container and cover as appropriate. (See page 73.) In six to twelve months, the wine will be ready for bottling. During this time frame the wine will be clearing, and should be siphoned from the lees into another clean glass jar about once every three months. When sufficiently clear, the wine may be siphoned into sterilized wine bottles and corked. Enjoy immediately, or store your wine on its side for later consumption.

## *Gorse*

Gorse

**When to Collect.** Year-round, sometimes more abundant in winter months.

**Where to Collect.** Thickets along the Pacific coast of Oregon and California.

**Wine Color.** Yellow.

**Wine Flavor.** Mellow.

**Wine Aroma.** Mousy, but improves with age. In spite of its unfavorable aroma, the taste of the wine is very good.

## Wild Plant Collection Tip

Gorse (*Ulex europaeus*) is a dense, thorny shrub that does not welcome the innocent flower picker. This eight-foot-tall shrub has yellow pea-shaped flowers that bloom almost year-round, even in the winter. Be cautioned: You must wear your most protective clothing to tackle gorse flower collection, since the blooms are interspersed within the densely spiny branches. Despite your best efforts to ward off the painfully sharp thorns, you will inevitably be pricked. The individual flowers are moderately sized, so collecting the amount needed for this recipe is fairly quick.

## GORSE FLOWER WINE

1 gallon (about 16 cups) gorse flowers, unrinsed

1 gallon boiling water

7 cups sugar

2 cups raisins

¼ teaspoon wine yeast

1. In a large food-grade bucket, combine the flowers with the boiling water. Cover with a porous lid, and allow to soak for forty-eight hours.

2. Strain the liquid through cheesecloth into a large nonreactive pot. Bring to a boil over high heat; then remove from the heat immediately.

3. Return the heated liquid to the bucket. Add the sugar and raisins, and use a long nonreactive spoon to stir until the sugar is dissolved.

4. When the liquid has cooled to lukewarm, sprinkle the yeast on top. Cover with a nylon stocking and a loose-fitting lid, and allow to ferment for at least fourteen days.

5. Strain the liquid into a clean glass container and cover as appropriate. (See page 73.) In six to twelve months, the wine will be ready for bottling. During this time frame the wine will be clearing, and should be siphoned from the lees into another clean glass jar about once every three months. When sufficiently clear, the wine may be siphoned into sterilized wine bottles and corked. Enjoy immediately, or store your wine on its side for later consumption.

**Hawthorn**

# *Hawthorn*

**When to Collect.** April and May.

**Where to Collect.** Meadows, hillsides, and along streams in sunny locations throughout most of the United States.

**Wine Color.** Dark amber, nearly tea-colored.

**Wine Flavor.** Hints of vanilla.

**Wine Aroma.** Sweet.

## Wild Plant Collection Tip

Hawthorn (*Crataegus monogyna*) is a shrublike thorny tree that grows up to twenty feet in height, and bears clusters of cream-colored flowers. Hawthorn petals do not separate easily from the branches as a whole flower, but the five small, rounded petals will float off if you tickle them over a bowl or collection container. The petals that do not detach readily are telling you that it's too soon for them to be removed, and you can try again in a day or two. Be especially alert to pollinating bees, as they may not be friendly toward your plant-collecting efforts, and be sure to avoid this tree's protruding thorns.

To remove the tiny spiders and insects hiding in the petals, leave your collection bowl alone on a counter for a few minutes, and most of the "critters" will climb to the top of the petal heap, where they can be easily removed. It is definitely time-consuming to gather the necessary amount of petals for this recipe. Unless you find a tree where the blossoms are easy to reach, you may wish to reduce the quantity of wine you make.

## HAWTHORN FLOWER WINE

3 quarts (about 12 cups) hawthorn
flowers, unrinsed

1 gallon boiling water

6 cups sugar

3 cups raisins

¼ teaspoon wine yeast

1. Place the flowers in a large food-grade bucket, and pour the boiling water over them. Cover with a porous lid, and allow to soak for forty-eight hours.

2. Strain the liquid through cheesecloth into a large nonreactive pot. Bring to a boil over high heat; then remove from the heat immediately.

3. Return the heated liquid to the bucket. Add the sugar and raisins, and use a long nonreactive spoon to stir until the sugar is dissolved.

4. When the liquid has cooled to lukewarm, sprinkle the yeast on top. Cover with a nylon stocking and a loose-fitting lid, and allow to ferment for at least fourteen days.

5.  Strain the liquid into a clean glass container and cover as appropriate. (See page 73.) In six to twelve months, the wine will be ready for bottling. During this time frame the wine will be clearing, and should be siphoned from the lees into another clean glass jar about once every three months. When sufficiently clear, the wine may be siphoned into sterilized wine bottles and corked. Enjoy immediately, or store your wine on its side for later consumption.

# *Oregon Grape*

Oregon Grape

**When to Collect.** March through May.

**Where to Collect.** Borders of forests west of the Cascade Mountains from Washington to California.

**Wine Color.** Cinnamon-colored.

**Wine Flavor.** Strong and pleasant.

**Wine Aroma.** Strong and pleasant.

## Wild Plant Collection Tip

The Oregon grape plant (*Mahonia nervosa* or *Berberis nervosa*) is a short, erect, unbranched evergreen shrub that seldom grows more than three feet in height. Although it can survive in thick woods, any shrub located in the shade may not be flowering. You will have more success collecting the bright yellow flowers by finding plants that are growing in at least partial sunlight. The flowers grow densely on long, upright racemes, and separate from the mother plant with a slight tug. The leaves of this plant are holly-like with pointed tips, but you can easily avoid the prickles when you collect these flowers. Because the flower clusters are dense, it is a simple task to collect the amount of blossoms required for this wine.

## OREGON GRAPE FLOWER WINE

1 gallon (about 16 cups) Oregon grape flowers
and/or flower buds, unrinsed

1 gallon boiling water

6 ¾ cups sugar

2 cups raisins

¼ teaspoon wine yeast

1. Place the flowers and buds in a large food-grade bucket, and pour the boiling water over them. Cover with a porous lid, and allow to soak for forty-eight hours.

2. Strain the liquid through cheesecloth into a large nonreactive pot. Bring to a boil over high heat; then remove from the heat immediately.

3. Return the heated liquid to the bucket. Add the sugar and raisins, and use a long nonreactive spoon to stir until the sugar has dissolved.

4. When the liquid has cooled to lukewarm, sprinkle the yeast on top. Cover with a nylon stocking and a loose-fitting lid, and allow to ferment for at least fourteen days.

5. Strain the liquid into a clean glass container and cover as appropriate. (See page 73.) In six to twelve months, the wine will be ready for bottling. During this time frame the wine will be clearing, and should be siphoned from the lees into another clean glass jar about once every three months. When sufficiently clear, the wine may be siphoned into sterilized wine bottles and corked. Enjoy immediately, or store your wine on its side for later consumption.

## Ox-Eye Daisy

Ox-Eye Daisy

**When to Collect.** May through August.

**Where to Collect.** Roadsides, disturbed ground, and open fields in the northern half of the United States.

**Wine Color.** Yellow.

**Wine Flavor.** Sweet, excellent.

**Wine Aroma.** Hints of chrysanthemum.

## Wild Plant Collection Tip

Ox-eye daisies (*Chrysanthemum leucanthemum*) are the familiar one- to two-foot tall herbaceous plants with white flower petals surrounding a yellow disc—the same blooms used to play "he loves me, he loves me not." Often, you will see a field of white when the blossoms have newly opened, with the flowers covering a meadow like a blanket of snow. Collect the flowers midday after the dew has lifted, plucking the flower heads from their stems with a simple pull. When ox-eye daisies are growing densely, you can very often grab a handful of flower tops with just one tug. Remember that you want to make your wine out of the whole flower head, and not just the petals.

## OX-EYE DAISY WINE

1 gallon (about 16 cups) ox-eye daisy flowers
(entire flower heads, including the yellow central disc
and the white petals), unrinsed

1 gallon hot (not boiling) water

6 cups sugar

¼ teaspoon wine yeast

1. Place the flowers in a large food-grade bucket, and pour the hot water over them. Cover with a porous lid, and allow to soak for forty-eight hours.

2. Strain the liquid through cheesecloth into a large nonreactive pot, squeezing the flowers to extract all of the flavor and the juice. Bring just to a boil over high heat; then remove from the heat immediately.

3. Return the heated liquid to the bucket. Add the sugar, and use a long nonreactive spoon to stir until the sugar is dissolved.

4. When the mixture has cooled to lukewarm, sprinkle the yeast on top. Cover with a nylon stocking and a loose-fitting lid, and allow to ferment for at least fourteen days.

5. Strain the liquid into a clean glass container and cover as appropriate. (See page 73.) In six to twelve months, the wine will be ready for bottling. During this time frame the wine will be clearing, and should be siphoned from the lees into another clean glass jar about once every three months. When sufficiently clear, the wine may be siphoned into sterilized wine bottles and corked. Enjoy immediately, or store your wine on its side for later consumption.

**Wild Rose**

# *Wild Rose*

**When to Collect.** May through August.

**Where to Collect.** Wet or dry, shady or sunny locations throughout the United States.

**Wine Color.** Yellow.

**Wine Flavor.** Rose.

**Wine Aroma.** Pleasant, but not roselike.

## Wild Plant Collection Tip

The petals of the wild rose plant (*Rosa* species) can be collected whenever this shrub is flowering, and before the petals begin to turn brown. Wild roses are a thorny bunch, and care must be taken to avoid the prickly protrusions. As a rule, the blossoms grow on arching canes that can be easily collected without entering the bramblelike mass. The colorful pink parts of the petals can be easily separated from the greenery by grasping the petals with the fingers of one hand while pulling the green plant part away with the other hand.

If you want to avoid foraging for wild roses, and are thinking of using cultivated roses instead, be aware that these two plants are quite dissimilar. The wild rose is more delicately scented and colored than any cultivated rose, so use of cultivated roses would produce a very different wine.

## WILD ROSE PETAL WINE

6 cups sugar

1 gallon boiling water

¼ teaspoon wine yeast

1 to 1½ quarts (4–6 cups) fresh wild rose petals, unrinsed

1. Place the sugar in a large food-grade bucket, and pour the boiling water over it. Using a long nonreactive spoon, stir to dissolve.

2. When the mixture has cooled to lukewarm, sprinkle the yeast on top. Cover with a porous lid, and allow to ferment for forty-eight hours.

3. Stir the wild rose petals into the liquid. Cover with a nylon stocking and a loose-fitting lid, and allow to continue fermenting for at least fourteen more days.

4. Strain the liquid into a clean glass container and cover as appropriate. (See page 73.) In six to twelve months, the wine will be ready for bottling. During this time frame the wine will be clearing, and should be siphoned from the lees into another clean glass jar about once every three months. When sufficiently clear, the wine may be siphoned into sterilized wine bottles and corked. Enjoy immediately, or store your wine on its side for later consumption.

## *Scotch Broom*

**When to Collect.** April through June.

**Where to Collect.** Open areas from Washington to California.

**Wine Color.** Dark orange-amber.

**Wine Flavor.** Full-bodied.

**Wine Aroma.** Mousy and sour, but improves with age. In spite of its unfavorable aroma, the taste of the wine is very good.

Scotch Broom

### Wild Plant Collection Tip

Scotch broom (*Cytisus scoparius*) is a common roadside plant with bright yellow (or red-tinged yellow), pea-like flowers. This shrub grows like a fanned bouquet of four- to ten-foot-tall flowered sticks, with the foliage appearing only after the blooms have been spent. By grasping the lower stem of the scotch broom plant and pulling upward, you can collect a gallon of flowers in a very short amount of time.

## SCOTCH BROOM FLOWER WINE

1 gallon (about 16 cups) Scotch broom flowers, unrinsed

1 gallon boiling water

6 ¾ cups sugar

1 cup raisins

¼ teaspoon wine yeast

1. Place the flowers in a large food-grade bucket, and pour the boiling water over it. Cover with a porous lid, and allow to soak for forty-eight hours.

2. Strain the liquid through cheesecloth into a large nonreactive pot. Bring to a boil over high heat; then remove from the heat immediately.

3. Return the heated liquid to the bucket. Add the sugar and raisins, and use a long nonreactive spoon to stir until the sugar is dissolved.

4. When the mixture has cooled to lukewarm, sprinkle the yeast on top. Cover with a nylon stocking and a loose-fitting lid, and allow to ferment for at least fourteen days.

5. Strain the liquid into a clean glass container and cover as appropriate. (See page 73.) In six to twelve months, the wine will be ready for bottling. During this time frame the wine will be clearing, and should be siphoned from the lees into another clean glass jar about once every three months. When sufficiently clear, the wine may be siphoned into sterilized wine bottles and corked. Enjoy immediately, or store your wine on its side for later consumption.

Snowbrush

# *Snowbrush*

**When to Collect.** May through August.

**Where to Collect.** In forest openings where there is poor soil, from Washington to central California, and east to South Dakota.

**Wine Color.** Apple juice-colored.

***Wine Flavor.*** Reminiscent of Beechnut gum.

***Wine Aroma.*** Fragrant but not flowery.

## Wild Plant Collection Tip

Although snowbrush (*Ceanothus velutinus*) is primarily considered to be a shrub, it appears tree-like when it attains a height of about fifteen feet. Look for snowbrush in forest openings where there is poor, gravelly soil. The plants growing in areas of greater sunlight seem to be graced by more prolific flowering clusters. The plant's white flowers grow in irregular racemes that can be easily snapped off from their branches. Snowbrush got its name from its dense clusters of small white flowers, and the entire flowering mass can be used for winemaking. Because the blossoms contain saponin, a soapy compound, they lather when fermented, so don't be surprised if your must appears foamier than expected.

## SNOWBRUSH FLOWER WINE

1 gallon (about 16 cups) snowbrush flower clusters, unrinsed

1 gallon boiling water

8 cups sugar

3 cups raisins

¼ teaspoon wine yeast

1. Place the flowers in a large food-grade bucket, and pour the boiling water over them. Cover with a porous lid, and allow to soak for forty-eight hours.

2. Strain the liquid through cheesecloth into a large nonreactive pot, squeezing the flowers to extract all of the liquid. Bring to a boil over high heat; then remove from the heat immediately.

3. Return the heated liquid to the bucket. Add the sugar and raisins, and use a long nonreactive spoon to stir until the sugar is dissolved.

4. When the mixture has cooled to lukewarm, sprinkle the yeast on top. Cover with a nylon stocking and a loose-fitting lid, and allow to ferment for at least fourteen days. At this time, the liquid may appear sudslike. This is normal and will not affect the wine.

5. Strain the liquid into a clean glass container and cover as appropriate. (See page 73.) In six to twelve months, the wine will be ready for bottling. During this time frame the wine will be clearing, and should be siphoned from the lees into another clean glass jar about once every three months. When sufficiently clear, the wine may be siphoned into sterilized wine bottles and corked. Enjoy immediately, or store your wine on its side for later consumption.

# *Wild Violet*

**Wild Violet**

**When to Collect.** March through June for common blue violets, and April through June for yellow wood violets.

**Where to Collect.** Both blue and yellow violets are found in damp woods. Blue violets grow throughout most of the United States, and yellow violets grow from Alaska to California and east to Montana.

**Wine Color.** Amber- to cider-colored, depending on color of violets. Yellow violets create a lighter-colored wine, while blue violets produce a deeper shade.

**Wine Flavor.** Sweet, strong, and pleasant.

**Wine Aroma.** Citrusy.

## Wild Plant Collection Tip

Common blue violet (*Viola papilionacea*) and yellow wood violet (*Viola glabella*) are herbaceous, perennial plants that have heart-shaped leaves with scalloped margins. The flowers are irregularly shaped; common blue violets have purple flowers and yellow wood violets have yellow flowers. Collect on a dry day after the dew has evaporated by plucking the flowers from their ground-hugging stems. The flowers are somewhat small and delicate, and because they rest so close to the ground, a good deal of bending and stooping is required. You may wish to make a smaller batch of wine to accommodate a lesser amount of plant matter. *Caution:* The common household plant African violet *cannot* be used as a substitute for wild violets, as it is a toxic and inedible violet species.

## VIOLET FLOWER WINE

1 gallon (about 16 cups) wild violet flowers, unrinsed

1 gallon boiling water

6 cups sugar

Juice and rind from ½ lemon

Juice and rind from ½ orange

¼ teaspoon wine yeast

1. Place the flowers in a large food-grade bucket, and pour the boiling water over them. Cover with a porous lid, and allow to soak for forty-eight hours.

2. Strain the liquid through cheesecloth into a large nonreactive pot. Bring to a boil over high heat; then remove from the heat immediately.

3. Return the heated liquid to the bucket. Add the sugar, citrus juice, and citrus rind, and use a long nonreactive spoon to stir until the sugar is dissolved.

4. When the liquid has cooled to lukewarm, sprinkle the yeast on top. Cover with a nylon stocking and a loose-fitting lid, and allow to ferment for at least fourteen days.

5. Strain the liquid into a clean glass container and cover as appropriate. (See page 73.) In six to twelve months, the wine will be ready for bottling. During this time frame the wine will be clearing, and should be siphoned from the lees into another clean glass jar about once every three months. When sufficiently clear, the wine may be siphoned into sterilized wine bottles and corked. Enjoy immediately, or store your wine on its side for later consumption.

# *Wisteria*

Wisteria

**When to Collect.** April through June.

**Where to Collect.** Close to streams in partial shade, primarily in the southeastern United States, but they can be found elsewhere.

**Wine Color.** Cider-colored.

**Wine Flavor.** Strong and sweet.

**Wine Aroma.** Hints of the flower's fragrance.

## Wild Plant Collection Tip

Chinese wisteria (*Wisteria sinesis*) and Japanese wisteria (*Wisteria floribunda*) can be used interchangeably. Both have pastel purple blooms and grow in full, drooping, dense racemes, making it easy to collect large quantities of flowers in a short amount of time. Wild wisteria is actually an escaped plant of cultivated gardens, and the vines may grow to a length of thirty feet. In the wild, this plant forms a mound unless there are nearby taller plants to support its twining nature.

## WISTERIA FLOWER WINE

1 gallon (about 16 cups) wisteria flowers, unrinsed

4½ quarts boiling water

6¼ cups sugar

2¼ cups raisins

¼ teaspoon wine yeast

1. Place the flowers in a large food-grade bucket, and pour the boiling water over them. Cover with a porous lid and allow to soak for five days, stirring the mixture daily with a long nonreactive spoon.

2. Strain the liquid through cheesecloth into a large nonreactive pot. Bring to a boil over high heat; then remove from the heat immediately.

3. Return the heated liquid to the bucket. Add the sugar and raisins, and stir until the sugar has dissolved.

4. When the mixture has cooled to lukewarm, sprinkle the yeast on top. Cover with a nylon stocking and a loose-fitting lid, and allow to ferment for at least fourteen days.

5. Strain the liquid into a clean glass container and cover as appropriate. (See page 73.) In six to twelve months, the wine will be ready for bottling. During this time frame the wine will be clearing, and should be siphoned from the lees into another clean glass jar about once every three months. When sufficiently clear, the wine may be siphoned into sterilized wine bottles and corked. Enjoy immediately, or store your wine on its side for later consumption.

Yucca

# *Yucca*

**When to Collect.** April through July.

**Where to Collect.** Sandy open areas, abandoned fields, and pine barrens of the southwestern United States.

**Wine Color.** Amber.

**Wine Flavor.** Full, but not too strong.

**Wine Aroma.** Fruity with a hint of citrus.

## Wild Plant Collection Tip

The flowers of the *Yucca baccata*, the fleshy fruited variety of yucca, and the *Yucca glauca*, the dry fruited variety, can be used interchangeably. Yucca flower stalks are several feet high and surrounded by slightly shorter, sword-like leaves with fraying edges. These perennial herbaceous plants are densely burdened with large cream-colored flowers that grow atop an erect, leafless stalk. It is simple to collect the flowers needed in a short amount of time.

# YUCCA FLOWER WINE

1 gallon (about 16 cups) yucca flowers, unrinsed
1 gallon boiling water
6 cups sugar
Juice and rind from 1/2 lemon
Juice and rind from 1/2 orange
1/4 teaspoon wine yeast

1.  Place the flowers in a large food-grade bucket, and pour the boiling water over them. Cover with a porous lid, and allow to soak for forty-eight hours.

2.  Strain the liquid through cheesecloth into a large nonreactive pot. Bring to a boil over high heat; then remove from the heat immediately.

3.  Return the heated liquid to the bucket. Add the sugar, citrus juice, and citrus rind, and stir with a long nonreactive spoon to dissolve the sugar.

4.  When the liquid has cooled to lukewarm, sprinkle the yeast on top. Cover with a nylon stocking and a loose-fitting lid, and allow to ferment for at least fourteen days.

5.  Strain the liquid into a clean glass container and cover as appropriate. (See page 73.) In six to twelve months, the wine will be ready for bottling. During this time frame the wine will be clearing, and should be siphoned from the lees into another clean glass jar about once every three months. When sufficiently clear, the wine may be siphoned into sterilized wine bottles and corked. Enjoy immediately, or store your wine on its side for later consumption.

# 11

# *Leaf Wines*

L eaves have a wonderful advantage over many other wild plant parts. You can collect the foliage when it is available, and then dehydrate it for wine-making later in the year. Dried leaves may be brewed during any season, but are particularly convenient when winter is upon you and there are fewer varieties of wine to create. Not only can most leaf wines be made from dehydrated leaves, but the dried leaves actually produce a more desirable finished product. In fact, fresh leaves are recommended for only three of the recipes in this chapter—chickweed, wild grape, and oak leaf wines.

## *Aniseroot*

**When to Collect.** April through October.

**Where to Collect.** Shady woods throughout most of the United States, but not in the arid Southwest.

**Wine Color.** Amber.

**Wine Flavor.** Sweet and delicate.

**Wine Aroma.** Herbal.

Aniseroot

## Wild Plant Collection Tip

Aniseroot (*Osmorhiza longistylis*) leaves can be collected when positive identification can be made. The flowers are white and lacy, growing in delicate umbels during May and June. The appearance of the flowers may aid in identification, but the leaves can be collected whenever they are visible. Aniseroot leaves are oval with deep lobes and fine teeth, and the branchlets can be snipped with a pair of scissors or plucked by hand from these one-foot-tall plants. The fragrant anise-scented leaves can be used fresh, or can be dried on a screen or dehydrator until they are brittle, and then stored in a glass jar for future winemaking.

## ANISEROOT LEAF WINE

4 cups fresh aniseroot leaves, unrinsed,
or 1 cup dried aniseroot leaves

1 gallon boiling water

6 cups sugar

3 cups raisins

Juice and rind from 1 orange

Juice and rind from 1 lemon

¼ teaspoon wine yeast

1.  In a large food-grade bucket, combine the aniseroot leaves and boiling water. Cover with a porous lid, and allow to soak for twenty-four hours.

2.  Strain the liquid through cheesecloth into a large nonreactive pot. Bring to a boil over high heat; then remove from the heat immediately.

3.  Return the heated liquid to the bucket. Add the sugar, raisins, citrus juice, and citrus rind, and use a long nonreactive spoon to stir until the sugar has dissolved.

4.  When the liquid has cooled to lukewarm, sprinkle the yeast on top. Cover with a nylon stocking and a loose-fitting lid, and allow to ferment for at least fourteen days.

5.  Strain the liquid into a clean glass container and cover as appropriate. (See page 73.) In six to twelve months, the wine will be ready for bottling. During this time frame the wine will be clearing, and should be siphoned from the lees into another clean glass jar about once every three months. When sufficiently clear, the wine may be siphoned into sterilized wine bottles and corked. Enjoy immediately, or store your wine on its side for later consumption.

Blackberry

# *Blackberry*

**When to Collect.** March through August, ending later in mild climates.

**Where to Collect.** Fields and clearings throughout the United States.

**Wine Color.** Pale amber.

**Wine Flavor.** Like lemon-flavored blackberry leaf tea.

**Wine Aroma.** Like lemon-flavored blackberry leaf tea.

## Wild Plant Collection Tip

Blackberry (*Rubus allegheniensis*) canes are arching and up to eight feet in length with downward facing thorns. The leaves are alternate (lined up in a staggered pattern on each side of the branch), oval, and toothed, and grow in groups of five. Do not collect blackberry leaves that have begun to change color in preparation for autumn. The youngest leaves are most desirable, so earlier springtime collection is preferred. Just snap off the end growth leaves, or those leaf clusters growing along the thorny canes. Blackberry canes are usually thorny masses, so wear protective clothing when you are collecting. The leaves can be dried on a screen until they are brittle, and then crumbled for more compact storage.

# BLACKBERRY
# LEAF WINE

4 cups fresh blackberry leaves, unrinsed,
or 1 cup dried blackberry leaves

1 gallon boiling water

6 cups sugar

Juice and rind of ¼ lemon

¼ teaspoon wine yeast

1. In a large food-grade bucket, combine the blackberry leaves and boiling water. Cover with a porous lid, and allow to soak for twenty-four hours.

2. Strain the liquid through cheesecloth into a large nonreactive pot. Bring to a boil over high heat; then remove from the heat immediately.

3. Return the heated liquid to the bucket. Add the sugar, citrus juice, and citrus rind, and use a long nonreactive spoon to stir until the sugar is dissolved.

4. When the mixture has cooled to lukewarm, sprinkle the yeast on top. Cover with a nylon stocking and a loose-fitting lid, and allow to ferment for at least fourteen days.

5. Strain the liquid into a clean glass container and cover as appropriate. (See page 73.) In six to twelve months, the wine will be ready for bottling. During this time frame the wine will be clearing, and should be siphoned from the lees into another clean glass jar about once every three months. When sufficiently clear, the wine may be siphoned into sterilized wine bottles and corked. Enjoy immediately, or store your wine on its side for later consumption.

# *Chickweed*

Chickweed

**When to Collect.** Year-round, or during the months that are snow-free. These hearty plants can withstand light frosts.

**Where to Collect.** Meadows and disturbed areas throughout the United States.

**Wine Color.** Colorless.

**Wine Flavor.** Oddly pleasant with a residual aftertaste of the chickweed plant that dissipates with age.

**Wine Aroma.** Pleasant and full.

## Wild Plant Collection Tip

Chickweed (*Stellaria media* and *Alsine media*) is a weak-stemmed herbaceous plant. Because of its sprawling nature, it seldom appears taller than several inches, although the leaning stems may actually be up to one foot long. The lime green leaves are opposite (lined up on the branch in opposite pairs, like butterfly wings), smooth, and ovate with prominently pointed tips. The white five-petaled flowers are nearly inconspicuous due to their small size. Because the petals are so deeply lobed, the flowers give the appearance of having ten petals. Gather chickweed by grasping any emerging part of the plant, and giving a gentle pull. If the root remains attached to the plant when this is done, just pinch it off with your fingers. All above-ground plant parts may be used, including the stems, leaves, and flowers. The root is the only part of chickweed that is not edible, which is not a great loss, as it consists of a tiny cluster of thread-like filaments.

## CHICKWEED WINE

1 quart (about 4 cups) fresh chickweed,
swished in some cold water to remove debris

1 gallon boiling water

8 cups sugar

Juice and rind of 1 lemon

Juice and rind of 1 orange

¼ teaspoon wine yeast

1.  In a large food-grade bucket, combine the chickweed and the boiling water. (Note that all above-ground plant parts may be used.) Cover with a porous lid, and allow to soak for twenty-four hours.

2.  Strain the liquid through cheesecloth into a large nonreactive pot. Bring to a boil over high heat; then remove from the heat immediately.

3.  Return the heated liquid to the bucket. Add the sugar, citrus juice, and citrus rind, and use a long nonreactive spoon to stir until the sugar is dissolved.

4.  When the liquid has cooled to lukewarm, sprinkle the yeast on top. Cover with a nylon stocking and a loose-fitting lid, and allow to ferment for at least fourteen days.

5.  Strain the liquid into a clean glass container and cover as appropriate. (See page 73.) In six to twelve months, the wine will be ready for bottling. During this time frame the wine will be clearing, and should be siphoned from the lees into another clean glass jar about once every three months. When sufficiently clear, the wine may be siphoned into sterilized wine bottles and corked. Enjoy immediately, or store your wine on its side for later consumption.

## *Dead Nettle*

**Dead Nettle**

**When to Collect.** April through October.

**Where to Collect.** Waste and cultivated areas throughout the United States.

**Wine Color.** Pale amber.

**Wine Flavor.** Like lemon-flavored dead nettle leaf tea.

**Wine Aroma.** Like lemon-flavored dead nettle leaf tea.

### Wild Plant Collection Tip

The six-inch-tall herbaceous annual dead nettle (*Lamium purpureum*) is a member of the mint family, and sports the trademark square stems. The leaves are heart-shaped and narrowly toothed. The lower leaves are green, while the uppermost leaves are lavender. Dead nettle flowers are small, lavender, and irregularly shaped, and bloom from April through October, which aids in identification. All above-ground plant parts, including the flowers (which are minute) and leaf stems, may be procured with the leaves to make this wine. Dead nettle can be used fresh or can be dried on a screen or in a dehydrator until brittle, and then crumbled for more compact storage.

## DEAD NETTLE LEAF WINE

4 cups fresh dead nettle leaves, unrinsed
(flowers and stems may be included),
or 1 cup dried dead nettle leaves

1 gallon boiling water

6 cups sugar

Juice and rind of ¼ lemon

¼ teaspoon wine yeast

1. In a large food-grade bucket, combine the dead nettle leaves and the boiling water. Cover with a porous lid, and allow to soak for twenty-four hours.

2. Strain the liquid through cheesecloth into a large nonreactive pot. Bring to a boil over high heat; then remove from the heat immediately.

3. Return the heated liquid to the bucket. Add the sugar and the lemon juice and rind, and use a long nonreactive spoon to stir until the sugar is dissolved.

4. When the liquid has cooled to lukewarm, sprinkle the yeast on top. Cover with a nylon stocking and a loose-fitting lid, and allow to ferment for at least fourteen days.

5. Strain the liquid into a clean glass container and cover as appropriate. (See page 73.) In six to twelve months, the wine will be ready for bottling. During this time frame the wine will be clearing, and should be siphoned from the lees into another clean glass jar about once every three months. When sufficiently clear, the wine may be siphoned into sterilized wine bottles and corked. Enjoy immediately, or store your wine on its side for later consumption.

*Fennel*

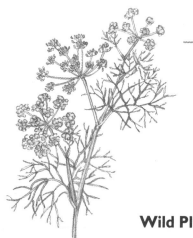

Fennel

**When to Collect.** May through September.

**Where to Collect.** Along roadsides and in fields west of the Sierra Nevada and Cascade Mountains.

**Wine Color.** Golden orange.

**Wine Flavor.** Tastes of fennel.

**Wine Aroma.** Herbal and sweet.

### Wild Plant Collection Tip

The leaves of the wild fennel plant (*Foeniculum vulgare*) can be collected throughout the growing season. To aid in identification, the yellow flowers bloom in flat-topped umbels from May through September on this tall perennial herbaceous plant. The leaves are threadlike, feathery plumes. In spite of this, it is easy to collect the needed amount of leaves in a short period of time because of the plant's tall height and prolific leafing. Wild fennel is the same as cultivated fennel, although you will not see the mature seven-foot-tall plant for sale at the grocer. The leaves can be used fresh or dried on a screen or dehydrator until they are brittle, and then crumbled for more compact storage.

## FENNEL LEAF WINE

2 cups fresh fennel leaves, unrinsed,
or ½ cup dried fennel leaves
1 gallon boiling water
6 cups sugar
3 cups raisins
¼ teaspoon wine yeast

1.  In a food-grade bucket, combine the fennel leaves and the boiling water. Cover with a porous lid, and allow to soak for twenty-four hours.

2.  Strain the liquid through cheesecloth into a large nonreactive pot. Bring to a boil over high heat; then remove from the heat immediately.

3.  Return the heated liquid to the bucket. Add the sugar and raisins, and using a long nonreactive spoon, stir until the sugar is dissolved.

4.  When the liquid has cooled to lukewarm, sprinkle the yeast on top. Cover with a nylon stocking and a loose-fitting lid, and allow to ferment for at least fourteen days.

5.  Strain the liquid into a clean glass container and cover as appropriate. (See page 73.) In six to twelve months, the wine will be ready for bottling. During this time frame the wine will be clearing, and should be siphoned from the lees into another clean glass jar about once every three months. When sufficiently clear, the wine may be siphoned into sterilized wine bottles and corked. Enjoy immediately, or store your wine on its side for later consumption.

## *Fireweed*

**When to Collect.** May through September.

**Where to Collect.** Along roadsides throughout most of the United States, but less common in the eastern states.

**Wine Color.** Pale amber.

**Wine Flavor.** Like lemon-flavored fireweed leaf tea.

**Wine Aroma.** Like lemon-flavored fireweed leaf tea.

Fireweed

## Wild Plant Collection Tip

Fireweed (*Epilobium augustifolium*) is named for its tendency to grow in areas that have been ravaged by fire. Its leaves can be collected throughout the growing season from May through September, although the younger leaves are more desirable. This tall herbaceous plant has lavender flowers that grow in a cone-shaped formation atop five-foot-tall stems. The spear-shaped leaves are easy to strip from their stems by starting at the top of the plant and peeling the leaves downward. The leaves can be dried on a screen or in a dehydrator until they are brittle, and then crumbled for more compact storage.

# FIREWEED
# LEAF WINE

4 cups fresh fireweed leaves, unrinsed,
or 1 cup dried fireweed leaves

1 gallon boiling water

6 cups sugar

Juice and rind of ¼ lemon

¼ teaspoon wine yeast

1. In a large food-grade bucket, combine the fireweed leaves and the boiling water. Cover with a porous lid, and allow to soak for twenty-four hours.

2. Strain the liquid through cheesecloth into a large nonreactive pot. Bring to a boil over high heat; then remove from the heat immediately.

3. Return the heated liquid to the bucket. Add the sugar and the lemon juice and rind, and use a long nonreactive spoon to stir until the sugar is dissolved.

4. When the liquid has cooled to lukewarm, sprinkle the yeast on top. Cover with a nylon stocking and a loose-fitting lid, and allow to ferment for at least fourteen days.

5. Strain the liquid into a clean glass container and cover as appropriate. (See page 73.) In six to twelve months, the wine will be ready for bottling. During this time frame the wine will be clearing, and should be siphoned from the lees into another clean glass jar about once every three months. When sufficiently clear, the wine may be siphoned into sterilized wine bottles and corked. Enjoy immediately, or store your wine on its side for later consumption.

# *Wild Grape*

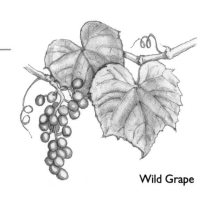

**Wild Grape**

**When to Collect.** May through October.

**Where to Collect.** Sunny locations throughout most of the United States.

**Wine Color.** Amber.

**Wine Flavor.** Full-bodied.

**Wine Aroma.** Strong and citrusy.

## Wild Plant Collection Tip

The leaves of the wild grape (*Vita* species) can be collected any time during the growing season, whenever positive identification can be made. It is more desirable, however, to use the early springtime leaves rather than the late season foliage. While some of these tendril-bearing plants prefer dry habitats, others flourish in damp soil. The toothed, heart-shaped or maple-like leaves are four to eight inches across, and can be easily stripped from their shreddy vines. Due to the leaves' large size, it is quick and easy to collect the amount needed for this recipe.

## WILD GRAPE LEAF WINE

1 gallon (about 16 cups) fresh wild grape leaves, unrinsed

1 gallon boiling water

6¾ cups sugar

Juice from 1 orange

Juice from ½ lemon

¼ teaspoon wine yeast

1. In a large food-grade bucket, combine the fresh wild grape leaves and the boiling water. Cover with a porous lid, and allow to soak for twenty-four hours.

2. Strain the liquid through cheesecloth into a large nonreactive pot. Add the sugar and citrus juices, and bring to a boil over high heat, stirring with a long nonreactive spoon to dissolve the sugar. Boil for ten minutes; then remove from the heat.

3. When the mixture has cooled to lukewarm, sprinkle the yeast on top. Cover with a nylon stocking and a loose-fitting lid, and allow to ferment for at least fourteen days.

4. Strain the liquid into a clean glass container and cover as appropriate. (See page 73.) In six to twelve months, the wine will be ready for bottling. During this time frame the wine will be clearing, and should be siphoned from the lees into another clean glass jar about once every three months. When sufficiently clear, the wine may be siphoned into sterilized wine bottles and corked. Enjoy immediately, or store your wine on its side for later consumption.

New Jersey Tea

# *New Jersey Tea*

**When to Collect.** May through July.

**Where to Collect.** Open woods and clearings in the eastern half of the United States.

**Wine Color.** Pale amber.

**Wine Flavor.** Like lemon-flavored New Jersey tea leaf tea.

**Wine Aroma.** Like lemon-flavored New Jersey tea leaf tea.

## Wild Plant Collection Tip

The leaves of the New Jersey tea plant (*Ceanothus americanus*) can be picked throughout the growing season, but are best collected when the plant is in bloom to ensure proper identification. New Jersey tea flowers from May through July. The blooms are five-petaled and white, growing in one-inch oval clusters. This three-foot-tall plant has alternate, oval, toothed leaves that are sharply pointed with prominent, nearly parallel veins. Another name for this plant is soapbloom, so don't be surprised if your fermenting liquid produces a little suds. The leaves can be plucked from this shrub and used fresh, or can be dried on a screen or in a dehydrator until they are brittle, and then crumbled for more compact storage.

## NEW JERSEY TEA LEAF WINE

4 cups fresh New Jersey tea leaves, unrinsed,
or 1 cup dried New Jersey tea leaves

1 gallon boiling water

6 cups sugar

Juice and rind of ¼ lemon

¼ teaspoon wine yeast

1. In a large food-grade bucket, combine the New Jersey tea leaves and the boiling water. Cover with a porous lid, and allow to soak for twenty-four hours.

2. Strain the liquid through cheesecloth into a large nonreactive pot. Bring to a boil over high heat; then remove from the heat immediately.

3. Return the heated liquid to the bucket. Add the sugar and the lemon juice and rind, and use a long nonreactive spoon to stir until the sugar is dissolved.

4. When the liquid has cooled to lukewarm, sprinkle the yeast on top. Cover with a nylon stocking and a loose-fitting lid, and allow to ferment for at least fourteen days.

5. Strain the liquid into a clean glass container and cover as appropriate. (See page 73.) In six to twelve months, the wine will be ready for bottling. During this time frame the wine will be clearing, and should be siphoned from the lees into another clean glass jar about once every three months. When sufficiently clear, the wine may be siphoned into sterilized wine bottles and corked. Enjoy immediately, or store your wine on its side for later consumption.

## Oak

Oak Leaf

**When to Collect.** May through October.

**Where to Collect.** Deciduous forests throughout the United States.

**Wine Color.** Amber.

**Wine Flavor.** Pleasantly sweet.

**Wine Aroma.** Potent.

### Wild Plant Collection Tip

Oak (*Quercus* species) leaves can be collected from the lower hanging branches of this mighty tree any time the leaves are present and have not yet changed color in preparation for autumn. White oak leaves are best for winemaking. Black and red oak leaves have higher amounts of tannin, which may make your finished wine too astringent. White oak leaves have rounded lobes, while black and red oak leaves have pointed lobes. It is best to collect the leaves in the springtime, when they are new and fresh. Tannins are naturally occurring in oak, and this in one reason oak leaf wine is so superb. You can find a variety of acorn-bearing oak trees growing throughout the United States, with their habitat varying by region.

## OAK LEAF WINE

1 gallon (about 16 cups) fresh oak leaves, unrinsed

1 gallon boiling water

6½ cups sugar

Juice of 2 oranges

Juice of 1 lemon

¼ teaspoon wine yeast

1. In a large food-grade bucket, combine the oak leaves and the boiling water. Cover with a porous lid, and allow to soak for twenty-four hours.

2. Strain the liquid through cheesecloth into a large nonreactive pot. Add the sugar and the citrus juices, and bring to a boil over high heat, stirring with a long nonreactive spoon to dissolve the sugar. Boil for ten minutes and remove from heat.

3. Return the heated liquid to the bucket. When the liquid has cooled to lukewarm, sprinkle the yeast on top. Cover with a nylon stocking and a loose-fitting lid, and allow to ferment for at least fourteen days.

4. Strain the liquid into a clean glass container and cover as appropriate. (See page 73.) In six to twelve months, the wine will be ready for bottling. During this time frame the wine will be clearing, and should be siphoned from the lees into another clean glass jar about once every three months. When sufficiently clear, the wine may be siphoned into sterilized wine bottles and corked. Enjoy immediately, or store your wine on its side for later consumption.

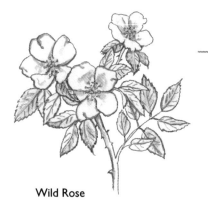

Wild Rose

# *Wild Rose*

**When to Collect.** May through August.

**Where to Collect.** Wet or dry, shady or sunny locations throughout the United States.

**Wine Color.** Pale amber.

**Wine Flavor.** Like lemon-flavored rose leaf tea.

**Wine Aroma.** Like lemon-flavored rose leaf tea.

## Wild Plant Collection Tip

Leaves of the wild rose (*Rosa* species) can be picked throughout the growing season, but are best collected when in bloom to ensure proper identification. Wild roses bloom from late spring through early summer, and the flowers range from pale pink to dark pink. Roses are a thorny bunch and care must be taken to avoid the prickly protrusions, so wear gloves when collecting. As a rule, wild roses grow as arching shrubs; however the shiny, oval, toothed leaves can be stripped fairly easily without entering the bramble-like mass. The leaves can be plucked from this shrub and used fresh, or can be dried on a screen or in a dehydrator until they are brittle, and then crumbled for more compact storage.

## WILD ROSE LEAF WINE

4 cups fresh wild rose leaves, unrinsed,
or 1 cup dried wild rose leaves

1 gallon boiling water

6 cups sugar

Juice and rind of ¼ lemon

¼ teaspoon wine yeast

1. In a large food-grade bucket, combine the wild rose leaves and the boiling water. Cover with a porous lid, and allow to soak for twenty-four hours.

2. Strain the liquid through cheesecloth into a large nonreactive pot. Bring to a boil over high heat; then remove from the heat immediately.

3. Return the heated liquid to the bucket. Add the sugar and the lemon juice and rind, and use a long nonreactive spoon to stir until the sugar is dissolved.

4. When the liquid has cooled to lukewarm, sprinkle the yeast on top. Cover with a nylon stocking and a loose-fitting lid, and allow to ferment for at least fourteen days.

5. Strain the liquid into a clean glass container and cover as appropriate. (See page 73.) In six to twelve months, the wine will be ready for bottling. During this time frame the wine will be clearing, and should be siphoned from the lees into another clean glass jar about once every three months. When sufficiently clear, the wine may be siphoned into sterilized wine bottles and corked. Enjoy immediately, or store your wine on its side for later consumption.

# *Self-Heal*

**When to Collect.** May through September.

**Where to Collect.** Shaded, moist ground and fields throughout the United States.

**Wine Color.** Pale amber.

**Wine Flavor.** Like lemon-flavored self-heal tea.

**Wine Aroma.** Like lemon-flavored self-heal tea.

Self-Heal

## Wild Plant Collection Tip

Leaves of the self-heal plant (*Prunella vulgaris*) can be picked throughout the growing season, but are best collected when the plant is in bloom, from May through September. This eight-inch-tall perennial herbaceous plant is another member of the mint family, and the characteristic square stem is a good plant identifier. The leaves are opposite, lance-shaped to oval, and obscurely toothed. Ants seem to like the nooks and crannies of the pink flower heads, so be sure you shake them out before you proceed with winemaking. All above-ground plant parts can be used, including the flowers, leaves, and stems. This herb can be used fresh, or it can be dried on a screen or in a dehydrator until brittle, and then crumbled for more compact storage.

# SELF-HEAL
# LEAF WINE

4 cups fresh self-heal leaves, unrinsed,
or 1 cup dried self-heal leaves

1 gallon boiling water

6 cups sugar

Juice and rind of ¼ lemon

¼ teaspoon wine yeast

1.  In a large food-grade bucket, combine the self-heal leaves and the boiling water. Cover with a porous lid, and allow to soak for twenty-four hours.

2.  Strain the liquid through cheesecloth into a large nonreactive pot. Bring to a boil over high heat; then remove from the heat immediately.

3.  Return the heated liquid to the bucket. Add the sugar and the lemon juice and rind, and use a long nonreactive spoon to stir until the sugar is dissolved.

4.  When the liquid has cooled to lukewarm, sprinkle the yeast on top. Cover with a nylon stocking and a loose-fitting lid, and allow to ferment for at least fourteen days.

5.  Strain the liquid into a clean glass container and cover as appropriate. (See page 73.) In six to twelve months, the wine will be ready for bottling. During this time frame the wine will be clearing, and should be siphoned from the lees into another clean glass jar about once every three months. When sufficiently clear, the wine may be siphoned into sterilized wine bottles and corked. Enjoy immediately, or store your wine on its side for later consumption.

# *Silverweed*

Silverweed

**When to Collect.** May through August.

**Where to Collect.** Moist, open ground throughout most of the United States.

**Wine Color.** Amber.

**Wine Flavor.** Like lemon-flavored silverweed leaf tea.

**Wine Aroma.** Like lemon-flavored silverweed leaf tea.

## Wild Plant Collection Tip

Leaves of the silverweed (*Potentilla anserina*) can be collected from this creeping, herbaceous, perennial plant from May to August, when silverweed is flowering, so that proper identification can be made. Once you recognize the foliage of this plant, it can be collected earlier in the year, before the flowers bloom. The shiny, five-petaled, bright yellow flowers emerge from the center of the lime green foliage. The leaves resemble the teeth of a shark, and there are between seven and twenty-five leaflets on each foot-long leaf stem. Silverweed can be found in strawberry-like tufts with runners, so a silverweed patch may be quite large, making the amount of plant material needed very easy to collect. Just grasp the leaves close to the plant base and pull.

## SILVERWEED LEAF WINE

4 cups fresh silverweed leaves, unrinsed,
or 1 cup dried silverweed leaves

1 gallon boiling water

6 cups sugar

Juice and rind of ¼ lemon

¼ teaspoon wine yeast

1. In a large food-grade bucket, combine the silverweed leaves with the boiling water. Cover with a porous lid, and allow to soak for twenty-four hours.

2. Strain the liquid through cheesecloth into a large nonreactive pot. Bring to a boil over high heat; then remove from the heat immediately.

3. Return the heated liquid to the bucket. Add the sugar and the lemon juice and rind, and use a long nonreactive spoon to stir until the sugar is dissolved.

4.  When the liquid has cooled to lukewarm, sprinkle the yeast on top. Cover with a nylon stocking and a loose-fitting lid, and allow to ferment for at least fourteen days.

5.  Strain the liquid into a clean glass container and cover as appropriate. (See page 73.) In six to twelve months, the wine will be ready for bottling. During this time frame the wine will be clearing, and should be siphoned from the lees into another clean glass jar about once every three months. When sufficiently clear, the wine may be siphoned into sterilized wine bottles and corked. Enjoy immediately, or store your wine on its side for later consumption.

Snowbrush

# *Snowbrush*

**When to Collect.** May through August.

**Where to Collect.** In forest openings where there is poor soil from Washington to central California, east to South Dakota.

**Wine Color.** Pale amber.

**Wine Flavor.** Like lemon-flavored snowbrush leaf tea.

**Wine Aroma.** Like lemon-flavored snowbrush leaf tea.

## Wild Plant Collection Tip

An evergreen shrub, snowbrush (*Ceanothus velutinus*) grows along forest fringes from Washington to central California, and east to South Dakota. The leaves can be collected year-round, but to aid in identification, you should wait until the flowers bloom from May through August. The white flower clusters grow in irregular racemes, and the leaves are shiny and oval with parallel leaf veins and tiny teeth. Because of its sticky leaves, older snowbrush foliage often has years of debris attached, such as feathers, dust, and cobwebs. For this reason, it is more desirable to collect the shiny new green growth, which should be dirt-free. These new-growth leaves can be collected in July and August, and can be dried on a screen or in a dehydrator until brittle. Crumble the dried leaves and place in glass jars for more compact storage. Because this plant contains saponin, suds may form during fermentation.

## SNOWBRUSH LEAF WINE

4 cups fresh snowbrush leaves, unrinsed,
or 1 cup dried snowbrush leaves

1 gallon boiling water

6 cups sugar

Juice and rind of ¼ lemon

¼ teaspoon wine yeast

1. In a large food-grade bucket, combine the snowbrush leaves and the boiling water. Cover with a porous lid, and allow to soak for twenty-four hours.

2. Strain the liquid through cheesecloth into a large nonreactive pot. Bring to a boil over high heat; then remove from the heat immediately.

3. Return the heated liquid to the bucket. Add the sugar and the lemon juice and rind, and use a long nonreactive spoon to stir until the sugar is dissolved.

4. When the liquid has cooled to lukewarm, sprinkle the yeast on top. Cover with a nylon stocking and a loose-fitting lid, and allow to ferment for at least fourteen days.

5. Strain the liquid into a clean glass container and cover as appropriate. (See page 73.) In six to twelve months, the wine will be ready for bottling. During this time frame the wine will be clearing, and should be siphoned from the lees into another clean glass jar about once every three months. When sufficiently clear, the wine may be siphoned into sterilized wine bottles and corked. Enjoy immediately, or store your wine on its side for later consumption.

## *Wild Strawberry*

**When to Collect.** April through June.

**Where to Collect.** Shaded woods or sunny fields throughout most of the United States.

**Wine Color.** Pale amber.

**Wine Flavor.** Like lemon-flavored strawberry leaf tea.

**Wine Aroma.** Like lemon-flavored strawberry leaf tea.

**Wild Strawberry**

## Wild Plant Collection Tip

Wild strawberry (*Fragaria virginiana*) grows as an herbaceous creeping plant with runners, and its ground-hugging nature means that your knees will get a workout during collection. The plant has five-petaled white flowers that bloom from April through June, aiding in identification. The leaves—oval, toothed, and growing in threes—can be collected before the plant flowers, but the plants are easier to locate and identify when the blossoms are present. When you find a patch, you can return year after year, as wild strawberry grows as a perennial plant. The leaves can be plucked and used fresh, or can be dried on a screen or in a dehydrator until brittle, and then crumbled and stored for later use.

## WILD STRAWBERRY LEAF WINE

4 cups fresh wild strawberry leaves, unrinsed, or 1 cup dried wild strawberry leaves

1 gallon boiling water

6 cups sugar

Juice and rind of ¼ lemon

¼ teaspoon wine yeast

1. In a large food-grade bucket, combine the wild strawberry leaves and the boiling water. Cover with a porous lid, and allow to soak for twenty-four hours.

2. Strain the liquid through cheesecloth into a large nonreactive pot. Bring to a boil over high heat; then remove from the heat immediately.

3. Return the heated liquid to the bucket. Add the sugar and the lemon juice and rind, and use a long nonreactive spoon to stir until the sugar is dissolved.

4. When the liquid has cooled to lukewarm, sprinkle the yeast on top. Cover with a nylon stocking and a loose-fitting lid, and allow to ferment for at least fourteen days.

5. Strain the liquid into a clean glass container and cover as appropriate. (See page 73.) In six to twelve months, the wine will be ready for bottling. During this time frame the wine will be clearing, and should be siphoned from the lees into another clean glass jar about once every three months. When sufficiently clear, the wine may be siphoned into sterilized wine bottles and corked. Enjoy immediately, or store your wine on its side for later consumption.

# 12

# *Other Wines*

Fruit, leaves, roots, and flowers aren't the only plant parts you can turn into wine. Plant spikes, shoots, bark, and sap are just a few of the other parts that can be used to make delicious libations. And some of these plants are wonderfully easy to find, as well. Cattails, for instance, are so common that almost anyone in the country can locate them, no matter where they live. Maple trees—the source of sweet maple sap—are also common, being found in many deciduous forests throughout the United States. In fact, learning how to tap a tree for its sap can be both fun and educational. Even if you decide not to make wine, you can always boil the sap down for syrup!

## *Cattail*

**When to Collect.** May through July.

**Where to Collect.** Perimeter of freshwater marshes throughout the United States.

**Wine Color.** Amber.

**Wine Flavor.** Full-bodied and strong.

**Wine Aroma.** Full-bodied.

### Wild Plant Collection Tip

Spikes of the cattail—*Typha latifolia*, which is the common cattail, and *Typha augustifolia*, which is the narrow-leaved cattail—are best collected in the spring and early summer. At that point, the upper male spike is green, tight, and perhaps still partially sheathed beneath its green leafy covering, like a cob of corn with its kernels hidden under a leafy cloak. Later in the season, when the male spikes expand and dry, releasing their pollen onto the lower female spikes, the plant is

Cattail

unsuitable for winemaking. These plants are common not just along freshwater marshes, but also along roadsides in ditches. However, roadside spikes are likely to have been exposed to fumes from car exhaust, and should not be collected.

## CATTAIL SPIKE WINE

5 pounds (about 24 cups) cattail spikes
(upper male flower spike), unrinsed

4½ quarts cold water

8 cups sugar

1½ cups raisins

1½ cups kibbled maize, dried corn kernels,
or coarsely ground cornmeal

Juice of 1 orange

Juice of 1 lemon

¼ teaspoon wine yeast

1. In a large nonreactive pot, combine the cattail spikes with the cold water. Bring to a boil over high heat. Then reduce the heat to low and simmer for five minutes.

2. Strain the liquid through cheesecloth into a large food-grade bucket. Add the sugar, raisins, kibbled maize, and citrus juices, and use a long nonreactive spoon to stir until the sugar is dissolved.

3. When the mixture has cooled to lukewarm, sprinkle the yeast on top. Cover with a nylon stocking and a loose-fitting lid, and allow to ferment for at least fourteen days.

4. Strain the liquid into a clean glass container and cover as appropriate. (See page 73.) In six to twelve months, the wine will be ready for bottling. During this time frame the wine will be clearing, and should be siphoned from the lees into another clean glass jar about once every three months. When sufficiently clear, the wine may be siphoned into sterilized wine bottles and corked. Enjoy immediately, or store your wine on its side for later consumption.

## *Japanese Knotweed*

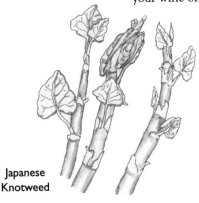

**Japanese
Knotweed**

**When to Collect.** April through June.

**Where to Collect.** Waste places and roadsides in shade or sun throughout the United States.

**Wine Color.** Dark amber.

**Wine Flavor.** Hearty.

**Wine Aroma.** Not detectable.

## Wild Plant Collection Tip

The shoots of Japanese knotweed (*Polygonum cuspidatum*) are best collected when the plants are less than twelve inches in height. When mature, Japanese knotweed is a tall, jointed plant that reaches a height of about seven feet. The blossoms are delicate white clusters, but by the time you see this herbaceous plant in bloom, it will be far too late in the season to gather young shoots. Just note the location of the plant, and return next year for earlier collection. Japanese knotweed shoots can be snapped off with the hand, but the plant matter is a little stringy, so it is best to cleanly sever them with a small pocketknife. At this stage of growth, the leaves will be tightly clasping the top of the knotweed stalk, as the foliage will not unfurl until the plant attains a greater height later in the growing season.

## JAPANESE KNOTWEED SHOOT WINE

3 pounds (about 9 cups) young Japanese knotweed shoots
(less than 12 inches tall), rinsed with cold water
and cut into 2-inch lengths

1 gallon cold water

8 cups sugar

1½ cups raisins

1 cup barley

¼ teaspoon wine yeast

1. Purée the shoots by putting two to four cups of Japanese knotweed into a blender at a time. Add just enough of the cold water to cover, and blend to a puréed consistency. Repeat with the remaining shoots. This process will extract the greatest amount of flavor from the shoots.

2. In a large food-grade bucket, combine the purée with the rest of the cold water. Cover with a porous lid, and allow to soak for twenty-four hours.

3. Strain the liquid first through a colander and then through cheesecloth into a large nonreactive pot, squeezing the water from the puréed knotweed. Bring the liquid to a boil over high heat; then remove from the heat immediately.

4. Return the heated liquid to the bucket. Add the sugar, raisins, and barley, and use a long nonreactive spoon to stir until the sugar is dissolved.

5. When the liquid has cooled to lukewarm, sprinkle the yeast on top. Cover with a nylon stocking and a loose-fitting lid, and allow to ferment for at least fourteen days.

6. Strain the liquid into a clean glass container and cover as appropriate. (See page 73.) In six to twelve months, the wine will be ready for bottling. During this time frame the wine will be clearing, and should be siphoned from the lees into another clean glass jar about once every three months. When sufficiently clear, the wine may be siphoned into sterilized wine bottles and corked. Enjoy immediately, or store your wine on its side for later consumption.

**Madrone Bark**

# *Madrone Bark*

**When to Collect.** Year-round, but bark becomes more accessible in July, when it curls from the trunk.

**Where to Collect.** Hot, rocky slopes west of the Cascade crest.

**Wine Color.** Dark amber.

**Wine Flavor.** Sweet and pleasant.

**Wine Aroma.** Full-bodied.

## Wild Plant Collection Tip

Pacific madrone (*Arbutus menziesii*) grows as a sparsely branched, exotic-looking tree. Although the autumnal clusters of orange-red, single-seeded, warty berries aid in identification, the bark is easiest to harvest in July. The bark of this tree peels in thin layers. On mature trees, the lower bark is rough, furrowed, and firmly attached, but the higher rust-colored bark curls like fragile cinnamon sticks. Rub the tree with the palm of your hand, and the loose bark will fleck away like tissue paper into your collection container. Further drying is not necessary, as the bark will be thoroughly dry at this stage of growth.

## MADRONE BARK WINE

2 cups madrone bark

1 gallon boiling water

6 cups sugar

1 cup prunes

¼ teaspoon wine yeast

1. In a large food-grade bucket, combine the madrone bark and boiling water. Cover with a porous lid, and allow to soak for twenty-four hours.

2. Strain the liquid through cheesecloth into a large nonreactive pot. Bring to a boil over high heat; then remove from the heat immediately.

3. Return the heated liquid to the bucket. Add the sugar and prunes, and use a long nonreactive spoon to stir until the sugar is dissolved.

4. When the liquid has cooled to lukewarm, sprinkle the yeast on top. Cover with a nylon stocking and a loose-fitting lid, and allow to ferment for at least fourteen days.

5. Strain the liquid into a clean glass container and cover as appropriate. (See page 73.) In six to twelve months, the wine will be ready for bottling. During this time frame the wine will be clearing, and should be siphoned from the lees into another clean glass jar about once every three months. When sufficiently clear, the wine may be siphoned into sterilized wine bottles and corked. Enjoy immediately, or store your wine on its side for later consumption.

*Maple Sap*

**When to Collect.** January through April.

**Where to Collect.** Deciduous forests throughout most of the United States.

**Wine Color.** Amber.

**Wine Flavor.** Strong, unusual.

**Wine Aroma.** Nutty.

Maple Leaves

## Wild Plant Collection Tip

Maple trees (*Acer* species) grow in deciduous forests throughout most of the United States. Any maple can be tapped for sap, but the sap from the sugar maple (*Acer saccharum*) is the sweetest. The palm-shaped, deeply lobed maple leaf is identifiable to most people, and appears on the Canadian flag. Be aware, though, that the trees will be leafless between January and April, when the sap is flowing.

Tap your tree when the nighttime temperatures are in the twenties, and the daytime temperatures are in the forties. Drill a quarter- to half-inch hole, two to three inches deep between knee and shoulder height, on the sunniest side of the tree. Insert a short length of quarter- to half-inch plastic tubing, not quite all the way into the hole. Then hammer a sturdy nail into the tree below the hole and hang your collection container from the nail, placing the free end of the plastic tubing in the container. When the sap is flowing at its peak, one or two gallons can be collected from a single hole in a single tree on a single day.

## MAPLE SAP WINE

1 gallon maple tree sap
6 cups sugar
3 cups raisins
¼ cup almonds
¼ teaspoon wine yeast

1. Place the sap in a large nonreactive pot, and bring to a boil over high heat. Then remove from the heat immediately.

2. In a large food-grade bucket, combine the heated sap with the sugar, raisins, and almonds. Using a long nonreactive spoon, stir until the sugar is dissolved.

3. When the liquid has cooled to lukewarm, sprinkle the yeast on top. Cover with a nylon stocking and a loose-fitting lid, and allow to ferment for at least fourteen days.

4. Strain the liquid into a clean glass container and cover as appropriate. (See page 73.) In six to twelve months, the wine will be ready for bottling. During this time frame the wine will be clearing, and should be siphoned from the lees into another clean glass jar about once every three months. When sufficiently clear, the wine may be siphoned into sterilized wine bottles and corked. Enjoy immediately, or store your wine on its side for later consumption.

# Wild Oat

**When to Collect.** May and June.
**Where to Collect.** Roadsides, cultivated ground, and waste areas throughout most of the United States.
**Wine Color.** Light amber.
**Wine Flavor.** Strong, whiskey-like.
**Wine Aroma.** Full-bodied.

## Wild Plant Collection Tip

Wild oats (*Avena fatua*) can be collected in May or June when the grain is mature—that is, when the oat berry is full and ripe. You'll know that the oats are mature when these annual herbaceous plants are half green and half brown as they begin their seasonal decline. Look for wild oats along roadsides, in cultivated ground, and in waste places throughout most of the United States, up to an eleva-

Wild Oat

tion of 7,500 feet. The three-foot-tall oat grass is most visible on a breezy day when the weighed-down, arching sheaves are swaying in the wind. Oat berries can be collected by grasping the uppermost portion of the oat grass and stripping the seed heads from the plant. Crush the dry outer covering with leather-gloved hands, and winnow out the chaff to ready the oats for winemaking. The outer sheath of the oat grain can be difficult to remove, so you may want to try this recipe when you're a more experienced winemaker.

## WILD OAT WINE

5 quarts boiling water

9 cups sugar

6 cups raw wild oats

Juice and rind of 2 oranges, cut in half

Juice and rind of 2 lemons, cut in half

¼ teaspoon wine yeast

1. In a large food-grade bucket, combine the boiling water with the sugar. Using a long nonreactive spoon, stir until the sugar is dissolved. Add the wild oats and the citrus juice and rinds.

2. When the liquid has cooled to lukewarm, sprinkle the yeast on top. Cover with a nylon stocking and a loose-fitting lid, and allow to ferment for at least fourteen days.

3. Strain the liquid into a clean glass container and cover as appropriate. (See page 73.) In six to twelve months, the wine will be ready for bottling. During this time frame the wine will be clearing, and should be siphoned from the lees into another clean glass jar about once every three months. When sufficiently clear, the wine may be siphoned into sterilized wine bottles and corked. Enjoy immediately, or store your wine on its side for later consumption.

## *Wild Rice*

Wild Rice

**When to Collect.** August and September.

**Where to Collect.** In shallow ponds in the Midwest and eastern portions of the United States.

**Wine Color.** Dark cider-colored.

**Wine Flavor.** Strong and rich.

**Wine Aroma.** Full-bodied and fruity.

## Wild Plant Collection Tip

Wild rice (*Zizania aquatica*) can be collected from this aquatic plant for a short period of time in late summer or early autumn. Simply bend the rice sheaves over a canoe or other boat, and beat or shake out the ripened seeds onto a sheet arranged over the boat's floor. When wild rice is ripe, it can very easily be detached from its mother plant. A good deal of the grain is lost when it lands in the freshwater depths, becoming future wild rice plants. Dry and then bake the rice grains in a low-heat oven until the husks are dry. Wearing leather gloves, rub the grains together between your hands until the husks are removed, and then winnow out the chaff. Your wild rice is ready to use.

Be aware that wild rice is very different from the white and brown rices that most of us eat. In fact, wild rice is not a rice at all, but a grass. If you don't want to forage for this plant, store-bought wild rice can be used instead with good results.

## WILD RICE WINE

5 quarts boiling water

7 cups sugar

4 cups raw wild rice

1½ cups raisins

¼ teaspoon wine yeast

1. In a large food-grade bucket, combine the boiling water with the sugar. Using a long nonreactive spoon, stir until the sugar is dissolved. Add the wild rice and raisins.

2. When the mixture has cooled to lukewarm, sprinkle the yeast on top. Cover with a nylon stocking and a loose-fitting lid, and allow to ferment for at least fourteen days. (Note that the wine may not finish fermenting for up to one month.)

3. Strain the liquid into a clean glass container and cover as appropriate. (See page 73.) In six to twelve months, the wine will be ready for bottling. During this time frame the wine will be clearing, and should be siphoned from the lees into another clean glass jar about once every three months. When sufficiently clear, the wine may be siphoned into sterilized wine bottles and corked. Enjoy immediately, or store your wine on its side for later consumption. The amount of wild rice wine you end up with is relatively small in comparison to the greater amount of discarded solids (the spent rice and raisins). Still, it is a wine worth making.

# Glossary

**Acid.** A substance with a pH less than 7. Too little acid causes the wine to have a dull taste, while too much acid makes the wine overly tart. The four major acids found in wine are tartaric, malic, lactic, and citric.

**Aerobic.** Living or occurring in the presence of oxygen.

**Aftertaste.** A flavor or odor that lingers in the mouth after a wine is swallowed.

**Aging.** Holding wines for a period of time in barrels, tanks, or bottles to modify the character of the finished product. All wines age differently and at different rates.

**Airlock.** A device that allows carbon dioxide to escape from fermenting wine while preventing airborne contaminants from getting in.

**Alcohol.** A natural by-product of fermentation caused by yeast metabolizing sugar. Most wines range from 7 to 14 percent alcohol by volume. Alcohol affects the taste, aroma, and mouthfeel of wine.

**Anaerobic.** Occurring without the presence of oxygen. When this term is used to describe fermentation, it means that fermentation occurs without exposure to air, such as in a closed container or a carboy with an airlock.

**Appellation.** A winegrowing region, such as Napa Valley.

**Aroma.** A wine's fragrance or scent. Some experts use this term to describe only young wines, and use "bouquet" to describe a more aged wine.

**Balance.** The sense you get from a wine when all of its components—fruitiness, acidity, tannin, and sweetness—are in harmony.

**Bloom.** A waxy or powdery whitish to bluish coating on the surface of certain plants, such as plums and grapes. While some say that this bloom is composed of wild yeast cells, others say it is a waxy covering that protects the plant from water loss.

**Body.** The mouthfeel or weight of the wine on the palate, commonly described as full-, medium-, or light-bodied. The higher the alcohol content, the more full-bodied a wine typically is.

**Bouquet.** The complex aromas that develop with age in fine wines.

**Carbon dioxide.** A by-product of fermentation. This is the gas released when yeast reacts with sugar.

**Carboy.** A large container with a narrow neck used to ferment wines. Carboys are available in half-gallon, one-gallon, two-gallon, and five-gallon sizes.

**Character.** Refined, distinguished qualities in a wine that are a result of climate, soil, and the process of winemaking.

**Citric acid.** A natural acid found mainly in citrus fruits.

**Citrusy.** Resembling lemon, grapefruit, lime, or orange in the bouquet or aftertaste.

**Clearing.** A process after fermentation in which the wine is strained from the must, and then allowed to sit so that any remaining solids sink, leaving a clear beverage that can be siphoned into bottles.

**Dry.** A term used to describe a wine that is not sweet because all perceptible sugar was consumed during the fermentation process. This is a subjective description, as tasters may perceive sweetness to varying degrees.

**Earthy.** A term used to describe an almost soil-like wine smell or flavor, suggestive of the earth. Some earthiness is appealing; too much makes the wine coarse.

**Fermentation.** The chemical process whereby yeast converts sugar into alcohol and carbon dioxide.

**Filtering.** The process of removing particles from wine after fermentation.

**Fining.** The process of clarifying wine by removing sediment through the addition of a fining agent. Some common fining agents include bentonite (clay), egg whites, and gelatin.

**Floral/flowery.** Having an aroma suggestive of flowers.

**Fruity.** Having an aroma and/or flavor suggestive of fruit.

**Herbaceous.** Characteristic of a plant that has stems and leaves which die at the end of the growing season.

**J-Tube.** A stiff plastic tube that turns up at one end, suggesting the letter "J." This tube allows you to siphon wine from one container to another without disturbing the lees and drawing up sediment.

**Lees.** Wine sediment made up of plant solids and spent yeast cells.

**Malic acid.** The organic acid found in apples.

**Malolactic fermentation.** A secondary bacterial fermentation in a wine that can occur either intentionally or accidentally.

**Mature.** Fully developed wine, ready to drink.

**Mousiness.** A negative aftertaste resulting from a wine's low acidity.

**Mouthfeel.** The in-mouth impression of a wine's "texture," which may be described as smooth, thin, heavy, etc.

**Must.** In the case of wild wines, the mixture of wild plant matter, water, and sometimes dried fruit, citrus fruit, or grains that is fermented into wine.

**Musty.** A stale, moldy, or mildewy smell that may be caused by a poor cork, moldy plant matter, or improperly cleaned fermentation containers.

**Nose.** The smell of a wine, which includes the aroma and the bouquet. Wine can be said to have either a "good nose" or an "off-nose," meaning a defective odor. To nose a wine is to smell it.

**Oxidized.** A term used to describe wine that's been overexposed to oxygen. Oxidized wine may have a dull, brownish appearance and a spoiled flavor.

**Palmate.** Having three or more veins, leaflets, or lobes radiating from one point, like a hand with its fingers extended.

**Peak.** The time at which a wine is at its best. This is a subjective determination.

**Pectin.** A gelatin-like substance found in fruit, and often used as a thickening agent in jams and jellies.

**Perennial.** A plant that lasts for three years or more.

**pH.** The measurement of the acidity or alkalinity of a substance. The lower the pH, the more acidic the wine.

**Pulp.** The soft moist part of the plant matter.

**Raceme.** A stalk on which fruits or flowers are borne on small individual stems.

**Racking.** Siphoning wine from one container to another for the purpose of separating the cleared wine from the settled lees.

**Rich.** Full flavor, body, and aroma.

**Rosé.** A pale pink wine.

**Rosette.** A circular arrangement of leaves.

**Runner.** A horizontally growing stem that often bears small plantlets along its length or at its tip.

**Sediment.** The residue of solids in a bottle of wine that forms as the wine matures. This is considered a negative quality, and can be separated from a well-aged wine by transferring the wine to another container.

**Settling.** The sinking of suspended particles in wine, causing it to become clear.

**Siphon.** A tube used to transfer wine during racking and bottling.

**Smooth.** A term used to describe wine that is velvety, rich, and soft in texture and body.

**Sparkling wine.** A wine that contains bubbles of carbon dioxide gas. Sparkling wines can be created intentionally, or can be produced accidentally by bottling a still-fermenting wine. The fermenting gases have nowhere to go, and the bubbles get trapped in the bottle.

**Sulfur dioxide.** The antioxidant, antibacterial agent added to wine to inhibit the growth of unwanted microorganisms and prevent browning. Small amounts of sulfur dioxide naturally occur as a by-product of fermentation, but more of the substance is usually added to extend the shelf life of the product.

**Tannin.** A substance, found in many plants, that acts as a natural preservative and causes a drying, astringent feeling on the tongue. Particularly large amounts of tannin are found in oak leaves, acorns, wood from oak trees, and the seeds and stems of grapes.

**Thin.** A term used to describe a wine that is lacking in substance and body.

**Umbel.** A rounded or flat-topped flower in which the individual flower stalks arise in a cluster from the same point, as in Queen Anne's lace (wild carrot).

**Vineyard.** A place where grapes are grown.

**Vintage.** The year a wine was produced. Vintages appear only on bottles of wine that was produced from grapes, not on wine produced from other fruits or plants.

**Winery.** A place where wine is made.

**Yeast.** A one-celled fungus that is used in winemaking to transform juice into wine.

**Yeasty.** The odor of yeast present in wine. It is pleasing if not excessive.

# Resources

While it's easy to make wild wines at home, you do need an understanding of the process, as well as a stock of simple plant-gathering and winemaking supplies. In this book, I've tried to provide you with all the basic information you need to make delicious wild wines. But there's a lot to learn about wild and organic wines! That's why this section was created—to guide you towards further information, as well as a variety of companies that offer wine- and winemaking-related products. And if you occasionally prefer to buy your wine rather than making it yourself, you'll even find a list of organic vineyards and wineries. (For more detailed information on these wineries, see page 199.)

## BIODYNAMICS

**Demeter Association Inc.**
25844 Butler Road
Junction City, OR 97448-8525
Phone: (541) 998-5691
Fax: (541) 998-5694
Website: www.demeter-usa.org
*A national independent nonprofit corporation committed to assuring that biodynamic foods in the United States continue to be grown with the strictest care and highest integrity. Provides biodynamic certification for food growers, processors, and handlers.*

## CITRUS FRUIT TREES

**Ty Ty Nursery**
4723 U.S. Highway 82 W.
PO Box 130
Ty Ty, GA 31795
Phone: (800) 972-2101
Website: www.tytyga.com
*A supplier that sells citrus trees, including the Meyer lemon tree.*

## FRUIT-FLY TRAPS

**Bio-Logic Resources, Inc.**
PO Box 22815
Milwaukie, OR 97269-0815
Fax: (503) 653-1303
Website: www.bugtraps.com
*A supplier that sells "Natural Catch Fruit Fly Traps," which successfully eliminate fruit flies during wine fermentation. This product can also be found at hardware stores.*

# FRUIT-PICKING SUPPLIES

**R.H. Shumway's**
Catalog Fulfillment Center
334 W. Stroud Street
Randolph, WI 53956-1274
Phone: (800) 342-9461
Fax: (888) 437-2733
Website: www.rhshumway.com
*A supplier that sells fruit pickers to allow easier access to hard-to-reach fruit from higher limbs.*

# ORGANIC CERTIFICATION

**California Certified Organic Farmers (CCOF)**
2155 Delaware Avenue, Suite 150
Santa Cruz, CA 95060
Phone: (831) 423-2263
Fax: (831) 423-4528
Website: www.ccof.org
*Promotes and supports organic food and agriculture through an organic certification program, also a USDA Accredited Certifying Agent (ACA) for organic growers, processors, and handlers in North America.*

**The National Organic Program**
USDA-AMS-TM-NOP
Room 4008, South Building
Ag Stop 0268
1400 Independence Avenue, SW
Washington, DC 20250-0020
Phone: (202) 720-3252
Website: www.ams.usda.gov/nop
*Ensures that agricultural products marketed as organic meet consistent, uniform standards. Regulations specific to organic standards and labeling can be obtained from this agency.*

**Northeast Organic Farming Association of New York (NOFA)**
840 Upper Front Street
Binghamton, NY 13905
Phone: (607) 724-9851
Fax: (607) 724-9853
Website: www.nofany.org
*A nonprofit educational organization of consumers, gardeners, and farmers, NOFA is also a USDA Accredited Certifying Agent (ACA) for organic growers, processors, and handlers in the Northeastern United States.*

**Oregon Tilth**
470 Lancaster Drive, NE
Salem, OR 97301
Phone: (503) 378-0690
Fax: (503) 378-0809
Website: www.tilth.org
*A nonprofit research and education organization dedicated to biologically sound and socially acceptable agriculture. Composed mostly of organic farmers, gardeners, and consumers, Oregon Tilth is also a USDA Accredited Certifying Agent (ACA) for organic growers, processors, and handlers internationally.*

**Washington State Department of Agriculture**
1111 Washington Street, SE
PO Box 42560
Olympia, WA 98504-2560
Phone: (360) 902-1924
Website: www.agr.wa.gov
*Supports the agricultural community and promotes consumer and environmental protection, also a USDA Accredited Certifying Agent (ACA) for organic growers, processors, and handlers.*

# ORGANIC WINE IMPORTER

**Organic Wine Company**
1592 Union Street #350
San Francisco, CA 94123
Phone: (888) 326-9463
Fax: (415) 256-8888
Website: www.theorganicwinecompany.com

# ORGANIC VINEYARDS AND WINERIES

**Amity Vineyards**
18150 Amity Vineyards Road
Amity, OR 97101
Phone: (888) 265-8966
Website: www.amityvineyards.com

**Badger Mountain Vineyard**
1106 S. Jurupa Street
Kennewick, WA 99338
Phone: (800) 643-9463
Fax: (509) 627-2071
Website. www.badgermtnvineyard.com

**Barra of Mendocino**
10801 East Road
PO Box 196
Redwood Valley, CA 95470
Phone: (707) 485-8771
Fax: (707) 485-0147
Website. www.barraofmendocino.com

**Brick House Vineyards**
18200 Lewis Rogers Lane
Newberg, OR 97132
Phone/Fax: (503) 538-5136
Website: www.brickhousewines.com

**Ceago Vinegarden**
PO Box 3017
Nice, CA 95464
Phone: (707) 274-1462
Fax: (707) 274-9736
Website: www.ceago.com

**Chateau Lorane**
27415 Siuslaw River Road
PO Box 47
Lorane, OR 97451
Phone: (541) 942-8028
Fax: (541) 942-5830
Website: www.chateaulorane.com

**China Bend Winery**
3751 Vineyard Way
Kettle Falls, WA 99141
Phone: (800) 700-6123
Email: winery@chinabend.com
Website: www.chinabend.com

**Cooper Mountain Vineyards**
9480 SW Grabhorn Road
Beaverton, OR 97007
Phone: (503) 649-0027
Fax: (503) 649-0702
Website: www.coopermountainwine.com

**Coturri Winery**
6725 Enterprise Road
PO Box 396
Glen Ellen, CA 95442
Phone: (707) 525-9126
Fax: (707) 542-8039
Website: www.coturriwinery.com

**Fetzer Vineyards**
12901 Old River Road
PO Box 611
Hopland, CA 95449-0611
Phone: (800) 846-8637
Fax: (707) 744-1439
Website: www.fetzer.com

**Fitzpatrick Winery**
7740 Fair Play Road
Fair Play, CA 95684
Phone: (800) 245-9166
Fax: (530) 620-6838
Website: www.fitzpatrickwinery.com

**Four Chimneys Organic Winery**
211 Hall Road
Himrod, NY 14842
Phone: (607) 243-7502
Fax: (607) 243-8156
Website: www.fourchimneysorganicwines.com

**Frey Vineyards**
14000 Tomki Road
Redwood Valley, CA 95470
Phone: (800) 760-3739
Fax: (707) 485-7875
Website: www.freywine.com

**Frog's Leap**
8815 Conn Creek Road
PO Box 189
Rutherford, CA 94573
Phone: (800) 959-4704
Fax: (707) 963-0242
Website: www.frogsleap.com

**Hallcrest Vineyards**
379 Felton Empire Road
Felton, CA 95018
Phone: (800) 699-9463
Fax: (408) 335-4450
Website: www.hallcrestvineyards.com

**Handley Cellars**
3151 Highway 128
PO Box 66
Philo, CA 95466
Phone: (707) 895-3876
Fax: (707) 895-2603
Website: www.handleycellars.com

**Heller Estate**
69 W. Carmel Valley Road
PO Box 999
Carmel Valley, CA 93924
Phone: (800) 625-8466
Fax: (831) 659-6226
Website: www.hellerestate.com

**King Estate Winery**
80854 Territorial Road
Eugene, OR 97405
Phone: (800) 884-4441
Fax: (541) 942-9867
Website: www.kingestate.com

**La Rocca Vineyards**
PO Box 541
Forest Ranch, CA 95942
Phone: (800) 808-9463
Fax: (530) 894-7268
Website: www.laroccavineyards.com

**Madonna Estate**
5400 Old Sonoma Road
Napa, CA 94559
Phone: (866) 724-2993
Fax: (707) 257-2778
Website: www.madonnaestate.com

**Nevada County/Our Daily Red/ Orleans Hill Winery/Heartswood**
11372 Winter Moon Way
Nevada City, CA 95959
Website: www.ourdailyred.com

**Robert Sinskey Vineyards**
6320 Silverado Trail
Napa, CA 94558
Phone: (800) 869-2030
Website: www.robertsinskey.com

**Staglin Vineyard**
PO Box 680
Rutherford, CA 94573
Phone: (707) 944-0477
Website: www.staglinfamily.com

**Yorkville Cellars**
25701 Highway 128
Box 3
Yorkville, CA 95494
Phone: (707) 894-9177
Fax: (707) 894-2426
Website: www.yorkville-cellars.com

## WATER QUALITY

**Air & Water, Inc.**
17335 Mount Wynne Circle
Fountain Valley, CA 92708
Phone: (800) 734-0405
Fax: (714) 200-0665

Website: www.air-n-water.com
*A supplier that sells a variety of water testing kits, including tests for hardness of tap water and undesirable metals and chemicals. Helps you decide if you want to use your faucet water for creating homemade wine.*

**U.S. Environmental Protection Agency**
Office of Ground Water and Drinking Water (4601)
Ariel Rios Building
1200 Pennsylvania Avenue, NW
Washington, DC 20460-0003
Phone: (202) 564-3750
Fax: (202) 564-3753
Website: www.epa.gov/safewater
*Responsible for protecting the public health by ensuring safe drinking water and protecting ground water. You can obtain statistics on the quality of your local drinking water, as well as a listing and description of contaminants found in your water source and violations that have occurred.*

## WINE LABELING

**Alcohol and Tobacco Tax and Trade Bureau (TTB)**
Department of the Treasury
1310 "G" Street, NW—3rd Floor
Washington, DC 20220
Website: www.ttb.gov
*Currently responsible for overseeing wine labeling and substantiation of labeling claims.*

## WINEMAKING SUPPLIES

**E.C. Kraus**
733 S. Northern Boulevard
PO Box 7850
Independence, MO 64054
Phone: (800) 353-1906
Fax: (816) 254-7051
Website: www.ECKraus.com

*Catalogue that sells home winemaking supplies including yeast, bottles, corks, fermentation containers, and testing equipment.*

## WINE-RELATED PRODUCTS

**The Wine Enthusiast**
103 Fairview Park Drive
Elmsford, NY 10523
Phone: (800) 356-8466
Fax: (800) 833-8466
Website: www.wineenthusiast.com
*Catalogue that sells products pertaining to wine such as wine racks, glasses, corkers, and wine-related gifts.*

## WINE AROMA KITS

**Artisans on Web**
Pier 23
Studio 1
San Francisco, CA 94111
Phone: (888) 216-6399
Fax: (415) 738-2471
Website: www.aoweb.com
*A supplier that sells wine aroma kits, ranging from about $100 to $399, depending on the complexity of the kit and the number of scents included. Over fifty kits are now available in English, Spanish, and French.*

# Evaluation of Organic Wineries

As you learned in Chapter 3, the term "organic" can mean a number of different things when printed on a bottle of wine. Fining agents of various types may or may not have been used; there's no way to tell from the label. Creosote-soaked end posts may have been employed in the vineyards—and the vintner doesn't have to tell you.

With this in mind, I contacted a number of organic vineyards and wineries, and asked them about their growing and winemaking processes. Although I couldn't get all the information I wanted from every winery, I did receive answers to most of my questions. It is my hope that the following table, which summarizes the information I found, will guide you to wines that are not only delicious, but also meet your own personal standards for healthy organic products. (For winery contact information, see page 195.)

| ORGANIC WINERY EVALUATION | | | | | | |
|---|---|---|---|---|---|---|
| Winery Name/Label | Certified "Organic" * | Certified "Made With Organically Grown Grapes" * | Sulfites Added | Fining Agent Used | Biodynamic Pruning and Harvesting | Creosote-Soaked End Posts Used in Vineyard |
| Amity Vineyards | No. | One variety, their sulfite-free pinot noir, is made with organically grown grapes from the Cattrall Brothers Vineyard in Amity, Oregon. | One variety, their sulfite-free pinot noir, is made without sulfites. All other varieties are made with sulfites. | Not stated. | No. | No. |
| Badger Mountain Vineyard/Powers Winery | Yes. | Yes. | No. | No. | No. | Yes, but the posts are wrapped in plastic so they don't touch the ground. |
| Barra of Mendocino/ Girasole Vineyards | No. | Yes. | Yes. | Bentonite. | Considering conversion to biodynamics. | The vineyard is in the process of conversion. Less than half the posts are creosote; the others are cement. |

## ORGANIC WINERY EVALUATION

| Winery Name/Label | Certified "Organic" * | Certified "Made With Organically Grown Grapes" * | Sulfites Added | Fining Agent Used | Biodynamic Pruning and Harvesting | Creosote-Soaked End Posts Used in Vineyard |
|---|---|---|---|---|---|---|
| Brick House Vineyards | No. | Yes. | Yes, although they have made some sulfite-free wine in the past. | Fining agents are rarely used. When used, agents are organic egg whites or organic milk. | Yes. Demeter certified since 2005. | No. |
| Ceago Vinegarden | No. | No. | Yes. | Egg whites are used for red wines only if needed. | Yes. | No. The vineyard uses only metal end posts. |
| Chateau Lorane | No. | Yes. | Not stated. | Not stated. | Not stated. | Not stated. |
| China Bend Winery | Yes. | Yes. | No. | No. | No. | Not stated. |
| Cooper Mountain Vineyard | No. | Yes. | Not stated. | Not stated. | Yes. | Not stated. |
| Coturri Winery | No. | Some vines are certified and some are not. | No. | No. | Some vines are in conversion to biodynamics and some are not. | No. The vineyard uses posts made of redwood or metal. |
| Fetzer Vineyards/ Bonterra Vineyards | No. | Yes. | Yes. | Organic egg whites. | Yes—at Bonterra Vineyards home ranch. | Not stated. |
| Fitzpatrick Winery | No. | Yes. | Yes. | Bentonite. | Incorporates many biodynamic practices, but is not certified. | No. |
| Four Chimneys Organic Winery | No. | Yes. | Yes. | Not stated. | Not stated. | Not stated. |
| Frey Vineyards | Yes. | Yes. | No. | Bentonite. | Some varieties state "biodynamic" on the label. | No. The vineyard uses all metal posts. |
| Frog's Leap | No. | 75% of their grapes are certified organic. | Yes. | Bentonite, Isinglass, and milk. | No. | No. |

| ORGANIC WINERY EVALUATION | | | | | | |
|---|---|---|---|---|---|---|
| Winery Name/Label | Certified "Organic" * | Certified "Made With Organically Grown Grapes" * | Sulfites Added | Fining Agent Used | Biodynamic Pruning and Harvesting | Creosote-Soaked End Posts Used in Vineyard |
| Hallcrest Vineyards | Yes. | Yes. | Yes. | Bentonite is sometimes used. | Follows some biodynamic practices. | No. |
| Handley Cellars | No. | Yes. | Yes. | Organic egg whites and milk. | No. | Not stated. |
| Heller Estate | No. | Yes. | Yes. | Bentonite and cream of tartar are used for white wines. | No. | No. The vineyard uses untreated or metal posts. |
| King Estate Winery | No. | Some wines are made with organically grown grapes; some wines are not organic because the grapes come from other, nonorganic vineyards. | Yes. | Different unspecified fining agents are used for different wines. | No. | Not stated. |
| LaRocca Vineyards | Yes. | Yes. | No. | Bentonite. | No. | No. |
| Madonna Estate | No. | Yes. | Not stated. | Not stated. | Not stated. | Not stated. |
| Nevada County Wine Guild— Our Daily Red, Orleans Hill Winery, Heartswork | Yes. | Yes. | No. | Bentonite is used only for white wines. | No. | No. |
| Robert Sinskey Vineyards | No. | Yes. | No, but the wine's natural sulfite level exceeds allowable amounts. | Not stated. | Yes. | Yes, but the vineyard is phasing out creosote and replacing with metal. |
| Staglin Vineyard | No. | Yes. | Yes. | Egg whites. | Follows some biodynamic practices. | Older posts have creosote; newer ones do not. |
| Yorkville Cellars— Randle Hill Vineyard and Rennie Vineyard | No. | Yes. | Yes. | Not stated. | No. | No. |

* This refers to standards established by the National Organic Program (NOP).

# Suggested Reading List

## Foraging Wild Plants

Angier, Bradford. *Field Guide to Edible Wild Plants*. Harrisburg, PA: Stackpole Books, 1994.

Brill, Steve. *Edible and Medicinal Plants*. New York: Hearst Books, 1994.

Crowhurst, Adrienne. *The Weed Cookbook*. New York: Lancer Books, 1972.

Domico, Terry. *Wild Harvest*. Blaine, WA: Hancock House Publishers, 1979.

Duke, James A. *Handbook of Edible Weeds*. Boca Raton, FL: CRC Press, 1992.

Elias, Thomas S. and Dykeman, Peter A. *Edible Wild Plants—A North American Guide*. New York: Sterling Publishing Co., Inc., 1990.

Elliott, Doug. *Wild Roots*. Rochester, VT: Healing Arts Press, 1995.

Fernald, Merritt Lyndon and Kinsey, Alfred Charles. *Edible Wild Plants of Eastern North America*. New York: Dover Publications, Inc., 1986.

Gibbons, Euell. *Stalking the Good Life*. New York: David McKay Company, Inc., 1971.

Gibbons, Euell. *Stalking the Healhful Herbs*. Chambersburg, PA: Alan C. Hood & Company, Inc., 1966.

Gibbons, Euell. *Stalking the Wild Asparagus*. New York: David McKay Company, Inc., 1962.

Gibbons, Euell and Tucker, Gordon. *Euell Gibbons' Handbook of Edible Wild Plants*. Virginia Beach, VA: The Donning Company Publishers, 1979.

Hall, Alan. *The Wild Food Trailguide*. New York: Holt, Rinehart & Winston, 1976.

Harrington, H.D. *Edible Native Plants of the Rocky Mountains*. Albuquerque, NM: University of New Mexico Press, 1996.

Kavasch, Barrie. *Native Harvests*. New York: Vintage Books, a Division of Random House, 1979.

Kindscher, Kelly. *Edible Wild Plants of the Prairie*. Lawrence, KS: University Press of Kansas, 1987.

Tilford, Gregory. *Edible and Medicinal Plants of the West*. Missoula, MT: Mountain Press Publishing Company, 1997.

Turner, Nancy. *Food Plants of Interior First Peoples*. Vancouver, Canada: UBC Press, 1997.

Young, Kay. *Wild Seasons*. Lincoln, NE: University of Nebraska Press, 1993.

## Plant Identification

Alden, Peter and Paulson, Dennis. *National Audubon Society Field Guide to the Pacific Northwest*. New York: Alfred A. Knopf, 1998.

Barash, Cathy Wilkinson. *Edible Flowers*. Golden, CO: Fulcrum Press, 1995.

Derig, Betty and Fuller, Margaret C. *Wild Berries of the West*. Missoula, MT: Mountain Press Publishing Company, 2001.

Kowalchik, Claire and Hylton, William H., Editors. *Rodale's Encyclopedia of Herbs*. Emmaus, PA: Rodale Press, 1987.

Little, Elbert. *National Audubon Society Field Guide to North American Trees—Eastern Region*. New York: Alfred A. Knopf, 1980.

Little, Elbert. *National Audubon Society Field Guide to North American Trees—Western Region*. New York: Alfred A. Knopf, 1996.

Newcomb, Lawrence. *Newcomb's Wildflower Guide*. Boston: Little, Brown and Company, 1977.

Niering, William A. and Olmstead, Nancy C. *National Audubon Society Field Guide to North American Wildflowers—Eastern Region*. New York: Alfred A. Knopf, 1979.

Spellenberg, Richard. *National Audubon Society Field Guide to North American Wildflowers—Western Region*. New York: Alfred A. Knopf, 1979.

Strickler, Dr. Dee. *Wayside Wildflowers of the Pacific Northwest*. Columbia Falls, MT: The Flower Press, 1993.

Taylor, Ronald J. *Northwest Weeds: The Ugly and Beautiful Villains of Fields, Gardens, and Roadsides*. Missoula, MT: Mountain Press Publishing Company, 1990.

Taylor, Ronald J. *Sagebrush Country*. Missoula, MT: Mountain Press Publishing Company, 1992.

Underhill. J.E. *Northwestern Wild Berries*. Blaine, WA: Hancock House, 1994.

Underhill, J.E. *Roadside Wildflowers of the Northwest*. Blaine, WA: Hancock House, 1999.

## Poisonous Plants

Kingsbury, John M. *Deadly Harvest*. Austin, TX: Holt, Rinehart and Winston, 1965.

Turner, Nancy J. and Szczawinski, Adam F. *Common Poisonous Plants and Mushrooms of North America*. Portland, OR: Timber Press, 1991.

# Index

## GOING WILD IN THE KITCHEN
### The Fresh & Sassy Tastes of Vegetarian Cooking
#### Leslie Cerier

Go wild in the kitchen! Venture beyond the usual beans, grains, and vegetables to include an exciting variety of organic vegetarian fare in your meals. *Going Wild in the Kitchen* shows you how. In addition to providing helpful cooking tips and techniques, this book offers over 150 kitchen-tested recipes for taste-tempting dishes that contain such unique ingredients as edible flowers; tasty sea vegetables; wild mushrooms, berries, and herbs; and exotic ancient grains like teff, quinoa, and Chinese "forbidden" black rice. Author Leslie Cerier encourages the creative instincts of novice and seasoned cooks alike, prompting them to "go wild" by adding, changing, or substituting ingredients in existing recipes. Lively illustrations and a complete resource list for finding organic foods complete this user-friendly cookbook.

*Going Wild in the Kitchen* is more than a unique cookbook—it's a recipe for inspiration. Excite your palate with this treasure-trove of distinctive, healthy, and taste-tempting recipe creations.

*$16.95 US / $25.50 CAN • 240 pages • 7.5 x 9-inch quality paperback • ISBN 978-0-7570-0091-1*

## EAT SMART EAT RAW
### Creative Vegetarian Recipes for a Healthier Life
#### Kate Wood

As the popularity of raw vegetarian cuisine continues to soar, so does the evidence that uncooked food is amazingly good for you. From lowering cholesterol to eliminating excess weight, the health benefits of this diet are too important to ignore. Now there is another reason to go raw—taste! In *Eat Smart, Eat Raw,* cook and health writer Kate Wood not only explains how to get started, but also provides kitchen-tested recipes guaranteed to delight even the fussiest of eaters.

*Eat Smart, Eat Raw* begins by explaining the basics of cooking without heat. This is followed by twelve chapters offering 150 recipes for truly exceptional dishes, including hearty breakfasts, savory soups, satisfying entrées, and luscious desserts. There's even a chapter on the "almost raw." Whether you are an ardent vegetarian or just someone in search of a great meal, *Eat Smart, Eat Raw* may forever change the way you look at an oven.

*$15.95 US / $21.95 CAN • 184 pages • 7.5 x 9-inch quality paperback • ISBN 978-0-7570-0261-8*

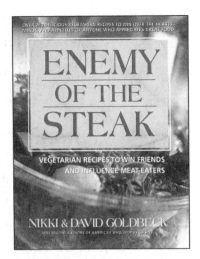

# ENEMY OF THE STEAK
## Vegetarian Recipes to Win Friends and Influence Meat-Eaters

### Nikki & David Goldbeck

Don't blame vegetarians for starting this. Who said "real food for real people"? Aren't asparagus, carrots, and tomatoes every bit as real as . . . that other food? To answer the call to battle, best-selling authors Nikki and David Goldbeck have created a wonderfully tempting new cookbook that offers a wealth of kitchen-tested recipes which nourish the body, please the palate, and satisfy even the heartiest of appetites.

*Enemy of the Steak* first presents basic information on vegetarian cooking. Then eight great chapters offer over 250 recipes for breakfast fare; appetizers and hors d'oeuvres; soups; salads; entrées; side dishes; sauces, toppings, and marinades; and desserts. A perfect marriage of nutrition and the art of cooking, *Enemy of the Steak* is for everyone who loves a good healthy meal. Simply put, it's great food for smart people. If you have to take sides, you couldn't be in better company.

*$16.95 US / $21.50 CAN • 248 pages • 7.5 x 9-inch quality paperback • ISBN 978-0-7570-0273-1*

# GREENS AND GRAINS ON THE DEEP BLUE SEA COOKBOOK
## Fabulous Vegetarian Cuisine from the Holistic Holiday at Sea Cruises

### Sandy Pukel and Mark Hanna

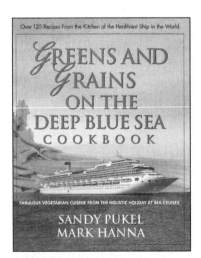

You are invited to come aboard one of America's premier health cruises. Too busy to get away? Even if you can't swim in the ship's pool, you can still enjoy its gourmet cuisine, because natural foods expert Sandy Pukel and master chef Mark Hanna have created *Greens and Grains on the Deep Blue Sea Cookbook*—a titanic collection of the most popular vegetarian dishes served aboard the Holistic Holiday at Sea cruises.

Each of the book's more than 120 kitchen-tested recipes has been designed to provide not only great taste, but also maximum nutrition. Choose from among an innovative selection of taste-tempting appetizers, soups, salads, entrées, side dishes, and desserts. Easy-to-follow instructions ensure that even the novice cook will have superb results. With *Greens and Grains on the Deep Blue Sea Cookbook,* you can enjoy fabulous signature dishes from the Holistic Holiday at Sea cruises whenever you desire—in the comfort of your own home.

*$16.95 US / $19.95 CAN • 160 pages • 7.5 x 9-inch quality paperback • ISBN 978-0-7570-0287-8*

# JUICE ALIVE
## The Ultimate Guide to Juicing Remedies
### Steven Bailey, ND and Larry Trivieri, Jr.

The world of fresh juices offers a powerhouse of antioxidants, vitamins, minerals, and enzymes. The trick is knowing which juices can best serve your needs. In this easy-to-use guide, health experts Dr. Steven Bailey and Larry Trivieri, Jr. tell you everything you need to know to maximize the benefits and tastes of juice.

The book begins with a look at the history of juicing. It then examines the many components that make fresh juice truly good for you—good for weight loss and so much more. Next, it offers practical advice about the types of juices available, as well as buying and storing tips for produce. The second half of the book begins with an important chart that matches up common ailments with the most appropriate juices, followed by over 100 delicious juice recipes. Let *Juice Alive* introduce you to a world bursting with the incomparable tastes and benefits of fresh juice.

---

*$14.95 US / $18.95 CAN • 272 pages • 6 x 9-inch quality paperback • ISBN 978-0-7570-0266-3*

# THE MISO BOOK
## The Art of Cooking with Miso
### John and Jan Belleme

For centuries, the preparation of miso has been considered an art form in Japan. Through a time-honored double-fermentation process, soybeans and grains are transformed into this wondrous food, which is both a flavorful addition to a variety of dishes and a powerful medicinal. Scientific research has supported miso's use as an effective therapeutic aid in the prevention and treatment of a range of disorders.

Part One of this comprehensive guide begins with miso basics—the different types, uses, and various manufacturing methods. A chapter called "Miso Medicine" then details this superfood's healing properties and role in maintaining good health. Easy directions for making miso at home are also provided.

Then Part Two offers over 140 healthy recipes in which miso is used in dips, spreads, soups, and much more. Whether you are in search of healthful foods or you simply want a delicious new take on old favorites, *The Miso Book* may be just what the doctor ordered.

---

*$15.95 US / $23.95 CAN • 192 pages • 7.5 x 9-inch quality paperback • ISBN 978-0-7570-0028-7*

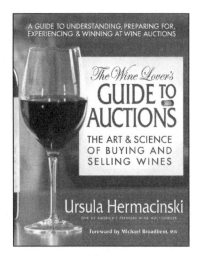

# THE WINE LOVER'S GUIDE TO AUCTIONS

## The Art & Science of Buying and Selling Wines

### Ursula Hermacinski

From America to Zanzibar, the popularity of wine has skyrocketed in recent years. While millions of people have come to appreciate wine's taste, a growing number of collectors also recognize it as a sound investment. For these savvy individuals, as well as top chefs and wine aficionados, the wine auction has become an important place to find superior wines. Now, renowned wine auctioneer Ursula Hermacinski has written *The Wine Lover's Guide to Auctions* to explain how wine auctions really work so that you, too, can become a successful player.

The guide begins by exploring the history of wine auctions. It then provides information on wine basics and details the auction process—for buyers *and* sellers. Rounding out the book are helpful hints on starting or expanding your wine collection, choosing the best auction house for your needs, and organizing your own wine tasting.

*$17.95 US / $22.50 CAN • 256 pages • 7.5 x 9-inch quality paperback • ISBN 978-0-7570-0275-5*

# THE GRAPES OF WINE

## The Fine Art of Growing Grapes and Making Wine

### Baudouin Neirynck, PhD

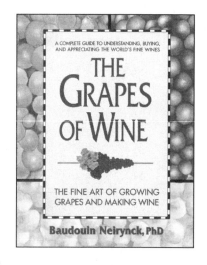

The ancient Greek philosophers called them elixirs of the gods. The Roman emperors used them to celebrate their victories. And today, fine wines are still being treasured and enjoyed. How and why these wines reach their zenith in color, flavor, and value is the focus of this beautifully illustrated book by wine connoisseur Baudouin Neirynck.

The book first looks at the activities of growing grapes and making wine. This is followed by a discussion of the twenty most popular white and black grapes responsible for great wines, from Chardonnay to Sangiovese. Included are chapters on investing in wines, storing and serving wines, matching wines with foods, reading wine labels, and even the health benefits of wine. Whether you are a wine expert or simply someone who enjoys an occasional glass of wine with your meals, *The Grapes of Wine* is as mesmerizing as a glass of the finest Cabernet Sauvignon.

*$29.95 US / $37.50 CAN • 224 pages • 9 x 12-inch hardback • ISBN 978-0-7570-0247-2*